P9-DIH-988

The United States and Malaysia

The
United States
and
Malaysia

James W. Gould

Harvard University Press

Cambridge, Massachusetts

1969

Distributed in Great Britain by Oxford University Press, London

Library of Congress Catalog Card Number 76–78518
SBN 674–92615–3

Printed in the United States of America

To the Peace Corps Volunteers
in Malaysia

Editor's Foreword

The American Foreign Policy Library was founded in 1945 by Sumner Welles, then Undersecretary of State, and Donald McKay, professor of history at Harvard but at the time on leave with the Research Analysis Branch of the Office of Strategic Services. Their aim was to produce a series of brief but authoritative handbooks which would enlighten the public on key countries or areas where the United States faced major foreign policy problems.

Fifteen volumes had been produced by 1959 when Crane Brinton, professor of history at Harvard, succeeded Professor McKay as editor of the series. At first he had with him as coeditor Lincoln Gordon, then professor of international economic relations at Harvard and subsequently American ambassador to Brazil. Under Professor Brinton's able leadership six new titles appeared. The present volume would have been the seventh, for Professor Brinton arranged for its writing and saw it through the earlier stages of publication; his death prevented him from seeing fulfillment of the project.

Since foreign policy problems keep changing, a Foreign Policy Library can never be completed. Earlier books must be revised and brought up to date or supplanted by new efforts. For example, revised editions of five books were published during Professor Brinton's editorship. Whenever possible, gaps in coverage should be filled and new problem areas treated. I hope that in the task of editing this series, I can maintain the high standards set by my distinguished predecessors.

Malaysia has long constituted a serious gap in this series. It is distant from the United States, not very large (about the size of Montana), and small in population for Asia (only about twelve million). On it, however, focus many of the great problems of our time. In the two thirds of the world that we call either less developed or developing, Malaysia stands out among the leaders in economic and institutional growth. Among the former colonial parts of the world, no region has made faster progress toward parliamentary democracy. But divided three ways among almost equal numbers of Malay peoples and Chinese as well as a substantial Indian minority, no region faces graver problems of racial, linguistic, cultural, and religious diversity. Put together from various colonial pieces of territory and divided today into three separate political units, Malaysia faces sharp problems of national identity.

Malaysia also lies at the core of the security problems of the whole Southeast Asian area, for it dominates crucial water routes and in Singapore contains the great entrepôt of Southeast Asian trade and the once dominant naval base of the region. At a time when the United States is rethinking and attempting to readjust its whole role in the Southeast Asia, the present realities and future possibilities of Malaysia are matters of vital concern to Americans. It is fortunate that Professor Gould's careful and detailed analysis of these problems has become available at this time.

Edwin O. Reischauer

Author's Preface

The Malaysian region contains three political units. Two of these, Singapore and Brunei, have been closely tied with the largest nation, Malaysia. Malaysia has great importance to the United States and the world. The obvious strategic significance of its position on the world's sea lanes, and its value as the greatest supplier of tin and rubber, are less important than its remarkable society. By its peaceful transition from colonial status to full independence it has shown that violent revolution is not essential to freedom, and that ex-colonies need not be paranoid about their former masters. This viable democracy has successfully combined the dynamism of capitalism with the humanity of social welfare. And its model development administration has provided so much economic impetus that many economists are confident that Malaysia will "take off" into sustained economic growth.

Malaysia has been a leader in international cooperation, first showing how separate colonies can be brought together in a democratic federalism, then leading its neighbors into regional organization, and always giving effective support to the United Nations and its agencies. But the most significant thing is that Malaysia has found a way to encourage three ancient cultures to exist together in peace, and to get them to cooperate politically and culturally.

It is the purpose of this book to show how this remarkable development came about, to tell how Americans have contributed to it, and to suggest how the United States can best assure that the development will continue.

It is important to clarify the meaning of some terms that sound and look alike: Malaya, Malaysia, Malay, Malaysian.

Malaya is the geographical region comprising the southeasternmost peninsula of Asia. In 1948 the British combined their colonies in Malaya—the Federated Malay States, the unfederated Malay States, and the Straits Settlements—into the Federation of Malaya. This federation excluded only one part of Malaya: the colony of Singapore. In 1957 the Federation of Malaya became an independent nation, and in 1963 formed the core of a new nation, Malaysia. Since 1966 Malaya has been called West Malaysia. (East Malaysia encompasses Sabah and Sarawak).

Malaysia was long used to describe the region lying north of Indonesia. In 1963 the name Malaysia was adopted by the nation which combined the former Federation of Malaya and the British colonies of North Borneo (renamed Sabah), Sarawak, and Singapore. This new state of Malaysia included all of the Malaysia region except Brunei, which did not join; in 1965 Singapore broke away from Malaysia and formed an independent republic.

A *Malay* is a member of a racial and cultural group which has inhabited the Malaysian region for well over 3000 years. The Malay language is the lingua franca of the area, and is the national language of Malaysia, Brunei, and Singapore. The term *Malaysian* refers broadly to an inhabitant of the Malaysia region, no matter what race.

This book is about Malaysia in the broad sense of the term— including Malaysia, Brunei, and Singapore.

Contents

The United States and Malaysia

1
The Natural Setting

If you fly halfway around the world in a somewhat southerly bearing from North America, you come to Malaysia. If you choose the route across the Atlantic, Europe, and India, you arrive first at West Malaysia, the long Malayan peninsula that is the southeastern tip of Asia. If you go across the Pacific, you will come first to East Malaysia, which is the northern quarter of Borneo, the third largest island in the world.

Malaysia lies to the north of the great chain of islands called Indonesia. They are both geographically and culturally part of the same archipelago, which can be called with equal justice Malaysia or Indonesia. Only an accident of colonial history separated the countries. The East Indies were divided arbitrarily in 1824, when the British left their Dutch ally with the southern Netherlands India, while the northern part stayed with British India. When the Dutch East Indies became independent in 1945, the nationalist leaders chose one of the names that had been applied to this whole area, Indonesia. When the British territory achieved independence in 1963 it chose the name Malaysia. We will be constantly reminded of the similarity, and indeed the unity, of Malaysia-Indonesia.

Malaysia is not a small country. Its land mass measures 130,000 square miles. This is ten times the size of Formosa and considerably larger than Nepal, Cambodia, Laos, and both Koreas. Malaysia extends over more area than the Philippines and only slightly less than Japan. It is 1350 miles from Chinchin Point on the northwest tip of Langkawi Island on the Indian Ocean to Hog

Point on the Sibutu Passage between the Sulu Sea and the Celebes
Sea. West Malaysia, known as Malaya until 1966, is nearly 500
miles long; East Malaysia, 750 miles.

These two wings are separated by 400 miles of the South China
Sea, measured at the nearest points at the southeastern tip of Asia,
Tanjung Penyusuh, to the westernmost tip of Sarawak at Tan-
jung Datu. The wingspread between the northern tips is over a
thousand miles, if measured between the cities of Kota Kinabalu
(Jesselton) and Kota Bharu.

These two parts of Malaysia have much geographical unity in
spite of the separation by the sea. Both sections are on the Sunda
Shelf, a shallow ocean platform only 120 feet deep in the south.
And the same flora and fauna are found in the east as in the west.
Naturalists have long recognized the unity of this area by calling
it Malaysia.

The political separation is greater; the intervening islands, the
Natuna and Anambas groups, belong to Indonesia. In fact, instead of Malaysia surrounding Indonesia, as Sukarno used to say,
it is almost the other way around. For 500 miles on its west
Malaysia faces the Indonesian island of Sumatra across the Strait
of Malacca. This strait narrows to twenty-eight miles off Batu
Pahat, then to ten miles off the southern tip of Johore. Indonesia
is clearly visible from the quays of Singapore, whose southern-
most islands are only a couple of miles from the nearest Indonesian ones. On the east, Malaysia shares with Indonesia a rugged
Borneo frontier of about 900 miles.

In contrast with this 1900-mile frontier with Indonesia, Malaysia's northern borders are short. The Malayan Peninsula is separated from Thailand by a mountainous frontier of 250 miles at
the Kra Isthmus. The sea border with the Philippines is only 375
miles as it jogs between the coral reefs of the Sulu Sea. The rest
of the northern frontier is the South China Sea, with Vietnam
225 miles northwest of Kota Bharu and China's Hainan 975 miles
north of Kota Kinabalu. Cambodia and Burma are near neighbors, within 300 miles to the north. In the other direction,
Australia is only 1200 miles distant.

Malaysia has been an important crossroad throughout history.

It lies athwart the shortest sea routes from the Far East to Indonesia, India, and Europe. Travelers and trade between India and China have had to go either across the Malay Peninsula or around it through the Straits of Malacca. From the arrival of the Portuguese in 1509 until today, the sea route from Europe to China has gone through Malaysia. It lay on the "lifeline" of the British Empire, and will undoubtedly be important to naval officers and seamen as long as there are ships. In this air age, Singapore is a nodal point of air traffic between Australia and the continents of Asia and Europe.

Now that we have found our location, let us look at the appearance of the country. More than half of Malaysia is steep and mountainous, covered with thick tropical forest. Dominant in Borneo is the Western Cordillera and Border Range, which extends for 500 miles into Indonesian Kalimantan. It continues north for the length of Sabah as the Crocker Range. The highest peak in Malaysia, and in all of Southeast Asia, is Mount Kinabalu, soaring 13,455 feet, as high as the Jungfrau or Mauna Loa. This magnificent mountain, sacred to the peoples of Sabah, rises above the clouds in a series of jagged pinnacles. Rarely visible from sea level after late morning, the blue peak is a beautiful sight for the early riser.

The highest mountain in Sarawak is Gunung Murud, at the southern tip of Sabah, which rises to 7950 feet. Many of the spur ranges which branch off into Sarawak like giant ribs have peaks nearly as high as Murud.

Like Borneo, mainland Malaya also has a spine of mountains in the Central Range which extends 300 miles from the Thai border to Tampin near Malacca. This range is old and worn. Its tallest peak, Gunung Korbu, in the Cameron Highlands above Ipoh, is 7162 feet tall.

These mountain spines and their ribs cut the country into segments which are difficult to reach except by sea. The basins between ridges mark natural regions, and the rivers usually give their names to the states of Malaysia.

The heavy tropical rains of the highlands run off steeply over waterfalls and rapids; the rivers then level out at the coastal plains. Rivers are relatively short; the longest in Malaysia, the Rajang, flows 350 miles from its source in the Iran Mountains of Sarawak to the South China Sea. Typical of the river courses of Malaysia, it jogs at right angles around the mountain spurs, over rapids above Belaga at Pelagus, and then runs straight in a long navigable stretch and finally through a myriad of delta meanders into the sea.

Nearing the sea, the drop of the rivers is almost imperceptible. The result is that the lower deltas of the rivers are flooded much of the year. In some places silting is causing the deltas to move out at the rate of thirty feet a century. Often one can walk out great distances in shallow water. Not far from Kuala Lumpur the water is still only 18 feet deep some 26 miles off shore.

The process of land building is assisted by the mangrove tree which thrives in the tidal mudflats of the deltas. Its prop roots branch out from the lower trunk above the highwater line and burrow into the surrounding mud, catching vegetable debris and soil that comes down the river. The mangrove covers only one percent of Malaysia, but it is a conspicuous fringe, a striking sight for visitors arriving in port. As the mangrove advances, behind it follows the nipah palm, growing in the brackish water of the meanders. Its fronds shoot ten or twelve feet straight out of the water. From the leaves of this tree the Malaysians make thatching for roofs and house walls, and weave baskets and bags. Behind the nipah grows the taller nibong palm, used for fishing stakes and poles. Most of the west coast of Malaya is lined with mangrove and nipah, as are the great deltas of Sarawak and much of the east coast of Sabah.

Behind the mangrove and nipah are large freshwater swamps that cover about a tenth of the country. Some of the more fertile clay soils of the swamps have been converted to wet rice plantings, as in Kedah, Kelantan, and the east coast of Sabah. In Sarawak large parts of the swamp are devoted to the sago palm from whose pith flour is made. Undeveloped parts of the swamp contain a variety of valuable timber trees like the meranti and alan.

Most of Malaysia's South China Sea coast is lined with white sand which has been piled up as beaches by the heavy monsoon waves and strong sea currents. Rows of the aru (casuarina) trees, which look something like a feathery pine, line many of the beaches. Farther inland there are often successive rows of dunes, called *permatang*, on which coconut trees grow. Common is the sight of a tall coconut leaning out over the gleaming sand. Off the eastern coasts are coral-girt islands whose beaches have a wonderful profusion of colorful seashells.

Tropical rain forest covers three quarters of Malaysia. Like a great green carpet it spreads from the lowland swamps up to the 9000 foot level. The canopy consists of several layers. At the tallest, reaching some 150 feet above the ground, are the light-hogging giants of the forest; most important of them are the dipterocarps, like meranti, which provide the best timber. Many trees have girths of fifteen feet and rise up as straight smooth pillars for a hundred feet. Some have strong buttresses at the base that support their immense weight. There is a great variety of trees of the fig family, some of which send snaky runners down the sides of another tree, eventually choking the host tree to death like a great boa. Others of the family, like the banyan or India rubber tree, send streamers down from the branches. These take root and swell into trunks, so that a small thicket is created by one tree. There is a profusion of epiphytes living in the branches of the forest trees: orchids of amazing variety of color, lovely ferns, and leafy basketlike plants. There are long trailing lianas like the spiny rattan, from which furniture is made, and the bauhinia whose stems when cut yield pure drinking water.

Under the shady canopy, the forest floor is quite dark. Little grows there except for a few shrubs, seedlings, shade-loving ferns, and low palms like the pinang, from which comes the betel nut for chewing. The luxuriant growth above does not mean that the soil is fertile. Most of the soils of Malaysian uplands are quite poor, except on the slopes of some old volcanoes in the Upper Pahang Valley and Tawau in eastern Sabah.

Above 4000 feet the forest changes. It is some fifteen degrees cooler; cloudiness and rainfall increase. The dipterocarps disappear and are replaced by an immense variety of oaks and laurels. The canopy lowers, and we begin to see tree ferns. Epiphytes become more profuse. Above 9000 feet, on the heights of Mount Kinabalu, for example, there is a mist forest zone where rhododendrons, pines, and other temperate zone plants grow. At the mountain's peak there are no trees at all, but an Alpine-like flora of dwarf shrubs and wind-blown grasses.

Altogether Malaysia has the richest variety of flora in the world, with over 8000 species. In some places over two hundred kinds of plants have been found in an area of only four acres.

The great forest mass that covers Malaysia is occasionally broken by limestone cliffs, the remnants of once submerged seas. These white outcrops are strung like a pearl necklace on the green landscape from Perlis to the northwest down through Ipoh and Kuala Lumpur and back up through Pahang to Kelantan. In a typical landscape these limestones form fantastic and beautiful pinnacles that remind one of a Chinese painting. In the Langkawi Islands the limestone and marble peaks provide some of the most exciting scenery in the world. Elsewhere great caves have been hollowed out by waves or by subterranean rivers. Some of these contain famous Hindu shrines, such as the Batu Caves near Kuala Lumpur or the Buddhist monasteries near Ipoh. Traces of early man have been found in the Niah caves in Sarawak.

The climate of Malaysia, which lies just above the equator, is very warm, muggy, and rainy; there are no extremes of temperature. Aside from local variations of rainfall, most of lowland Malaysia has a similar climate. We can generalize by saying that it has about a hundred inches of rain a year, well distributed, with a tendency toward drier spells in the "summer" months. The sky is more than three-quarters covered with cloud. Almost daily rains keep the temperature down. The mean temperature is only 80°F. It is a rare day that the thermometer goes above ninety, and a rare night below seventy. But it is sticky; the humidity averages about 85 percent. The only variations in this pattern are associated with the monsoon winds.

The basic influencing factor in Malaysia's climate is the two monsoons. These are caused by the pressures over Asia and Australia. When it is winter in the northern hemisphere, there is a high pressure area over China and Siberia, with a corresponding low over the hot deserts of Australia. The winds move from the high pressure areas to the low, southward across the equator. When it is summer in the northern hemisphere, the process is reversed, and the Asian desert low draws the winds northward from the southern continent.

The effect of this is to give Malaysia two seasons. The Northeast monsoon lasts from November to March, as the winds blow down the China Sea. Since this is the greatest sweep of ocean to which the country is exposed, this season is the rainiest. It first strikes the north and east coasts of Malaysia. The east coast of Malaya, all of Sarawak and Brunei, on up to southern Sabah, and the Sandakan Residency get more than 120 inches of rain a year. In Sarawak this season is called the Landas—one of floods. Floods are frequent in these months all along the China Sea; disastrous ones swept Kelantan and Trengganu in 1966.

This is also the coolest time of the year except in the northwest corner of West Malaysia. This area, shielded from the wet monsoon by the Thai mountains, suffers a dry season during the "winter." The little state of Perlis, the island of Langkawi, and the Padang Terap district of north Kedah have long droughts, when the countryside turns gray and dusty; in this season the thermometer may go over a hundred. The highest temperature ever recorded for Malaysia is 103°F., recorded on the island of Langkawi in March 1931.

The "summer" monsoon comes when the winds reverse direction across the equator and blow from the southwest across Indonesia. The high mountains of Sumatra and Borneo catch much of the rain, so that this is a relatively dry season for most of Malaysia. July is usually the driest month throughout the country.

The high mountains receive heavy rainfall during the southwest monsoon. Since they also get the northeast rains, they have the heaviest rainfall in Malaysia. In the mountains of northern Perak, as Maxwell Hill, the most rain in Malaya is recorded, over two hundred inches each year. Even wetter is the Tama Abu Range of Sarawak, where Long Akah on the Baram River averages 236 inches. This is only about 150 miles from the driest place in Malaysia, the Interior District of Sabah between Tenom and

Tambunan, which gets only 60 inches of rain annually because it is shielded by surrounding mountains.

Twice a year, in April and October, when the monsoon winds are changing direction, there are about five to eight weeks of unstable weather. It usually rains more often from cumulus clouds that cover the sky. These great storm clouds, so typical of the tropics, often build up into great mushrooms reaching heights of 30,000 feet within an hour. As they begin to push into the higher cold air they start to form cloud waves, which level off into giant anvils of cumulonimbus. Thunderstorms are more frequent during these times between monsoons, but there can be quiet doldrums of windless weather.

The changes in the direction of the monsoons do not bring very distinct changes in the monotony of warmth and humidity, so that the daily routine of weather is more important than the seasons. Each sunrise is a new springtime, cool and fresh, when work can be done until the sun heats the earth to midday summer. The air is nearly saturated in the morning, but as the temperature rises the humidity falls quickly to only 65 percent at noon. It is common throughout Malaysia for rain to fall between two and four in the afternoon, as the great cumulus clouds pile up moisture until they can hold it no longer. The skies darken and thunder, and suddenly the rain will pour down, often more than three inches an hour. But the rain seldom lasts long; the skies clear quickly. The sun is often shining nearby during a shower, and one city block can be drenched while the next one still bakes in the sun. The rain has cooled the atmosphere, but brought a rise in humidity. The steam can be seen rising from the wet surfaces of the ground and streets. There is a definite relief at the end of the day when the sun goes down and the air cools again.

The most important influence of the climate is its enervating effect. The perpetual mugginess is uncomfortable. Since muscular effort causes perspiration anything energetic is discouraged. This, more than anything else, makes people of all races less active during the heat of the day; heavy work is postponed until the cool of evening and early morning.

Man shares this environment with an extraordinary variety of animals. Nearly two hundred species of mammals have been found in Borneo alone, and there are as many species of snakes in Malaysia. Nearly six hundred species of birds have been found, many of them by American collectors. The identification of insects has barely begun. The Straits of Malacca are one of the greatest fishing grounds of the world, and the sea life varies from huge whales to numerous kinds of shells and corals.

So much of Malaysia is covered with tall forest that half of the animals live in trees. Not only is there a great variety of bats and birds, but squirrels, lemurs, snakes, lizards, geckos, and even frogs glide through the air on special "wings." Most of the animals living in trees are vegetable eaters, but those which live on the ground include predators such as the tiger and bear. Crocodiles, pythons, and cobras are also a danger to man, but the greatest enemies of mankind are the disease-bearing insects. Among these is the anopheles mosquito which carries malaria and filariasis, and the chigger which is host to scrub typhus. The endemic nature of such diseases has been a major factor in the lack of human energy.

Not all animal life is hostile to man. Primitive tribes still live on game like wild pig, deer, and buffalo. The seas teem with edible fish, sharks, shrimp, and lobsters. The beaches have fine clams and edible turtle eggs. The rocks provide juicy oysters and big crabs. On land, the trees often have huge honeycombs hanging from their limbs, and the ceilings of many limestone caves are lined with edible birds nests that have been a delicacy in China for centuries. Man has found no end of joy in the beautiful feathers and beaks of birds like the hornbill. He has stolen the tusks from the elephant and the horn from the rhino until these animals are nearly extinct.

This was Malaysia at the dawn of modern times: a rugged, forest-clad land, with a humid, warm climate. The soils were poor except in a few places, but there was a thin topsoil to permit farming, and enough game and fruit on land and plenty of fish in the sea to support a population comfortably.

2
The Malaysian People

Malaysia is the home of three races: Chinese, Indian, and Malaysian. Each is the proud inheritor of its own ancient civilization. Each has its own virtues and strengths, from which the others have borrowed. Each has weaknesses which the others may perceive with hatred that can cause communal riots and even bloody massacres. Here is a potential melting pot like America, or an explosive mixture. This is the fascination of Malaysia: it could be the scene of bloody race riots and communal slaughter, or it can hold out to the world an example of the future, how three proud cultures can live together in harmony and appreciation of each other.

Malays and related groups are nearly equal in size to the Chinese community; both constitute about 40 percent of the total population of greater Malaysia. But the Chinese so predominate in Singapore that it seems a Chinese city. The Malays and related groups are about half of the population of both Malaya and of the nation of Malaysia (see Appendix, Table 2). The Indians make up about 10 percent of the population of greater Malaysia.

In his study of national character of Englishmen, Frenchmen, and Spaniards, the Spanish diplomat and poet Salvador de Madariaga perceived that every nationality accentuated one facet of a universal human character. It helps to understand some of the differences of the Malaysian races to say that the Malay shows a Latin temperament, the Chinese is more like a north European, and the Indian has a French touch.

The Malay

As with the Spanish, the closest Malay social unit is the family. An old Malay proverb says, "What good is the thatch on someone else's roof?"

In the Malay home the first thing a child is taught is that he must not dishonor his family. His father says: "Spit in the air, and it will land on your nose." He learns a dozen such proverbs which remind him not to talk about what goes on in the family, lest he disgrace it.

Next to the family, the most important social unit is the kampong, or village. A Malay's parents will want him to marry within the village, and eventually to return there if he must travel. Malays cannot be easily persuaded to join the diplomatic service; it is almost like going into exile.

Though the community is the center of life, the Malay does not want to be stacked on top of his neighbor like the Chinese. One of the underlying causes of the terrible Singapore riots in 1964 is believed to have been the attempt to move Malays out of their single-family houses into apartments. The Chinese, like the New Yorker or Londoner, may feel comfortable in close quarters, but the Malay insists on privacy.

If the community is less important than the family, the state is a concentric ring even farther removed. The Malay feels some vague loyalty to a ruler like the sultan of Pahang or Brunei. This attachment to the local state is like the Spaniard's—it makes federation the only natural political system; a sense of nationhood has been difficult to create. Before 1957 there never had been a Malay nation, only local sultanates and British colonial inventions called Federated Malay States and the like. The problem of loyalty is even greater with Malaysia, a state created only in 1963. Beyond the nation, the Malay has a vague humanistic sympathy with mankind as a whole, but the world is a long way from the kampong.

While the Malay is individualistic, he is not egotistical. There is a strong sense of equality expressed in his proverb "When we stand, we're equally high; when we sit we're equally low."

The most controversial, and probably the most misunderstood, part of the Malay's character is his attitude toward work. The debate has raged for years between the European planter who firmly insists that the Malay is lazy, particularly compared with the Chinese, and the Malay's defender who points to the debilitating climate, the endemic diseases like malaria, or the lack of incentives in the economic system. The apologist may deny the accusation entirely, pointing to the fact that Malay tradesmen are up before dawn while the European is still abed. By the time the vigorous European gets to work he sees the Malay relaxing for a chat. In the heat of day only "mad dogs and Englishmen" are charging about while the Malay sleeps, a habit that most old-timers in the tropics sensibly adopted. And, the defender continues, the Malay puts in another day's work in the afternoon. Just imagine the effort of plowing a flooded rice paddy with the mud up to your hips and the equatorial sun beating down on your head. Or try hauling in a net with thousands of pounds of fish. Then decide if the Malay is lazy.

Both sides miss the point. Even the Malays admit that they are often lethargic. *Utusan Melayu*, the leading Malay language daily of Malaysia, points this out periodically. "Malays customarily blame [the government] for their backwardness but seldom blame themselves . . . The theory that Malay backwardness is due to imperialism, capitalism, or foreigners in this country is 'stale' . . . A lot of opportunities are open to Malays . . . Are the imperialists to be blamed if the Malays themselves do not want to make use of such opportunities?" "Why is the Malay such a spendthrift?" asked the paper a few days earlier.[1] "It is difficult to contradict Malaysian cabinet member Ghaffar Baba when he says Malays spend more on wedding ceremonies, feasts, and the like than on the education of their children . . . It is this harmful mentality that our leaders should try to eradicate among the Malays."[2]

[1] Jan. 14, 1966; Dec. 30, 1965. Translations here and elsewhere unless otherwise specified are my own.

[2] *Utusan Melayu*, Dec. 30, 1965.

The prime minister of the state of Negri Sembilan, a distinguished Malay physician, recently listed the four ills that hinder rural progress: poverty, ill health, illiteracy, and the care-free attitude of the Malays.[3]

The same debate over conscientiousness will be heard about Mexican and Spanish peasants. Why is it always *mañana*—tomorrow? The reason, de Madariaga points out, is that the Spaniard lets life flow quietly onward until something arouses him to effort. It is the same with the Malay. He is content to enjoy life—the things that really count—his family, his children playing in the yard, a chat with friends on the front porch. The Malay enjoys a walk, the pleasure of which his language expresses so well: "to eat the wind." There is an unhurriedness expressed in many proverbs like: "If you take long strides you'll tear your pants." One observer called this attitude "tidapathy," from the Malay expression "tidak apa"—"who cares?"[4] Why not enjoy living? God gives abundant rain and food, and seldom lets anyone die of hunger.

Behind this carelessness is a great deal of fatalism which is reinforced by the Islamic religion to which almost all Malays belong. The very word Islam means surrender, to God. Religion really affirms what the Malay sees by living close to Nature: that there is very little he can do to change it.

There is an apparent contradiction in the behavior of both Malay and Spaniard when they are aroused. Once stimulated they go to extremes. The Malay proverb goes: "If you bathe, get wet; if you use ink, make it black." The history of the Atjehnese fight for independence, and the Indonesian's persistence in guerrilla warfare show how Malays can be strongly aroused to group dynamism. Individually, this has its counterpart in amok behavior. His hostility generated, the man must kill, even though it means his own death. Usually what has aroused him is an irreparable insult to his pride, that motivating force in Malay character. Rather dead than disgraced, says the Malay proverb.

The same sudden reaction can be seen in Malay politics. Out of a clear sky comes a dramatic and generous proposal that Malay-

[3] Dato Dr. Mohammed Said, in *Straits Times*, March 16, 1966.
[4] J. R. Audy, "Family Life," *Malayan Historical Journal*, 1.1 (May 1954): 47.

sia be formed. Equally dramatic and surprising was the sudden decision that Singapore and Malaysia could no longer live together. It was like a Malay marriage gone wrong: "If the thread snaps you can tie it, but charcoal is broken forever."

The important thing is not to misjudge Malay tranquillity. It can be turned to destruction as in Indonesia recently, or harnessed for power. It is this strength that the present leaders of Malaysia have so successfully directed into a constructive program of national development.

To the man of feelings, the things of the spirit are all-important and govern his life. Thus, the three things that count most in the world of the Malay are his traditional customs, his religion, and his means of expression through oral and written language.

Many observers have noticed how attached the Malays are to their traditions. Of course, all societies have their rituals and customs which bind individuals together. But in Malay society the force of conservatism seems particularly strong. The individual Malay will affirm how important *adat*, the body of custom, is to him. The old proverb goes: "Dead we are wrapped by earth; alive we are wrapped by custom."

At the heart of Malay custom is a deeply held belief in the spiritual quality of things. We can readily recognize a similarity to the medieval European world view before it became permeated with the physical explanation of all phenomena. One modern Malay professor observes that "the Malays are as much concerned with symbols as with reality."[5]

Fundamental to Malay ideas is the belief in *semangat*, or soulforce. This the Malay finds present in all things, both living and dead. He finds it in inanimate things like iron, which gives soulforce to the Malay knife. Semangat is found in rocks, trees, waterfalls, and other natural objects. Tall isolated trees, the *pokok rajah*—kings of the jungle—are often left standing when the forest is cleared because no workmen can be found to risk offending the spirit of the trees by cutting them down. Soon small spirit shrines will appear at the base of these giants. Above all, semangat

5 Wan Abdul Hamid, "Religion and Culture," in Wang Gungwu, *Malaysia: A Survey* (New York: Praeger, 1964), p. 180.

is present in rice, the staff of life. Malays, like all related Malaysians, carefully reap the heads of grain with a special knife, the *tuai,* which they hide in the palm of the hand so as not to frighten the soul of the plant.

Semangat is found also in parts of the body, even in discarded parts such as hair, fingernails, spittle, sweat, and placenta. There is spirit in one's shadow, in footsteps, in the water in which one has washed, even in one's spoken name. Thus, it is believed that another person can influence your actions by performing rituals over your possessions or traces.

It is thought that one's spirit can take off in dreams, as well as in death. Belief in ghosts, called *hantu,* is widespread even among educated Malays. This is one belief most criticized by Westerners (who forget about the large number of haunted houses in England). Malay ghosts can be both good and bad. Among the most dangerous is the *pontianak,* the ghost of a woman who has died in childbirth.

One story that had wide currency in the national capital last year shows the prevalence of such beliefs in a modern society. A motorist offered a ride to a pretty girl hitchhiking on the highway and drove her home. Finding that she had left her sweater in the car, he later called at her house. There he found her family mourning for her death, which they said happened days before. Obviously it was a ghost that he had picked up.

The Malays will give so much evidence of ghosts that it is impossible for a Westerner to disprove their existence. Objects that have disappeared unaccountably are too numerous. Too many people can tell you of objects that have flown off shelves in this earthquake-free country. Too many people have become sick or insane after an encounter with a spirit, or through the magic of an enemy, or because they have defied the prohibitions of custom.

In almost every Malay community there is a *bomoh* or *pawang,* someone who can deal with ghosts. He may use ordinary herbs and incantations, the latter interlarded with Arabic words as a concession to Islam. The expert Malay magician conducts a seance with incense, wands, and drumbeats. He stares into the flame of a candle to bring him into touch with the spirit world. The bomoh is called in for the blessing of the crop planting, the harvest, and for many other traditional ceremonies.

The belief in spirits, which is held by all Malaysian peoples, has been strongly reinforced by borrowings from other cultures, particularly Indian and Arabian. "Scratch a Malay Muslim and you will find a Hindu; scratch the Hindu and you will find an animist." This is not to say that the Malays are not serious about their religion—quite the contrary—but they are exceptionally tolerant and adaptive. Like many cultures, the Malay is syncretic. The layers of culture are probably more than three, but one is constantly impressed with the depth and persistence of the basic core of Malaysian beliefs.

Of the many outside cultures that have touched Malaysia, the Malays have known the Indian longest, for about 2000 years, and the influence of Hinduism on their beliefs and ceremonies is marked. What seems to have appealed to the Malays about Indian culture were its spiritual qualities and its explanation of the universe.

A large part of the attraction of Islam as it was brought from India must have been its mystical quality. It was introduced largely by Sufi mystics, who also brought with them many Hindu accretions such as pantheism, the worship of saints and their graves, and mystical incantations. These features undoubtedly made the acceptance of Islam easier, as did the Islamic tolerance of native customs as long as they did not conflict with its fundamental tenets. Early Christianity of course found this same secret, permitting such pagan rites as Easter.

The five pillars of Islam are the supports of Malay religious life: profession, prayer, fasting, pilgrimage, and almsgiving. Profession, or conversion to Islam, involves learning the basic tenets and prayers in Arabic, and declaring one's surrender to the faith. After induction, one continues the study of the Koran, and is recognized by wearing a velvet cap, the *songkok* or *kopiah,* usually black or a dark color.

The second requirement of Islam is the *do'a* or prayer. This is performed five times daily, at dawn, noon, late afternoon, sunset, and before the night's sleep. Friday afternoon at one o'clock each

adult, male Muslim who is able prays at the town mosque. This
is a rectangular building, usually open-sided for coolness. The
mosque is oriented so that a little apsidal niche (the mihrab)
about the height of a man jets out of the wall facing toward
Mecca, which in Malaysia is slightly north of west. Prayers are
performed facing the mihrab and Mecca. The interior of the
mosque is quite plain, with prayer rugs on the floor; the only
furniture is a minbar or pulpit at the right of the mihrab. The
imam stands in the minbar to read from the Koran. The men sit
crosslegged in the main hall with caps on; women are segregated
behind a screen and wear a special white prayer robe.

Outside the mosque there is a minaret used for the call to
prayer, now frequently done over a loudspeaker. In front, on the
east side of the mosque, there is a basin of running water where
the faithful wash themselves before entering the mosque for
prayer. The ritual requires three washings, first the face, hands,
and wrists, then the forehead and top of the hair, and finally
elbows, feet and ankles. On the front of the mosque is usually a
veranda from the eaves of which a long drum may be suspended;
this is beaten for summons to prayer.

The third requirement of a good Muslim is observance of
Puasa, the fast during the month of Ramadan, currently falling in
December. The majority of Malays observe it seriously. They are
not allowed to eat, drink, or smoke between sunrise and sunset of
this month; they are not supposed to swallow anything, even their
own saliva. After prayers the fast is broken by a big meal at 7:30
p.m. Food is eaten again before morning prayers (about 3:45 a.m.)
and this must sustain one all day. In the tropical heat such a long
time without food, added to the lack of sleep, leaves the fasters
exhausted. It is the merciful custom during Ramadan to stop
work by midday.

The end of the fasting month is the occasion for rejoicing. After
the twentieth night houses are lighted with oil lamps, which have
been replaced in the towns with Christmas tree lights. At this time
the women start preparing sweet cakes and rice for guests. The
fast finally ends with the biggest holiday in the Malay year, Hari
Raya Puasa. The day starts with bathing, prayers, and forgiveness

of one's elders. The family head pays his compulsory tax, the *fitrah,* a gallon of rice, or about U.S. thirty-three cents a person. The house is cleaned and painted. Everyone dons new clothes and goes calling on friends, bringing each a little gift. Enemies are forgiven, families reunite, and there is general joy and celebration for this happiest time of year.

The fourth demand of Islam, the hajj, or pilgrimage to Mecca, is obviously difficult to perform, since the Holy Land is 4000 miles away. However, it is made easier by government subsidy of annual pilgrimage ships to Jidda. Most Malay men have retired before they have saved enough money for the passage for themselves and their wives, whom they often take. The man who has made the hajj dons a white cap, which entitles him to special respect from his fellow villagers.

The fifth duty of the Muslim is to give his tithe, or *zakat.* This is collected by the state Religious Affairs Department and distributed to the poor and needy. This agency also supervises mosques, religious schools, and the Muslim courts (shari'a) which handle such matters as problems of marriage between Muslims.

The only part of the Malay wedding ceremony that is Muslim is the oath taken at betrothal and registration on wedding night, both performed before the *kathi,* or religious registrar. Custom requires that the spouse become Muslim if outside the faith. In the case of a woman this is simple enough, but for a man the laborious study of the Koran discourages intermarriage.

Although Muslim men are permitted to take four wives, polygamy is extremely rare in Malaysia because Malays take quite seriously the requirement that they treat wives equally. A minister of finance recently remarked: "One wife is an expense; two wives are a luxury." Another factor in reducing polygamy is the ease with which divorce is obtained, at least by the husband. All he need do is say to his wife on three separate occasions: "I divorce you." In general, Malay couples are probably faithful to each other; adultery is frowned upon, and is severely punished in the rural areas.

The various family ceremonies of the Malay have a religious

character. At birth, the child's father whispers his Arabic name in his ear. Circumcision is an important puberty rite, and marked by eating food giving life energy. The graves of holy men, known as *keramat*, are visited by people of many religions, who come with offerings of food and incense to the spirit of the saint. Flowers and strange pebbles are tied to the keramats, offerings that go back to Hindu rites and beyond to ancient Malaysian propitiation of spirits. There is, of course, belief in life after death.

With few exceptions the Malays live close to nature. Even in the large cities of Singapore and Kuala Lumpur, the Malays will be found living by preference in tree-shaded rural-style houses, where possible by the banks of a flowing stream. About 90 percent of Malaysia's Malays still live in rural areas, and usually close to the sea. The Malay settlements, or kampongs, reflect the influence of water. The largest water settlement, Kampong Ayer, literally "Water Town," is in old Brunei, where 16,000 people live over the water. This oriental Venice is a remarkable sight. Along the waterways are shops, schools, government buildings, and small factories. The houses are linked together by boardwalks, some leading to the mainland. Others can be reached only by boat.

The pattern of Kampong Ayer is repeated on a smaller scale all along the coasts of Malaysia, where Malays have built their houses on shallow places in the tidal rivers. Along the sandy beaches, facing the sea, settlements string out in a line along the dunes, under the shade of the coconut palms. Inland, the kampongs wind up the higher banks of the rivers. Even away from the rivers, on the rice plains, the villages sit on slight rises just above the flood plain.

The Malay house reflects the water environment. It is always built on log stilts about the height of a man. The base is protected from termites by a block of laterite or concrete. The floor is well above the flood level, away from wild animals and ground insects. The elevation also allows the breezes to blow through. An easy way to dispose of refuse and dishwater is between the floorboards. Some Malays use the area under the house for domestic animals such as chickens. Everyone uses it like a basement storeroom for ladders, fruit-picking poles, and boats. Or it can serve as a work-shop as it does for the batik makers and brass smiths of Treng-ganu.

The upper part of the house is made simply from local mate-rials. It is always a one-story timber frame, rectangular in shape. The pointed roof used to be covered with palm thatch that had to be replaced every few years, but lately people have been using corrugated iron, which eventually rusts in an ugly fashion. There is great local variation in roof forms, usually reflecting the tribal origin of the people, such as the horned roof of the Minangkabau of Negri Sembilan. Sides of Malay houses are made of single planks of bamboo woven in a variety of attractive patterns, though good weaving is now getting rare. Windows that close with shutters at night and siesta time stand just above the floor. The openings above the windows and doors are often carved in attractive floral patterns.

The interior consists of two or more rooms, one a living room, the rest bedrooms. There is little furniture, since people sit on the floor, having removed their shoes at the foot of the steps. The floors are covered with finely woven pandan mats.

The kitchen is tacked onto the back, often as a separate shed. The hearth is a raised clay platform on which a charcoal fire is built. The smoke goes up into the roof and finds its way out through the open eaves.

The staple of the Malay diet is boiled rice, to which one adds usually one dish of boiled or curried vegetable, fish, or meat. Dried fish, particularly minnows, add a nice salty flavor and a crunchy texture. Chicken, home-raised, is the most common meat; goat meat and beef from the water buffalo are eaten on special occasions. Frying is done in coconut oil and steaming in banana leaves. Spices are used frequently; the universal seasoning is red chili, usually mixed into a paste with soy sauce. Another favorite flavoring is *blachang*, fish or shrimp paste of sandwich-spread con-sistency and a smell stronger than Limburger.

Food is usually eaten while one is seated on the floor; men are served before women and children. Utensils are used only to ladle the food onto the rice. The Malay eats with his right hand, the left hand being considered unclean (for the same reason, the Malay gives and accepts gifts with the right hand). Before and after meals the hands are carefully washed; a belch is a polite way of expressing enjoyment of the meal.

Food probably sets the Malays apart from the other races more effectively than any other custom. Of all the observances of the Muslims, the Malay most universally obeys the prohibition of eating pork. This goes to the extent of not dining in restaurants where that meat is served. The religious requirement of slaughter of animals by cutting their throats is also taken seriously by older Muslims.

Other prohibitions of Islam are observed with less care. They will not touch a wet dog, nor allow it to lick them, but may have dogs about the house. Gambling is frowned upon by the orthodox, but is widely practiced. Ways have been found around the prohibition against taking interest on loans, and the ban on alcohol is flouted by many devout Muslims.

The exterior of the Malay's house reflects his appreciation of nature. There is usually a veranda in front, where the family relaxes in the evening. Typically, the house is surrounded by flowers and colorful leafy plants. The unplanted parts of the yard are neatly swept if not covered with grass. Fruit trees interspersed with coconuts might surround the house. These trees give welcome shade and provide the family with variety in its diet; they might include several kinds of citrus like the lime, orange, and grapefruit; the guava, jackfruit, mango, rambutan, duku, or mangosteen, and above all the favorite durian, which smells rotten to most Western noses, but which the Malays all think tastes like ambrosia. Near the Malay house are small garden plots for vegetables like chilies, sweet potatoes, beans, corn, okra, peanuts, cassava, and other things like sugar cane, bananas, and papayas. This home production makes the Malay household nearly self-sufficient in food. In addition they require rice, which many Malays grow. They may buy salt and spices. This self-sufficiency is the main reason that income statistics are so low for the Malays.

Lush vegetation around the Malay home gives it a fair amount of privacy. Most houses are set well back from the road or river, so there is a big front yard. A path will lead down to the river or well where the family bathes. The Malays are quite modest about bathing. Men and women wash separately, and care is taken that the body is never exposed naked. The one piece sarong worn by men and women is loosened in the water and the body washed beneath it. Children bathe naked. The family washing is also done in the river, and no one seems to worry that everyone upstream has his privy built over the river.

Although the Malay does not want to live on top of his neighbor, he is gregarious. Custom requires that the Malay help his neighbor, particularly in need, and that he live in peace and harmony with him. Though property is individually owned, community members are bound to work for the general welfare through *gotong-royong,* or cooperative labor. This may be for the building of community public works like dikes, paths, a mosque or town hall, or for individual projects like harvesting rice or putting up a house.

Matters of communal interest are discussed at length by the men in the town meeting (and at home by the women, who may really have the final say). In discussion an attempt is made to reach a unanimous decision so that everyone is satisfied, rather than imposing the will of the majority upon the minority. This concept of universal harmony strikes the Westerner as inefficient and favoring obstruction. It takes longer to reach a decision, of course, but in Malay life there is plenty of time for discussion of important things.

The leader of the Malay community is far from an autocrat. The headman is elected, usually from among the sons of the previous one, on the basis of merit and ability. A following develops around him; this will dissolve when he dies. The many proverbs like "If the chicken dies, so do its ticks" reflect the personalism of Malay politics, like the following of the Spanish caudillo.

Malay politics is a drama. The leader acts out a part that is expected of him. At the highest level, the sultan performs a number of dramatic ceremonies that go back to the propitiation of the spirits of the universe and the gods. A subject owes loyalty to the sovereign as the mediator of the universe. The basic political ethic is loyalty, shown in a dozen ways in the national epic the *Sejarah Melayu* and in histories like the *Pasai Chronicle.*

Social relationships are governed by elaborate rituals and courtesies. An important point of Malay hospitality is to offer a visitor something to eat and drink or, failing that, a chew of betel. Chewing this nut of the pinang tree is a widespread Malay custom, and special implements, often of ornate brass or silver, are kept in most houses. The routine is important. The host takes from a tray a leaf of pungent *sirih* and spreads on it a bit of lime (the mineral, not the fruit). To this he adds a pinch of pipe tobacco and gambier and a snip of the rind of the betel, which he has cut off with special clippers. Folded up, this morsel is popped into the mouth and chewed until the lime mixes well with the gambier to form a crimson red juice. One can spit any excess out the front door if he is lucky enough to be close, for the pungent mixture stimulates the saliva. The effect on the teeth of prolonged chewing of betel is disastrous. At first the betel forms a brown stain; the lime eats away the enamel, so that older Malays often have only ugly stumps of teeth. Although Malays habitually wash their mouths when they bathe, dental care is poor.

Perhaps the best indication of the Malay's enjoyment of the simple things of life is his clear pleasure in having children around him. Little children are really loved, and "the more the better" rule is beginning to cause a population explosion. If a Malay cannot have children of his own, he often adopts them. He will gladly do this as an obligation to relatives; for his own pleasure he might take in orphans and unwanted children of any race. According to Western notions Malay children are terribly spoiled. Fathers notoriously pamper their toddlers. Permissiveness begins with weaning, which is left up to the child, and is therefore often late. Children are seldom punished, and then not corporally.

Because of the Muslim restriction on pictorial representations, Malay arts are primarily practical and domestic. The most characteristic work of art is the *kris,* or dagger, which is believed to possess a soul or spirit of its own. The hilt has a vaguely human resemblance. Sometimes it will clearly represent a Hindu demon carved in wood or ivory. On some hilts the figure is merely a stylized head, which appears to be doubled over its shoulders in pain; this is called "the Javanese with a fever." The shape of the blade is usually wavy, the odd number of curves having a special magical significance. The beautifully laminated knife is cared for as though it did have a soul. Almost any Malay can tell you stories he has heard about the magical uses for the kris: these daggers have foretold the deaths of their owners, and warned of impending disasters. A kris is truly a piece of art, especially if the base of the hilt has precious stones set in gold, or the scabbard is made of silver or ivory. It is part of the Malay national costume. Worn by the sultans and the Malaysian chief of state, it becomes part of the royal regalia, with all of its traditional legitimizing function.

Brass objects are often invested with special spiritual qualities too, particularly the brass cannons with flared muzzle made by the craftsmen of Brunei for use aboard small sailing craft of pirates and traders. A well-made cannon that has struck down several enemies at a great distance might well take on a certain magical quality. But the remarkable thing about these guns is their ornamentation; baroque filigree sometimes covers the whole barrel. The same Malay brass founders make great rice pots, teapots, candelabra, lamps, and all kinds of objects that are so important for the social ceremonies of Malay life, such as the betel sets, with the lime boxes, holders for sirih leaves, and the snippers. These pieces are treasured and passed from generation to generation.

The remarkable thing about Malay arts is how much they are a part of the life of the people. This reminds one of the paradox which de Madariaga found in Spanish art. Artistry is individual, yet has a distinctly national character. A fine example is the typical Malay art of the batik. This textile design, which probably originated in Java, is done as a household industry in Kelantan and Trengganu. The cotton cloth is printed in the age-old method with hot wax by a handcarved woodblock. When the cloth is soaked in the dye vat, only the unwaxed portions are colored. The wax is then washed out, and another design and color can be printed on the same cloth. The process may be repeated as many times as desired. The finest batiks use only the traditional dark blue and brown colors. The woodblock designs often follow traditional patterns such as the mythical *garuda* bird of Hindu mythology.

Skillful handweaving is done in the countryside. One of the best fabrics is the *kain songket,* the handwoven silk laced with silver thread. The colors of the silk are black, blue, green, and purple. This is still woven in Brunei, Kota Bharu, and Kuala Trengganu for royal weddings. There are dozens of other kinds of Malay handwoven cloth, done by a number of ingenious processes—some by separate dyeing of each thread, some by printing metal leaf designs, and others by embroidery. Unfortunately, many of these types of weaving are dying out because the modern Malay girls have little interest in the skills of their mothers.

In many parts of Malaysia, the people still make their own baskets of the durable leaves of pandan. Fine mats are woven to cover the floors; and other utilitarian things such as purses, sun hats, and pouches are made. Occasionally one comes across one of the strange animal figures woven for the celebration of the rice harvest, a reminder of some pre-Hindu custom of propitiating the rice spirit.

Islam has discouraged the pictorial arts by its prohibition of idols, but some interesting figure painting has survived in the making of leather puppets used to tell the drama of the great Hindu epic of the Ramayana. Much patience is required to cut and punch out the intricate design of the traditional figures so they will be recognized in silhouette. Though the audience sees only the profile, the Malay artist paints his puppets in bright colors.

Malay woodcarving is often associated with some ancient belief. The fishing boats of Trengganu still carry the head of a strange long-necked bird. Until a few years ago a tremendous amount of work went into carving giant *garuda* birds to be caried in ceremonial processions. Palanquins and thrones also required the skills of the woodcarvers. The demand is declining, however, and these old arts are being lost. Much skill used to go into the decoration of houses, particularly of royalty. Since most of these were made of wood, there are few antique examples left, but one can still see the old palace in the Negri Sembilan capital of Sri Menanti, and the old public buildings in the Kedah capital of Alor Star.

Some of the rural Malay's best artistic skill comes out in adult games. One sport involves spinning large tops. Wooden tops as large as eight inches across are set spinning by a contestant; his rival tries to knock one or more of these from the ring by casting in his own top which must remain spinning. These tops are hand carved from fine woods. In some communities the men build giant kites that are lofted high into the sky. No plain diamonds are these, but artfully decorated with birds and designs and carry musical whistles.

The Malay language is particularly musical because of a high proportion of vowels, and it is well adapted to rhyming. Indeed poetry is a common literary form. At almost any public occasion someone composes a *pantun*. This is a four-line poem to be recited by two persons. The first two lines make some observation about nature, which one person expresses succinctly. The second person (usually of the opposite sex) finishes the pantun with some mundane subject which does not have to be related directly to the first two lines, but often alludes to them. For instance:

> Through driving rain sail for the isle,
> While flying ants swarm in the well.
> Whilst we have life, let's jest awhile;
> For, when we're dead, alone we swell.[6]

How well this expresses the Malay philosphy of life too. A kind of fatalism gets the response of *carpe diem*. Most pantuns are on the subject of love, which plays an important part in Malay thinking—happy love, unrequited love, unfaithful love, lovers reunited in the spirit world, love in all its myriad complications. Malay literature is full of the emotion of love. The chief of all Malay heroes, Hang Tuah, was a great lover, as was one of the most famous kings, Sultan Mansur.

6 A. W. Hamilton, *Malay Pantuns* (Singapore: Eastern Universities Press, 1959), p. 80.

One might expect that a people which enjoys expressing itself would find pleasure in theatricals, and so it is with the Malays. The most popular drama form is the *wayang kulit,* or leather show. The cast of the play is about a hundred leather puppets manipulated between a light and a white screen. The audience thus sees only the silhouette and shadow of the puppets. The storyteller recites the episodes of the Hindu Ramayana and imitates the voices of the various characters. The audience, old and young alike, loves the mimicry of the clowns and monkey gods; the whole village will stay up all night to listen to the tale they have heard many times.

There is also a traditional Malay *wayang orang,* performed by humans dressed in ancient Hindu costumes. More common is the folk drama, *ma'yong,* which combines dancing and music with a story. The Malay's sense of drama becomes apparent when he imitates—a monkey, a fool, an old woman. Often two men will get onto the stage and improvise a burlesque of two women or a wife and a henpecked husband.

The Malays have evolved their own musical instruments. The most famous is the *gamelan,* an orchestra of brass gongs ranging from the size of a teacup to that of a wagon wheel, played by groups of from one to twelve musicians with remarkable coordination. A sense of rhythm is highly developed in the Malay.

Malays love to dance, and do it with a natural grace. The most popular mixed dances today are the *joget* and *ronggeng,* where the couples follow each other's movements but never touch. There are solo dances by both sexes, and unison dances of one sex, like *tari piring,* where girls holding lighted candles on saucers spin around without putting out the lights. The favorite men's dance demonstration is the *bersilat,* a highly stylized demonstration of self-defense in which one man fends off another's attacks with arm, foot, and kris.

Most typical of the Malay sports is cock fighting, for blood and money. A Malay man will lavish endless hours upon some beautiful rooster that he has raised like a child. He will carry it for miles along some dusty road in a wicker cage to the scene of a fight. In the ring a sharp knife is tied to the rooster's spur, which the animal should bring down on his opponent's neck to win. The other blood sport of the Malay, which goes far back into history, is one he shares with the Spaniard: bullfighting.

Groups Related to the Malays

Despite minor cultural differences, ethnologists are continually impressed with the essential unity of the Malay-related peoples, not only in their common physical character, but in the similarity of the basic cultural patterns and languages. This is true not only in Malaysia but in the whole archipelago that stretches from the Philippines to the ends of Indonesia.

The Malay-like peoples are racially indistinguishable from Indonesians who have migrated for centuries across the Straits of Malacca, the Java and Celebes Seas, and the mountains of Borneo. Tom Harrisson, a former director of the Sarawak Museum who has lived among the Borneo peoples for years, has said: "If you mix up Kayan, Iban, Melanau, Dusun, Land Dayak, Malay and Sibu Chinese, take all young men of the same age, and line them up in an identity parade, it is doubtful that any anthropologist in the world could guess their 'races' even fifty percent correctly."[7] There is no such thing as a pure Malay race, any more than there are pure Anglo-Saxons. But there is a Malay type that is distinguishable racially from the Indians and Chinese. The main difference is skin color. The local variant of the Genesis story is that when God made the first man, he baked him too long, and turned out the Indian. On the second try he undercooked him, and made the Chinese. The third time he reached perfect golden brown, the Malay. Indeed, the Malays and their cousins are very handsome people. They are shorter than most Europeans. They have round faces, small noses, generous lips, teeth that stand out slightly, and dark brown eyes with only a trace of the Mongoloid eye-fold. Their hair is glossy black and straight; the men have light hair growth on their faces.

[7] Tom Harrisson, "The Peoples of North and West Borneo," in Wang Gungwu, *Malaysia*, p. 170.

We cannot possibly describe here all the bewildering variety of cultural variations, but it is important that we indicate the names and characteristics of some of the Malay cousins. Most of these are found in Borneo.

The largest group in East Malaysia is the Dayaks of Sarawak. The total of 300,000 is divided into two major tribes, Land Dayaks and Ibans or so-called Sea Dayaks. The Ibans were misnamed Sea Dayaks by the British who encountered their forces at the mouths of the Borneo rivers; they are actually land dwellers. Iban oral genealogies relate that, like the Land Dayaks, they migrated fairly recently to the Second and Third Divisions[8] from Indonesian Borneo. They have much in common with the Malays. Their language is a dialect of Malay.

Ibans could not be distinguished from Malays if it were not for the fish-tailed "T" the Iban men tattoo on their throats. The other thing that separates the Iban from the Malay is religion, for few have been converted to Islam. They still follow a way of life that is probably like that of most Malay peoples at an earlier stage of history. They live mainly by cultivating rice on dry hillsides, rather than by the more advanced irrigation method, although some Ibans have planted the wet rice, or paddy, in swampy areas.

Like most Borneo peoples the Ibans live in "longhouses," which are communal apartments with units facing a common veranda. Iban communities are democratically presided over by longhouse chieftains who are elected on merit. The magician is important in the Iban society: his role is to deal with the spirit world which surrounds men. Festivals typically include wine drinking, offerings to the spirits, singing, playing of music on gongs and drums, and elaborate dances. Like many of the Indonesian peoples the Ibans were once headhunters. Grisly trophies still can be seen hanging from the rafters of some of their longhouses. This practice seems to have stemmed from the superstition that a killer acquired the strength of his enemy by taking the seat of his soul, his head. Headhunting was offered as proof of a young man's

---

[8] Sarawak is divided politically into five Divisions, numbered from west to east, as they were acquired by the Brooke family.

masculinity. Since the suppression of fighting and headhunting Iban aggressiveness and dynamism has been turned to politics. For all their bumptiousness, the Ibans are well-liked for their good humor, generosity, and hospitality.

Milder in disposition are the Ibans' peaceful cousins the Land Dayaks. By reputation more easy-going, they nevertheless also engaged in headhunting for ritual purposes until recently. They are fewer in number, only 60,000 against the 240,000 Ibans. They have settled rather recently in the First (westernmost) Division of Sarawak after coming over the border from Indonesian Borneo. There are minor differences in house arrangement, dress, and ritual, but the Land Dayaks share most of the basic customs of Borneo Malaysians: cultivation of rice, the longhouse, the magician to exorcise illness, and respect for the spirits of nature.

In Sabah most of the non-Muslim peoples belong to the Dusun-Murut group, which numbers about 175,000 people. The largest tribe by far is the 150,000 Kadazans or Dusuns. Since dusun means orchard, which carries the connotation of "hick," some prefer to be called Kadazan. Though far removed geographically from the Dayaks of Sarawak, this tribe has much in common in house style, agricultural methods, religion, amusements; and they were also once headhunters. Closely related to them are the 28,000 Muruts of the highlands of Sabah and Sarawak. They live by hunting and farming hillsides that are abandoned when soil fertility is exhausted. This way of life may represent a primitive stage of society that preceded the Dusuns, for many of their customs are similar. A smaller tribe of northern Sarawak, the Kelabits, are also related to the Dusun-Murut group.

Then there are the para-Malays, about 220,000 people who are so closely related to the Malays that they would be indistinguishable except for variant languages or customs. They can be found in the interior of Malaya and along the coasts of Eastern and Western Malaysia. The largest tribe is the 60,000-member Bajau. The Bajaus were once sea nomads and pirates. Their claim of descent from a Borneo prince and the daughter of a Johore sultan suggests that they were Borneo peoples who wandered across the

South China Sea. Now quietly settled along the coasts of Sabah, they have taken up fishing and cattle raising. In the latter work they ride little Spanish ponies as skillfully as any Argentine gaucho. The Bajaus are Muslims and follow many Malay customs. Sabah has other near-Malay tribes, some which are purely local, such as the Tidong and Orang Sungei, and others which extend into the southern Philippines, like the once piratical Suluks, Ilanuns, and Bisayas.

Sarawak has a large quasi-Malay tribe almost as big as the Bajaus: 45,000 Melanaus. Most of them too are now Muslim, and have adopted Malay customs, but show interesting traces of the pre-Islamic practices of the Malays. They live in the northern lowland areas of Sarawak, earning a livelihood from fishing and making sago palm flour. The thing that distinguishes them from the Malays is their language, which is closely related to that of the Kenyah-Kayan tribes of the interior. The Kenyah-Kayans, who number about 16,000, are fine artists and ex-headhunters.

Brunei also has its para-Malay group in the Kedayans, who have about 28,000 members in all three Borneo states. Their traditions state that they come from Java; their customs indicate close relation to the Malays. Malaya's counterpart of the para-Malays of Borneo are the 30,000 aboriginal Malays. They are divided into a great number of tribes, ranging from converts to Islam and Malay customs, to pagans who live as sea gypsies or migrating rice cultivators of the interior. But basically all are Malay types whose tribal customs suggest the origins of many Malay institutions and the endless ingenuity of man in devising infinite variants on the basic cultural themes of appeasing spirits, conducting a meeting or wedding, burying a great chief, or weaving a basket.

There are some truly primitive tribes in Malaysia which may represent an earlier stage of civilization or a wave of peoples who migrated before the present Malays. In Malaya there are 60,000 Senoi who have many of the basic customs of the Malay-related peoples: the world of spirits, the medicine man, migratory rice cultivation, houses on stilts, and so forth. In Sarawak there are

4800 Punans who roam the highland forests, shooting game with the blowpipe—a Malay invention. The Punans weave some of the most beautiful designs into their black and white mats.

The only peoples of the area who cannot properly be called Malays or Indonesian cousins of the Malays are the 10,000 Negritos who live in the highlands of northern Malaya. Yet even these people have intermarried with neighboring Malay peoples, and follow similar customs. Although there is consciousness of tribal differences among these various groups, we can see the underlying racial and cultural similarity with the Malays.

The Chinese

If the Malay is the most Latin-like of the three Malaysian peoples, the Chinese is most like the northern European. Many Westerners who come to Malaysia find their own values closest to the Chinese. In part, of course, this is because the Chinese are the most Westernized of the three communities.

Above all, the characteristic that strikes the Malay as well as the European is the Chinese emphasis upon money, hard work, and saving. No group has the so-called Protestant ethic more deeply engrained than the Overseas Chinese. It is proverbial, and true, that many Chinese immigrants came from the homeland as penniless coolies and died millionaires. Even those who did not make a million worked long hours in the tin mines and on plantations, denying themselves comforts by living in shanties and garrets, eating only the poorest rice and the cheapest vegetables, saving every cent until they could buy their own businesses. Many a merchant started as an itinerant peddler, carrying on his shoulder, suspended from the two ends of a bamboo pole, a whole store or restaurant. Even when he could afford to rent a store, he continued to live simply, always saving for a bigger investment. Rags to riches in one generation is the frequent story among Malaysian Chinese.

Today most of the wealth in Malaysia that is not owned by Westerners belongs to Chinese. Ninety percent of all employers and business owners in Malaysia are Chinese. They own the large banks, some of the biggest rubber companies and plantations over 500 acres, the shipping lines, 40 percent of the tin production, and most of the timber industry, coastal fisheries, vegetable farms, and retail stores. Though the Chinese in West Malaysia almost equal the Malays in number, they make two and a half times as much money. When last figured, the annual income of the Chinese was (U.S.) $283 a year against the Malay's $119 and the Indian's $230. Chinese dominance of the Malaysian economy creates a major political problem for the country.

The economic activity of the Chinese, as in Western culture, is related to the high value placed upon material things. The Malay and Hindu emphasis upon spiritual things seems more akin to the medieval European world view which was gradually put aside in the later Middle Ages and Renaissance. In becoming more materialistic the European did not leave behind all appreciation of things spiritual, nor has the modern Chinese, who is quite able to appreciate the beauty of the Han dynasty bronze, a Sung landscape painting, or a T'ang horse. But, like a Medici patron, a Chinese is more likely to buy things of beauty for his collection than try to create them himself. There is appreciation for traditional Chinese theater, and music too, but there is little creativity in these old arts among the Overseas Chinese.

The worship in Chinese temples, of which there are many in Malaysia, is done largely by the lower classes who have come most recently from China, and are thus closer to the traditional religious customs. The middle and upper class Chinese tend to have less interest in traditional religion. If they are not outright atheists, they may have been attracted to Christianity, especially to American Methodism.

Of the three ancient value systems that make up the Chinese religious view—Taoism, Buddhism, and Confucianism—the philosophy of the Sage is the strongest among Malaysian Chinese. Confucianism provides a system of practical morality which governs the behavior of individuals and society. The Confucian emphasis upon solidarity of family and clan helps make these the most important social units among the Malaysian Chinese. The Confucian stress on filial piety and the reverence of ancestors leads to the most important ritual observances in the Chinese family: the maintenance of the family altar and the ancestral tablets.

The biggest festival of the year for the Chinese is New Year. Since everyone becomes a year older on this day, it is the universal birthday celebrated in a kind of Christmas and New Year spirit. All debts are settled, and packets of new money passed out to family and friends in red envelopes. The color red brings good luck, so strips of red paper are pasted on each side of the front door of houses. Homes are cleaned, and honors are done to the household gods, ancestors, and elders. Chinese New Year is a noisy occasion. Everyone sets off firecrackers; the ostentatious show off their wealth with long strings that explode for fifteen minutes and leave the street covered with red paper.

From Confucianism the Chinese derive their emphasis upon education which makes them so well attuned to the modern world of the West. As late as 1947, there were 50 percent more Chinese than Malays in school in Malaya, although the populations were roughly equal. Today there are more Chinese than Malay students at the universities.

From ancient China too comes the tradition of scholarly study in preparation for the civil service, an honored occupation. This has helped provide a corps of highly trained civil servants who are dedicated to public service. Malaysia was fortunate to have a small group of well-trained Malays at the core of its administration. Still, there are not enough Malays to staff government posts, and much of the bureaucracy is Chinese, particularly in scientific and technical areas like medicine and engineering.

An interest in science has made the Chinese the most modern element in Malaysian society. While the Malay university students tend to prefer linguistic and arts studies, the Chinese predominate in technology and science. This is related in part to their pragmatic attitudes, not only toward professions in which the most money can be made, but in the ancient Chinese tradition of scientific curiosity. The Overseas Chinese have shown remarkable ingenuity in applying technology to industry, as demonstrated in their use of the gravel pump in tin mines.

The Chinese share another characteristic with the modern northern European in their preference for city life. The Chinese are by far the most urban of the three races, over three quarters of all city dwellers in Malaysia being Chinese. While 70 percent of all Chinese live in cities, less than a quarter of the Malays do. This preference for urban living is even carried into the country, where the Chinese crowd into compact rows of shop-houses along the main streets of villages, just as the Malays spread out in rural-style kampongs in the city. The tiny cubicles in which many of the urban Chinese families live exceed the crowding of the slums of New York. And there does not seem much urge to get away from the mass of humanity to some rural idyll; the Chinese on vacation will show up at a "World," a recreation park full of light and noise and crowds.

Many of the social problems of the modern Western cities are being experienced by the Chinese. Housing in smaller apartments has made it more difficult to accommodate the extended family. It is increasingly common to find that there is no room for the aged grandparents who must be cared for in old folks' homes. More Chinese women have jobs outside the home, particularly in industry, so that children are left to roam the streets if they cannot be placed in creches or nursery schools. Juvenile delinquency is beginning to appear in the crowded slums.

Voluntarism has marked the Chinese response to social problems of urbanization. From the earliest days in Malaysia the Chinese community banded together to establish charities such as orphanages, schools, and hospitals. Before World War II the main burden of Chinese education was born by private communities, and such efforts are still the mainstay of Chinese education in Borneo. One of the best hospitals in Singapore is supported by private contributions.

Community associations exist in as much variety as they do in the West. Secret societies were formed by the first large waves of Chinese immigrants in the nineteenth century. Many of them took on the character of fraternal organizations like the Masons, with secret initiations, ritual, and esoteric symbolism. Some had vague political connections with movements opposed to the

Manchu Dynasty in China, but their major function was as protective organizations, helping the new arrivals from China to settle in Malaysia. Some secret societies engaged in criminal activities and extortion like the Mafia. Others were wholly benevolent, particularly the clan organizations which cared for members of the same surname, or tribal groups which acted like guilds and chambers of commerce. The Chinese are such enthusiastic joiners that it is not surprising that they are attracted to American Rotary and Lions Clubs which are well represented in Malaysia.

Until the present century, the Chinese of Malaysia were divided into a half-dozen groups based upon language. Though they all came from south China, and had the same basic culture, Cantonese often battled Hokkien, and Hakka were despised by both, while the smaller Teuchiu and Hailam groups protected themselves by neutrality. Then suddenly in the twentieth century this tribalism was galvanized into an overall Chinese nationalism. Nationalism developed in the Chinese community long before it appeared among the Malays or Indians, perhaps in part because of the age-old belief in the superiority of Chinese culture. In part, also, it was a question of time sequence in the motherlands; nationalism developed in China before it became a force in India or Indonesia. Even after Indian and Malayan nationalism arose, they were mild compared to the intensity of Chinese chauvinism, still a dangerous factor in Malaysian politics.

Of the three races of Malaysia the Chinese have been the most sensitive to modern political ideologies of the West. Socialism has appealed more to Chinese city dwellers than any other class. The ruling party of Singapore, the Socialist People's Action Party, is predominantly Chinese, and West Malaysia's Socialist Front draws most of its support from the Chinese of Penang, Kuala Lumpur, Ipoh, and Malacca. The appeal of the communist version of Marxism has been confined almost exclusively to the Chinese in Malaya during the Emergency—the period 1948–1960 when the Communists rose in revolt and were met by a British declaration of emergency conditions—and in Sarawak's Clandestine Communist Organization. On the other hand, no more staunch defenders of the free enterprise system can be found than the Chinese capitalists.

The light skin of the Chinese makes them look most like whites, and the resemblance is accentuated by their adoption of modern dress. Malay men still cling to the sarong and cap, and many of the Indians still wear parts of the old dress, but the Chinese Revolution forever ended that distinctively Chinese hairstyle, the queue, and few Chinese own any traditional Chinese clothes. True, the Chinese women are a bit more conservative and wear the pajama-like *samfu* for work, but their grandmothers would be shocked to see the form-fitting dresses they wear on the city streets. The Chinese woman is probably the most modern of the three women of Malaysia, liberated in large part by education in Western ideas.

The Westerner and the Chinese are much alike in their incessant activity and restlessness, driven by a discontent with their present state to acquire more things and greater power, to explore the universe, and to change it rather than enjoy it as it is. This acquisitiveness certainly leads to a more aggressive attitude than is found in the Malay or Indian.

The Chinese is more like the Westerner in his awareness of history than those raised in the relatively unhistorical Hindu and Malay traditions. Chinese passion for chronologies, genealogies, and museums has given them a great storehouse of records of the past. This creates a consciousness of human experience and makes Man more important than some transcendental ideal. Even the concreteness of the Chinese written language, with its primarily visual nature, reveals the contrast between Chinese ways of thought and those of the more verbal traditions of Malaysia and India.

In emphasizing the modernity of Chinese culture in contrast to that of the Malay and Hindu, we must not overemphasize the similarities between Western and Chinese views. Western visitors will be constantly struck by the persistence of Chinese traditions of loyalty to the family, attempts to avoid giving offense to others by direct criticism, and deference to authority.

The Indians

The Indians are the smallest of the three racial groups of Malaysia, their one million members comprising less than 10 percent of the population. Like the Chinese and Malay communities, the Indian group is far from homogeneous, especially in language. The majority (over 80 percent) are Tamils from the southeast of India. About two thirds of them live in rural areas, mostly on rubber plantations, to which they were brought after the turn of the century. Most of them still live in these areas on the west coast, in Wellesley Province, in south Kedah, and around Klang in Selangor.

The center of Indian cultural life is the Hindu temple. This is used for prayer and worship of the gods of the Hindu pantheon. The temples are also used for social occasions such as weddings and community meetings, and as lecture halls for the teaching of the Hindu religion and Tamil culture. There is a strong interest in education in the Indian community, with a great pride in the ancient Tamil literary tradition.

The temples on rubber plantations are usually dedicated to the rural deities of South India. To these shrines the villagers bring offerings of food and toddy, an alcoholic beverage made from the coconut. After the ceremony the offerings are distributed to the worshipers, who often end up in a drunken state that causes quarrels in which the Indian's excitability is all too apparent.

The complexity of the Hindu religion followed by the Tamils contrasts sharply with the almost Spartan simplicity of Malay monotheism and the disorder of Chinese eclecticism. Hinduism furnishes a well-ordered social system in which predetermined caste gives each person his proper place. Since most of the Indians who came to Malaysia were from the lower castes, there is little caste differentiation among them, but there is a definite consciousness of their place at the bottom of the social scale. This caste position may be related to the docility which many observers have noted. Their reputed docility is perhaps related to the fact that Indians are usually the best plantation workers. They have been relatively inactive politically. They have been slow to develop a sense of nationalism and content to play a minor part in Malaysian politics since independence.

The Indian religious celebrations have developed their own character in Malaysia. The most important holiday of the year is Deepavali, the Festival of Lights, occurring in October or November; it is much like a New Year's celebration. This commemorates the coronation of King Vikram and the victory of the god Rama over the demon king Ravana. On this day the Indian family bathes and dresses in new clothes. Presents are given to the children and to the poor, and a family feast is held.

The next most important festival of the Indian year is Thaipusam, held in January or February. This is a glorification of human intelligence, celebrating the opening of the eye on the forehead of Lord Subramania by the god Shiva. Celebrations begin at the central Hindu temples where coconuts are broken at the altars, and other offerings made of incense, milk, and honey. The priest gives out ashes of burned cow dung which the devotees place on their foreheads to signify the third eye of wisdom. The crowd then follows the huge silver chariot bearing the image of Subramania, with its six heads and twelve arms, decked with flowers, fruit, and candles. The ox-drawn chariot proceeds to some sacred place of the god, in Penang at the Waterfall Gardens, in Kuala Lumpur to the Batu Caves, and in Singapore to the Chettiar Temple.

Among the devotees are penitents who have made vows during the year or who wish to show gratitude for the fulfillment of some prayer. These people afflict themselves with painful devices such as shoes with nails sticking upward into the soles of their feet. Most common is the *kavadi,* a heavy wooden arch which the penitent carries on his shoulders. The ornate decoration includes a portrait of the god Subramania surrounded by flowers. After ritual bathing, the bearer allows himself to be pierced by various metal implements, such as a silver skewer piercing his tongue and cheeks, fishhooks holding sour limes onto his back and sides, or long metal rods connecting to the kavadi. No blood is shed, and the penitent shows no pain. Often in a trance, he bears his torturous burden until he reaches the shrine of Subramania, which in the Batu Caves is reached only after climbing about 300 steep steps. At the shrine he makes his devotions to the god of wisdom.

The Indian emphasis upon knowledge is furthered by another important festival of the Malaysian Hindus, that devoted to Saraswati, the goddess of learning, speech, and eloquence. At this holiday of Navratri books are offered to the image of the goddess. At the end of the festival children begin school after being shown the first letter of the alphabet. Saraswati is also the goddess of music, and Hindu temples usually hold evening celebrations of South Indian music and dance. Like Indian music the dance is highly complex, and calls for thirty-six distinct movements of the head and foot, and hundreds of the hand, each motion possessing ritual significance.

The third of the Indians who live in the big cities are diverse in their languages and place of origin in India. Included are Tamils who work as common laborers in the railway or public works. Many of them live in government barracks along the railway lines at Sentul and Bungsar Road in Kuala Lumpur, next to which Indian cattle can be seen grazing.

The group of Malaysian Indians second in size to the Tamils is the Malayali from the Malabar (west) Coast of India; they number about 75,000. They have much the same customs and traditions as the Tamils who came from the Coromandel (east) Coast and north Ceylon, though they speak a different language and use another script. Most of the Malayali are lower caste also, and unskilled or semiskilled workers. They have provided many of the leaders of the vigorous Malaysian trade union movement. Most Malayalis are Hindus, but among them is a small group of "Old Christians," descendants of Indians who were converted to Christianity in the first centuries after Christ.

The third largest group are the Sikhs, Punjabi-speaking peoples from northeastern India and present-day West Pakistan. In contrast to the dark-skinned Dravidian peoples of south India, the Sikhs are quite fair and occasionally blond-haired. They follow their own religion, a blend of Islam and Hinduism. Most Sikh men adhere to the custom of letting their beards grow and wrap-

ping their uncut hair under a turban, and still wear the traditional iron bracelet, short drawers, and comb. The once-required
dagger is reduced to symbolic form by inlaying its model in comb.
Sikh women wear a long overblouse with flowing trousers. The
Sikhs are more prosperous than the south Indians. Originally
brought to Malaysia as policemen, watchmen, and militia for the
British regime, they continue as fierce-looking guards of the banks
of every town in Malaysia, and are often the top police officers.
Many Sikhs engage in moneylending in their spare time. Others
have gone into the dairy business in the suburbs of the big cities.

   The remainder of those classed as Indians represent a wide
range of tribes from the Indian subcontinent. From Ceylon there
are Buddhists as well as Hindu Tamils. From Afghanistan come
the fair-skinned Pathans. From Nepal are the former Gurkha
soldiers who sell jewels on the sidewalks. From East Pakistan are
the dark-skinned Bengalis who compete in trade with the Hindu
merchants from Gujarat and the Parsis and Jains from Bombay.

   The merchants are the wealthiest members of the Indian community; they are engaged in moneylending, foreign trade, and
retail trade, especially of cotton textiles, which they sell in shops
along the main streets of the big cities.

   In addition to the three major racial groups that have come
together in this crossroads of Malaysia, there are minorities of
Arabs and Japanese, representatives of almost every European
nationality, and over a thousand Americans and Canadians. To
add to the variety, most of the races have intermarried, producing
a small community of Eurasians as well as mixtures of Chinese
and Malays and Indian-Malays.

   Beneath a bewildering diversity of people in Malaysia there is
an underlying unity. Most of the people belong to one of the great
cultures, Malay, Chinese, or Indian. We have emphasized the
differences among these societies, but they have much in common. They are part of a wider Asian culture. For instance, they all
have as a staple of diet rice, which is also the mainstay of their agriculture. And all three groups have a deep respect and reverence
for the spirits of nature, whether expressed as Chinese geomancy

and spirit worship, as Malay semangat, or as Hindu polytheism. This common feeling is demonstrated when we see devotees of each religion worshiping at the same nature shrine, whether it be the grave of an Arab teacher, a giant tree of the forest, or a curiously shaped rock or cave. The three cultures have all experienced the influence of Buddhism, which is a reformed Hinduism. The Chinese revere Buddha, and there was a long Buddhist phase in Malaysian history which left deep marks. Islam came to Malaysia from India with strong influence from Hinduism. Tolerant Chinese do not totally reject Islam, and there are even a few Chinese Muslims living in Malaysia. These things serve as a reminder that the separate strands of Asian culture—which meet in Malaysia—have long intermingled and borrowed from each other.

3
History of the
Malaysian Peoples

At the crossroads of the Orient, Malaysia has received through the centuries the stimulus of many different civilizations, and in turn has developed individual cultural aspects which spread to other parts of the world.

There is evidence that manlike creatures lived in Malaysia as long as half a million years ago. The oldest remains of modern man discovered anywhere in Asia are those found in the Niah Cave of northern Sarawak. A skull dates back to 38,000 B.C. By 8000 B.C. Malaysian men were making tools of stone and clay pots, and decorating their cave walls with paintings. Between 4000 and 2500 B.C., at the same time the Late Stone Age people were settling Europe, present-day Malay types were moving down from southern China, bringing a Neolithic culture of polished stone tools, fine pottery, bracelets, and beads. Perhaps these people were the first farmers anywhere in the world, growing rice on the cleared hillsides.

During the two thousand years after 2500 B.C., when the Celts were settling western Europe and the Greeks were invading their present homeland, waves of Malay peoples were moving into Southeast Asia from China. They must have introduced many of the things associated with the Malaysian culture: houses built on piling; irrigated rice plantings; domesticated animals; skilled sea fishing required knowledge of navigation; a developed village democracy; communal property; worship of ancestors and forces of nature; artistry in metal, clay, and reeds as well as in music and poetry.

Hindu and Chinese Influences

For fifteen hundred years, from 100 B.C. to A.D. 1400, Malaysia was influenced by the cultures of India and China. As seafaring peoples the Malays may have made the first contacts with their neighbors. Malaysia had such a store of precious goods that as early as the first century B.C. the Chinese had begun to trade, buying the tropical spices, the fragrant gums and scented woods, and gold. In return the Malaysians bought Chinese pottery and textiles. The major contact was trade, and the great Han Empire of China made little effort to exert political or religious influence.

Indian culture, on the other hand, made a very deep and lasting impression upon Malaysia. Indian merchants played a major role, but the cultural exchange appears to have been encouraged consciously by Malaysian princes. They were trying to consolidate their power into units like the Aegean city-states. To legitimize their rule they introduced Indian religious sanctions conducted by Brahman priests. These included the coronation and court rituals still used today. Temples were built for the proper conduct of rites and offerings to the gods. The Sanskrit language was introduced as a medium for religious expression, as were Indian dances, plastic arts, and legend. New developments in India affected Malaysia. For instance, Buddhism had a profound influence.

During the Western Middle Ages the Malaysian area was dominated by the great maritime Empire of Srivijaya, with its capital near Palembang in south Sumatra. From Srivijaya the port of Singapore was settled in the seventh century. Well before that there was a thriving port in Kedah on the west coast of Malaya which traded with the Arab world. By the tenth century Arab merchants were calling at Brunei. Around the year 1000 the emperors of Srivijaya endowed Buddhist shrines and hostels in India; Malaysians making pilgrimages to them passed through the port of Kedah. At about this same time Malaysia became involved in international politics. In 1025 Kedah was conquered by an Indian king, jealous, perhaps, of the tolls and restrictions which Srivijaya placed on trade through the strategic straits. The

Indians went on to capture the capital of Srivijaya and the emperor himself. The invasion was repeated in 1068. Two centuries later a Malaysian prince attacked Ceylon. Shortly after this, in 1293, the Chinese made their first and only attempt to invade insular Southeast Asia; it was completely unsuccessful. A few shipwrecked sailors from this invading force were perhaps the first Chinese settlers in the region. In this period as today, Singapore was a multiracial town, with Chinese and Malays living in the shadow of the Buddhist monastery on Canning Hill.

Indian influence upon politics in the archipelago was especially marked because the Malaysian rulers had turned to Hinduism for sanctification. Thus, the Malay concepts of the ruler and the state are still basically Hindu. The higher structure of politics reflects Indian organization particularly in the adoption of Indian titles for such positions as commander-in-chief, minister of internal security, admiral, harbormaster, and ministers. Malay law also reveals Hindu influences; the similarity of Malay punishments to those in the Indian Code of Manu is striking.

The daily life of the Malays also shows the Indian imprint. As diverse things as the wedding rite and the names of most kitchen utensils are of Indian origin, as are many textile processes and the traditional decorating of steel and silver. Hindu religion left its mark in the ceremonies of the Malay magician, and Indian mythology lives on in the *wayang kulit,* in which puppets depict Hindu deities who tell the stories of the Mahabarata and the Ramayana.

Although Indian influence was important, we must not assume that Malay culture was purely passive and imitative. In adapting Indian forms Malays created new ones, such as its own temple architecture and a sculptural style that was unknown in India. The best example of this is the kris, the curved knife that is an original Malay art form, although it bears Indian designs.

Malacca and Islam

In the fifteenth century the Sultanate of Malacca achieved sudden and dazzling brilliance, and as suddenly disappeared. Much of its prosperity was based on international trade, for

Malacca was the Asian counterpart of Antwerp. Its importance as a trading center helped spread the Malay language so that it became the lingua franca of the archipelago. At its peak Malacca was the center of religious studies from which Islam spread throughout the Indonesian region.

This great port sprang from complete obscurity about the year 1400. Its founder, Parameswara, was an adventurer from Sumatra who was linked with the royalty of Java. Driven from his homeland by political troubles, he stopped briefly in Singapore, and finally settled at the site of Malacca, then no more than a fishing village on the west coast of Malaya. Parameswara's astute diplomacy had much to do with the rapid rise of the city. First he sought the protection of Thailand and paid it annual tribute. He also allied himself with China, whose navy frequently visited Malaysia during a remarkable period of exploration.

A major factor in Malacca's growth was the conversion of its rulers and people to Islam. Muslim merchants had traded in the area for centuries without particularly influencing the people religiously, but at this time mystics from India began to spread the teachings of Islam. The Malays were made more receptive to the new religion by the deterioration of the old political order and the degeneration of Hinduism into Tantric orgies. The social attraction of Islam must have been important since the wealthy traders of Malacca were Muslims, as were the visiting Chinese admirals and the Malaysian royalty across the straits in Sumatra.

Whereas the first ruler of Malacca had been a diplomat and the second, Megat Iskandar Shah, a promoter of trade, the third ruler, Mohammad, was a statesman. He gave the town the firm government that was so important to the security of commerce. His constitution successfully combined Hindu traditions with innovations from India, such as a cabinet in which each official was given a definite area of responsibility. By the end of Mohammad's reign in 1444 Malacca had a thriving trade with most of Asia.

When Mohammad died there was a struggle for succession between rival Hindu and Muslim court factions. The Islamic faction emerged victorious and placed Muzaffar Shah on the throne. He turned out to be the greatest of all Malacca's rulers, combining the qualities of warrior, diplomat, and politician. He repelled an attack by Thailand, then put down the civil war between the religious factions. He established a uniform code of justice and furthered commerce by fixing low customs duties, standardizing weights and measures, and defining the rules of discipline aboard ships. Muzaffar so improved the harbor of Malacca that it could accommodate 2000 craft; like Singapore today, Malacca became the great gathering point for the produce of the Indies. Ships of Gujerat in western India brought the goods of Europe and Africa; from India came textiles, from Burma rice. Malacca's link to the east was Brunei, for trade with Borneo and the Philippines. To Brunei and Malacca came Chinese junks with silks and porcelains; from the Ryukyus came Japanese copper. By 1450 Malacca was the hub of the trade of the Orient.

Muzaffar also built a strong army and a fleet that could control the strategic Straits of Malacca. These he put in the command of able leaders like the famous minister Tun Perak. A devout Muslim, Muzaffar saw that Islam was spread in the trading ports of Indonesia.

Although none of the succeeding sultans had the ability of Muzaffar, Malacca's influence and example continued to spread. The ruler of Brunei paid homage to Malacca, and was converted to Islam when he married a Muslim princess of West Malaysia. His claim to over half of Borneo, from Sebatik Island on the east to Sambas on the west, gave Malacca overlordship of an area greater than present-day Malaysia. This was the first time in history that a unit like Malaysia had been created; it retained much of its unity thereafter. This early Malaysian realm was similar to the modern one in its international and multiracial character. The second sultan of Brunei married a Chinese woman, from whom the present dynasty is descended. This followed the example of the sultan of Malacca who married daughters of an Indian merchant and the head of the Chinese community.

After 1475 Malacca declined under the rule of weak sultans. For a while Malacca was saved from the follies of its sultans by capable prime ministers, but in the end was ruined by a tyrannical ruler and an arrogant minister. Such were the men on hand for the great confrontation between East and West. In 1509 the first European vessel sailed into the harbor of Malacca under the command of the Portuguese Admiral Sequeira. The first encounter was unfortunate: the European gestures of honor were taken as insults, and the Malaccans imprisoned as many as they could surprise. Those who escaped returned the next year with a vengeance. A Portuguese fleet under Alfonso d'Albuquerque stormed Malacca and captured what the Portuguese called the richest seaport in the world. Malacca was not defeated because of technological inadequacy, for the Muslims had obtained artillery from the Turks. Rather the sultanate was brought to ruin by the disintegration and corruption of its administration.

Malacca's glory had been achieved under extremely capable leaders. The early kings had appreciated the value of Chinese friendship. They adopted the international religion of Islam, which opened the port to the trade of the world. Malacca's location on the sea lanes of the Straits was basically no better than the older ports like Palembang, Djambi, Kedah, or Pasai, and was less good than Singapore. The state's policies made the difference. The early rulers of Malacca fostered trade by providing stable maritime regulations and protection. When able leadership declined, so did the greatness of Malacca.

Although the Sultanate of Malacca lasted but a century, it marked an important phase in Malaysian history. The religion of Islam and the Malay language of the straits spread with Malaccan suzerainty. Malaysians proudly recall this classical era in their great national epics. The Sultanate of Malacca set the political pattern for the future; most Muslim states of Southeast Asia claim descent from it and follow the court ritual which commemorates the glory of the past.

The Response to the West

The fall of Malacca to the Portuguese did not mean the end of Malaysian independence, although European histories usually give that impression. The sultan of Malacca passed on to his decendants the bulk of the old empire, comprising southern Malaya, central Sumatra, and the islands between. This became known as the Sultanate of Johore since the capital was established at various places on the Johore River. Trade went on much as before with the Portuguese adding another source of supply and demand. Malacca became the focus for attacks as Asians from Sumatra, Java, and Johore attempted to free the port from European domination. Had the several Asian principalities joined together against the Portuguese they might have recaptured Malacca, but, as it was, their rivalry only weakened each other.

The Europeans were no more united, a fact which enabled the rulers of Brunei to bring that kingdom to its greatest power. The first Spaniards, members of Magellan's expedition, made a bad impression upon their arrival in Brunei in 1521 by pillaging Malaysian ships. This unfortunate policy was continued when the Spaniards established themselves in Manila and moved southward across the Philippines. They antagonized the Moros, as they called the Malaysian Muslims, and warfare lasted for the next three centuries. The Portuguese, on the other hand, took a conciliatory approach to Brunei, realizing that its friendship would protect their sea route to the Moluccas. They did not attempt to control either the sultan or his country, and in return their vessels and men were well treated. Eventually they were allowed to set up a trading station and a Catholic mission in Brunei. They strengthened Brunei's power by showing the sultan how to found the brass cannons for which the sultanate became famous.

Brunei's power was greatly expanded in the early sixteenth century under Sultan Bulkiah, who brought the coast of Borneo and most of the Philippines under his control and was strong enough to seize Manila. These conquests were made possible by a fleet comprised of native-designed ships which were as large as those in which Magellan's men circumnavigated the globe. Bulkiah was a racial mixture of Chinese, Arab, Malaccan, and Filippino. International in his interests as well as his blood, he encouraged the immigration of farmers from Java who are credited with improving rice growing in Borneo.

The arrival of the Iberians in the first decade of the sixteenth century tended to increase the warfare and rivalry in the area. Northern Europeans added to the confusion in the final decades.

The first Englishmen in Malaysia, who followed Drake's trip through the Indies in 1550, were unpopular because they pirated vessels of friend and foe alike. The Dutch came out to the East after 1596, largely for honest trade, but made no better impression than the English. Europeans added new rivalries to the tangle of Malaysian affairs, and Malaysian politics became a mirror of European intrigue and warfare. Thus the history of Malaysia in this period is like that of Europe—almost incessant international war. Johore got the worst of it with repeated devastation by Asians or Europeans. Brunei fared better under the able Sultan Hassan, who established a fine constitution that was to last to the nineteenth century.

Malacca was finally taken from the Portuguese in 1641 by the Dutch with Malaysian help. The transfer of power meant little to the Malaysians, for Portuguese power had never extended far beyond the town, and the Dutch proceeded to neglect the port in favor of Batavia. The hundred and thirty years of Portuguese occupation of Malacca left relatively little impression. Some cultural influence is indicated by the three hundred or so words that Malay had adopted from Portuguese. Many of these are household vocabulary such as eating utensils, clothing, furniture, and parts of the house. The most significant impact may have been the improvement of diet resulting from the introduction of foods from the New World like the banana, pineapple, papaya, and sweet potato. Christianity had a relatively small influence, although many of the few thousand Catholics in Malaysia are descendants of converts made by the great Saint Francis Xavier and other missionaries. Western music and instruments were also introduced to Malaysia through the church. Even these slight achievements were not popular with many of the local people and Christian activity only stimulated Islamic teachers to greater efforts.

Portuguese influence on economic life was minimal. They did set a pattern for the fortified trading post, or factory, and the mercantilist policy of state monopoly with licensing of shipping. Although there were a few Portuguese government terms (many with negative connotations such as executioner and torture) adopted by Malay, their political influence was not great.

The greatest mark left by the West was the introduction of scientific attitudes such as the measurement of time and the skillful application of technology. The Malaysians were apt students in making arms and fortifications, and improving their building and handling of naval vessels. Their aptitude for such skills is indicated by their own technological achievements. For example, in the seventeenth century they developed the Kinta Valley of Perak as the main tin producing area. They improved upon the age-old methods of sluicing tin ore into streams, and developed fairly accurate methods of prospecting by sampling the earth with bamboo poles. Where ore was found, a pit was dug and then kept free of rainwater by an ingenious bucket on a balanced boom. The Malays also developed ways of purifying the ore by washing it in sluice boxes and smelting it in clay furnaces between layers of charcoal.

The produce of the rich tin mines was the main attraction to the Europeans and the Americans who swarmed to these coasts in the seventeenth and eighteenth centuries. The Dutch tried unsuccessfully to monopolize the trade in tin. When their monopoly treaties were ignored they built forts along the Malaysian coast to prevent smuggling, but these, too, were evaded.

The Renaissance of Johore and First American Contacts

In the seventeenth and eighteenth centuries the old Malaccan dynasty revived its power and wealth under the name of Johore. The state began its comeback as an ally of the Dutch, who in 1637 built a strong fort at Johore. Though the Dutch did not hand Malacca back to the sultans, they did permit the trade of the Straits to go into Johore, which became an important entrepôt of the area. Ships were built by the Malaysians for sale to the Dutch, and trade was extended to Java and Sulawesi for spices, to Cambodia, Thailand, and northern Malaya for Chinese wares and foodstuffs. Pepper began coming in from Johore's vassal states in Sumatra, and Chinese and Indian merchants joined English, Dutch, and French trading there.

A key element in the Johore economy was the Chinese community which grew as refugees fled China after the fall of the

Ming Dynasty in 1644. Resistance to the Manchus was met by scorched-earth tactics which drove many south Chinese overseas. Some of these must have been farmers for in this period we find Chinese taking up farming in Malaysia for the first time. By the end of the seventeenth century there were about a thousand Chinese families growing pepper in Johore, and Chinese pepper planters and gold miners constituted half of the population of Kuala Trengganu. In eastern Malaysia, too, there were Chinese settlements in the port cities, and the Chinese held a near monopoly of the pepper trade. Thus by 1700 the multiracial character of the Malaysian economy and society had already been established.

It was at this time that the Americans became acquainted with Malaysia. The first native-born American visitor arrived in 1677. He was Captain Francis Davenport, born in Boston, navigating the English ship *Flying Eagle* through the Straits of Malacca on her voyage from India to Indochina, where he was to render the first American technical assistance, building a giant crane to lift a huge cannon onto the walls of the fort of the King of Tonkin in North Vietnam. Dozens of other Americans came to Malaysia toward the end of the seventeenth century, some as pirates, but many as "interlopers," or free traders who defied the East India Company monopoly by trading directly with Malaysia.

One such peaceful trader was Thomas Yale of Boston, who was active in the area in the business of his brother Elihu, the Boston-born president of the English fort at Madras in India. Elihu Yale had lived in India since 1672 and began a vigorous expansion of trade, most of it for his employer, the East India Company, but enough on his own account that he became a very wealthy man, enabling him to endow the university that bears his name. When the British lost their base in Java, Yale was instructed to look for a new one. He considered an island off Kedah, but chose Benkulen in west Sumatra, a decision that many British later regretted, for it was a century before British attention was turned away from the base in Sumatra to Kedah's island of Penang.

The American traders were penetrating an essentially Malaysian world, for Dutch and English trading posts were small and often ineffective forts on the mangrove shores. Malaysian princes of Brunei and Johore ruled most of the area. To the east, Brunei, on the decline because of prolonged civil war and dissolute rulers, continued its contacts with Johore through royal visits and inter-marriage. The long civil war resulted in a fateful decision that still plagues Malaysian-Philippine relations. One of the claimants to the throne of Brunei called on the aid of the neighboring Sultanate of Sulu. When this prince, Mauddin, was victorious in 1675, he had to live up to his kingly word and hand over to Sulu all of Sabah from the Kimanis River eastward and all of Brunei's islands in the southern Philippines. It is upon this cession in part that the Philippines claimed Sabah in 1963. During the civil war Brunei also lost control of the part of Borneo that is now Indonesia, as well as much of Sarawak, so that the sultanate was reduced to an area not much larger than its present size.

Four years after Brunei had paid off its eastern mercenaries, Johore delivered itself into the hands of a group of warriors from the east, the Bugis. These people, who hired themselves out like the Swiss mercenaries of contemporary Europe, came from the island of Sulawesi. They had been converted to Islam in the early seventeenth century. They roamed the Indonesian seas in their fast two-masted ships protected by cannons and suits of armor. When the capital of Johore was destroyed by a Sumatran prince, the Sultan of Johore called upon the Bugis. For their help in destroying the Sumatran capital, they were permitted to settle in the Johore realm which they dominated for the next century. From Riau, opposite Singapore, where the Johore capital was re-located, the Bugis sent colonists to Selangor. By 1740 they had established control over most of the area of modern Malaya.

Two remarkable Buginese viceroys were more than a match for the Dutch. The first, Daing Kemboja, reasserted Johore's control over east Sumatra and beseiged the Dutch in Malacca. Under him Riau became a thriving entrepôt for the whole area. Pepper came in from the Sumatran ports and tin was discovered in the Riau Islands, to supplement that mined in Malaya. Vegetable dye was grown by Chinese farmers. Ships came from India, China, Thailand, Java, and Europe for these goods. To encourage trade the Bugis followed many of the wise practices of Malacca: weights and measures were regulated; legal and maritime codes like Malacca's were strictly enforced; and a large fleet maintained the security of the sea lanes. As traders themselves, the Bugis appreciated that lack of tariffs would attract commerce and therefore created a free port at Riau. This scheme was borrowed by the British when they established Penang and was carried over to Singapore, which today enjoys prosperity as the fifth largest port in the world because of its free port status.

Daing Kemboja's successor as viceroy was a great military commander who might well have recaptured Malacca from the Dutch but for his own death before the walls of the town in 1784. Following his death the Dutch defeated the Buginese fleet and seized both the tin port of Kuala Selangor and the capital of Riau where they made the sultan of Johore their puppet for the next decade. But this was an empty victory, for the Dutch, too, were near the end of their power in Malaysia. Their homeland had been occupied by Napoleon, and the bankrupt Dutch East India Company collapsed. The Bugis recaptured the Dutch forts in Selangor, the ruins of which can be seen today, but the British snatched from them the prize of Malacca in 1795.

During the century of Bugis control of Johore, life for the ordinary Malaysian must have gone on as before, governed by the annual cycle of rice planting, weeding, and harvest. Europeans continued to import the same Indian cloths and trade goods that Asians had bought and sold for centuries, at prices which, if anything, were higher. The main difference in the seventeenth century was the rise in the level of violence. European accounts tell of many casualties, civilian as well as military, in the repeated pillaging of towns like Johore. Ports were often blockaded, which brought starvation. Many towns were burned. As European and American buccaneers preyed upon each other and upon Malaysians, the natives learned to practice piracy indiscriminately.

There was still no question of Malaysia being controlled by Europeans. The Bugis were the dominant power and they shaped the political framework of Malaya for the next century. Their greatest legacy was the demonstration of the success of the free port of Riau, which is the model for the present prosperous entrepôts of Penang and Singapore.

Merchants, Missionaries, and Men-of-War

Until 1874 most of Malaysia continued to be independent of European rule, though British influence was increasing. By that date the British had gained sovereignty over only one percent of Malaysia: the three offshore islands of Penang, Singapore, and Labuan, and the two coastal strips of Wellesley and Malacca. Though strategically important, these tiny posts did not give them control of the interior.

The main reason for the increase of British influence in Malaysia was the absence of any strong power in the area, either European or Malaysian. The large Malaysian "empires" tended to be short-lived and dependent on dynastic fortunes. Of course it was not the British interest to strengthen any native state; quite the opposite, they furthered the fragmentation of units that created much of the difficulty in unifying Malaysia today.

There was also the weakness of contested succession in Malaysian states. The practice of selecting the most able relative rather than the eldest had the great advantage of eliminating the weaklings, but it had the disadvantage of leaving disappointed candidates. It is not surprising that some turned to the British to support their claims to the throne. Another weakness of Malaysian politics was its dependence upon physical power. To seize power as well as to maintain it a Malaysian was strongly tempted to accept outside assistance, which the British were willing to lend. The price of such assistance might be a monopoly or a piece of territory.

The first British settlement in Malaysia was made in 1773 at Balambangan, an island just off the north tip of Sabah. The British were looking for a collecting point for East Indian spices as well as a place to repair ships and get water on the route to China. They obtained permission to settle Balambangan from a claimant to the throne of Sulu. After achieving his throne, he ceded to them all of Sabah and its offshore islands, some of which he did not actually possess. The founder of the British settlement, Alexander Dalrymple, foreshadowed Malaysia's triracial society by bringing in Indian soldiers and Chinese traders. The settlement was a failure, for in the same year that the Americans revolted against British rule the local Malaysians threw out this unwanted settlement of Europeans.

British attention now turned to the opposite end of Malaysia, to the island of Penang, where a successful settlement was finally made in 1786 under conditions of dubious legality. A British trader, Francis Light, obtained permission from the sultan of Kedah to rent Penang in exchange for military aid. Light could not obtain his government's support, but ran up the British flag anyway without either British or Kedah's permission. Once done the deed was hard to undo. When the sultan tried to drive him out, Light called upon the British navy for protection, and the sultan was forced to agree to a treaty.

Despite the shady circumstances of Penang's founding, it became the first place in Malaysia where British law was administered. The port was also opened up as a free port to ships of all nations on the model of Riau. Within the first year, a ship flying the American flag called at Penang. In the second year the first American consul in Asia, Major Samuel Shaw, called there as well as at the ports of Malacca and Kedah. By 1800 there was an American merchant permanently residing in Penang. Although it turned out to be a convenient port of call for the American trade—which was soon to rival that of the British in the Far East —Americans preferred going directly to Malaysian ports for trade. The United States government had considered acquiring bases or establishing an East India Company, but Congress rejected such direct government intervention. The trade was encouraged only by indirect measures like tariffs and shipping dues.

In 1800 the United States sent the warship *Essex* out to the Indies to protect American ships against depradations by Napoleon's navy. Such military protection was sporadic in the first quarter of the nineteenth century, and American traders had to rely on their own cannon and alertness to prevent seizure. The dangers they faced are shown by the capture of Nathaniel Bowditch's ship *Putnam* by pirates in the very harbor of Riau in 1805. This incident well illustrates how impotent the British were in these seas, a fact that pressed them to establish a firmer control of Malaysia. The French Revolutionary Wars provided another excuse for the gradual extension of British influence. This was mainly at Dutch expense. When Napoleon occupied the Netherlands in 1795 the British used this excuse to take over Malacca and put the Bugis back in Riau. They also seized the richest Dutch colony, Java, and used it as a base for extension of British interests in Borneo and Malaya.

The leader of this expansion was the remarkable Stamford Raffles. An energetic and restless man with great personal ambitions, he was none too scrupulous in his methods of achieving personal advancement or extension of British power. He learned to speak Malay fluently and won the respect of many Malaysians. He was one of the first Europeans to take a serious interest in Malaysian culture, and with the help of the American naturalist Dr. Thomas Horsfield explored the ancient ruins of Indonesia, founded a scientific society in Batavia, and studied the fascinating variety of flora, fauna, geology, archaeology, and ethnology of Indo-Malaysia.

Extension of British power in the area did not necessarily help American interests. The arbitrary impressment of American sailors into the British navy, for example, was a constant irritant in the Far East. Resentful young Americans got their revenge by serving on privateers during the War of 1812. Several of these ships made important captures of British ships in Malaysian waters. When one such raider was captured by the British and taken into Penang, the owners complained to the United States government. This was one of the factors which caused four American naval vessels to be dispatched to the Far East in 1814. Only one, the *Peacock,* got out to eastern waters. Its skirmish with the British off Java was the last battle not only of the War of 1812 but of the Napoleonic Wars as well.

American privateer and naval activity was one of the factors in British interest in acquiring a new naval base in the area. Forced to return Java and Malacca to the Netherlands by demands of

European politics, Raffles began the search for a more central base than Penang. His choice fell upon the island of Singapore, so strategically located at the confluence of the routes from India, China, and Europe. Contrary to the widespread myth, the island was not uninhabited, but had at least three Malay villages and thirty Chinese families settled on farms in the interior. When Raffles arrived in 1819 it was also important enough to be the home of the second-ranking official of the Sultanate of Johore, from whom he obtained the agreement to rent a trading post. When the sultan himself refused to ratify the agreement, Raffles found a pretender to the throne, and having made him sultan, had him sign the desired treaty. This illegal act had serious consequences for the future. Since the pretender had no control of the islands, Raffles in effect separated the Malayan part of the Johore domain from the Indonesian part, and forever partitioned the ancient empire, heir to Malacca and Srivijaya, which had always ruled a common cultural area on both sides of the Straits.

The terms of Raffles' treaty excluded settlements of other foreign countries at Singapore, specifically mentioning a major rival, the Americans. The trade of Singapore was slow in developing, in part because Raffles diverted attention to other ports, thinking he might find a better base nearer the American pepper ports in Sumatra. In part, too, the Americans and Dutch had no need of Singapore. The Americans had a well-established direct trade with Malay ports which, for example, brought twenty-two vessels into the Pepper Coast in the month following the founding of Singapore. Penang sufficed for emergency supplies.

Raffles' frequently expressed concern about this American competition is now amusing, but it was serious then. Experienced British officials like John Crawfurd noted that American success stemmed from their conciliatory conduct which contrasted with the squabbling Europeans who "invaded, conquered, and plundered those who have received them hospitably, quarrelled with and massacred one another."[1] This British diplomat and historian argued that thirty-five years of American trade with the Indies

[1] John Crawfurd, *History of the Indian Archipelago* (Edinburgh, 1820), III, 253.

clearly demonstrated the advantages of free trade over European monopolies. He was right in saying that the United States "has never connected itself with any political concern of the natives, never embroiled itself in their quarrels," but it did not neglect its traders. In 1819 it extended naval protection for the first time in peace by sending the frigate *Congress* out to Malaysian and Chinese waters.

Gradually the port of Singapore grew as the produce of the Indies began to come there instead of to Malacca and Riau. American ships found it convenient to call at Singapore to get supplies and to pick up the Straits produce, but the British decided to exclude the Americans on a legal technicality. For over a decade, from 1825 to 1837, Singapore merchants who wished to ship to the United States had to send their goods fifteen miles to the Riau Islands where Americans could anchor in the ports of the sultan of Johore.

The British increasingly intervened in native politics. One governor of Singapore, the aggressive Robert Fullerton, followed Raffles' example of expanding British interests by attempting to detach the northern Malay states from Thailand in 1825. Having acquired Malacca from the Dutch in the previous year, the British became involved in an inexcusable war on its borders in 1831.

Of far greater importance than these British activities on the fringes of Malaysia was the beginning of the economic development of the interior by the Chinese. Long before British rule, the Chinese had been interested in gold mining in Malaya and Borneo, and in the early nineteenth century were opening up tin mines in Malaya and antimony mines in Sarawak. These Chinese immigrants brought with them social institutions that were both constructive and destructive. In particular, Chinese secret societies like the Triad offered protection on the wild frontier, but they often turned to extortion and racketeering. Such activities inevitably evoked hostility, and the first recorded race riots in Malaysia occurred in 1828 following a Malay raid on the Triad Society treasury at the Lukut tin mines in Malaya. The raid initiated a round of retaliation which was not ended until a capable Malay ruler gave security to all groups.

The Chinese made many technological advances in the mining of tin. They installed water-driven pumps to drain water out of the pits, introduced California-style sluice boxes and improved smelting by using a new kind of bellows. Chinese farmers began moving into the interior of Malaya and Sarawak in the mid-1830's from the coastal areas which they had farmed since before 1700. Thus the Chinese settlement in Malaysia cannot be attributed to British rule which existed only on the fringes. Chinese came also to the British settlements, of course, which were often the staging points for their move to the interior. Where did they come from? Some migrated from the older Malay settlements like Malacca, Riau, Brunei, Sambas. Many more came directly from China, in a degrading passenger business that became known as the coolie trade. Most of the business was carried on by Chinese who "Shang-haied" poor victims aboard their crowded junks and sold them into virtual slavery for a year in Singapore.

Americans played an important role in the growth of the port of Singapore. In 1833 President Jackson's diplomatic agent for the Far East, Edmund Roberts, appealed to the British to open the port to American ships. Although the opening was delayed for three years, the American government did establish its first consulate in Malaysia in 1834, sending Joseph Balestier to open the post. Balestier became one of the outstanding civic leaders of the city of Singapore as a founder of the Chamber of Commerce and of the first agricultural society in Malaysia. As agent of his government Balestier ran a kind of information service by pro-viding the newspapers with news from America. He opened up a cotton plantation in what is now Balestier Plain, but later shifted to growing sugar. His son Revere set up the first sugar refinery in the city and established a tin smelter in Singapore. Consul Bales-tier continued to take a prominent part in the life of the city until 1847 when his sugar plantations were ruined by floods.

American missionaries also made an important contribution to the development of Singapore. Religious interest was first stimulated by the visit of Reverend David Abeel in 1831. In 1834 the American Board in Boston sent out its first resident mis-sionary, Reverend Ira Tracy, who began the printing of missionary tracts. He was followed by a medical missionary, Dr. Peter Parker, who set up the first dispensary in Singapore in 1835 and helped Tracy found the first free school in Malaysia. These two men also made one of the first proposals of a Peace Corps type of operation—an American missionary colony, as they called it—to teach the local people farming, industrial skills, and reading. The British encouraged this idea, but it did not appeal to the home office in Boston, which was content to send out skilled persons like doctors, printers, and teachers on a short-term basis. At one time the mission community reached seventeen, but health problems forced the station to close in 1841. One American from the group stayed on to continue educational work, becoming headmaster of Raffles Institution which American merchants supported. Printing work was taken over by a man from Britain whom the missionaries had sent to the United States for education. The direct successor of the mission press is still in operation in Singapore.

Americans from the mission station in Singapore took a great interest in other parts of Malaysia, then little known to Europeans. For instance, American merchants paid for an exploring expedition to Borneo and points east in 1837. At Brunei their offer of trade, doctors, books, and teachers was politely declined, perhaps because it was tied in with a Christian mission. About the only thing that came of the expedition was a more thorough knowledge of Borneo. The information gathered was presented in a book that was one of the first to use the present name of the area, *The Claims of Japan and Malaysia upon Christendom,* by G. T. Lay. At the time Borneo was still a wide-open frontier country with no European colonies whatever. There were a number of Chinese settlers who were engaged in farming and mining. The nominal ruler of the area, the sultan of Brunei, was troubled by dissident factions in his court who were willing to turn to foreigners for help. Some of the local Dayaks working in the Chinese mines were discontented with their relationship to Brunei and to the Chinese.

A British adventurer boldly stepped into this confused situation to establish his own private kingdom of Sarawak. This man was

James Brooke, a complex and contradictory personality. His
charm won him many friends, but he had strong racial prejudices.
Adamant in his insistence upon others obeying the law, he found
it difficult to adhere to legal niceties when they applied to him.
He was alternately elated and depressed, and in later life became
mentally unbalanced. Though generous in some respects, he was
an unmitigated egoist. A great admirer of Raffles, Brooke played
a conscious role of spreading British rule in Borneo. Upon his
arrival in Sarawak in 1839 he promised a local governor military
aid against rebels in return for the title of rajah. Acquiring an
armed ship, which he passed off as a British naval vessel, he helped
defeat some of the rebels. When the local official was unable to
deliver the title, Brooke brought pressure from the British. When
the sultan of Brunei finally consented to granting the title, Brooke
promised to be his subject, but proceeded to govern Sarawak as
his own private domain. With the aid of the British navy, Brooke
also intervened in court politics and eventually forced the sultan
to cede to Britain the island of Labuan and the right to control
piracy in the sultanate.

The United States was innocently a part of Brooke's designs.
The American frigate *Constitution* arrived at Brunei in 1845
seeking an agreement for trade and coal mining on Labuan.
Brooke used this as an excuse for intervention. A similarly inno-
cent visit by Joseph Balestier in 1859, traveling as a special envoy
aboard an American warship, was used by Brooke to obtain the
first international recognition of his rule. Even the British government was aware of Brooke's theoretical dependence upon Brunei
and refused to give recognition until it had taken Sarawak over
as a protectorate. While continuing to pay tribute to the sultan,
Brooke went on expanding his domain from the small area
around Kuching with which he started until he had taken over
nearly half of his sovereign's domain.

Much of Brooke's aggrandizement was accomplished under the
guise of extending the benefits of law and order. But his rule
was so chaotic that his claim to have brought peace was manifestly
false. Dayak patriots like Rentas and Balang carried on guerrilla
warfare against Brooke for years, and only British marines from

Singapore could put down the Melanau and Malay resistance. The Chinese, too, opposed Brooke and in 1857 occupied Kuching for a week and burned down the White Rajah's palace.

The sporadic lawlessness which gave the imperialists their excuse to rule now appears to have been part of a growing anti-imperialism among all of the Chinese of Southeast Asia, stimulated by the British wars against China. Frequent riots occurred even in those areas which were under supposedly peaceful British rule: in Singapore in 1846, 1851, 1854, 1857, 1863, and 1865; and in Penang. Hostilities between Chinese secret societies, particularly in the tin mining areas of Malaya, were used as an argument for extending the benefits of British government. By mid-century British policy had taken on a militancy that foreshadowed the coming intervention in 1874; British governor Cavenagh intervened with force in the affairs of several Malay states outside the British sphere.

While the British extended their influence, Americans carried on a highly profitable trade with Malaysia without any territorial base. By 1850 they became the world's largest shippers of Malaysian produce, lading the beautiful clipper ships at the British ports. During the American Civil War the operations of the Confederate cruiser *Alabama* in Malaysian waters gave a severe blow to this thriving trade. And after 1874 the American sailing ships disappeared as the merchants turned to the development of Western railroads and new industries of America. But the industrialization itself created a great demand for Malaysian produce like tin and rubber, so the United States continued to be one of the area's best customers, though the goods were now shipped in unromantic steel freighters driven by coal boilers.

The founding of the colony of North Borneo was an American contribution to Malaysian history. The first American consul stationed in Brunei, Claude Moses, obtained permission from the Sultan of Brunei to lease several bays on the west coast of Sabah. In 1865 the American Trading Company ran up the American flag over its post at Ellena on Kimanis Bay and cleared land for sugar, rice, and tobacco. The settlement had to be abandoned the next year, but the titles were sold eventually to British who formed the North Borneo Company, which ruled the area until 1942. The only reminder today of this American initiative is the grave at Kimanis of Thomas Harris, the first white man to cross the main range of Sabah and to visit the interior.

For nearly a century, from 1787 to 1874, the Americans had played an important role in the development of Malaysia. Without acquiring any territory, Americans pioneered in a number of fields, including industry, education, medicine, mining, and smelting, and in opening up of Borneo. American trade was second only to the British. The Americans established very friendly relations with Malaysians, and developed a deep affection for the peoples which they communicated to the United States, so that Malaysia was far from unknown. Successful relations depended, as so many Europeans pointed out, upon American refusal to become involved in politics or to establish colonies and bases. In contrast, during the same period, the British became more and more deeply involved. Still, in 1874 they held only five tiny coastal settlements, and most of Malaysia was still ruled by native rulers.

The British Century

Great Britain actually ruled Malaysia for less than a century, from 1874 to 1963, and it took nearly a third of that century to make British rule effective. Yet, that short period, being the most recent, has had the most immediate impact.

British conquest of Malaysia was not part of a plot or plan, and surprisingly began under the government of the great anti-imperialist Prime Minister Gladstone. Yet the British did not acquire Malaysia in a fit of absentmindedness. A large number of British citizens sincerely believed that the world would be better off under the Union Jack.

Foremost among the advocates of British expansion in Malaysia were the leading merchants of Singapore—persons like William Read, who headed one of the large agency houses that sold straits produce to the world. In the 1860's there was growing competition among these firms for tin concessions in the independent Malay states, as well as speculation in rights for telegraph lines between Australia and Europe. Securing these commercial interests through political control became a major concern of British merchants.

The principal obstacle to the extension of political control was the traditional British policy of nonintervention, which was reinforced by Singapore's subjection to the British government in India. Read led the campaign to shake free of this control. When this was achieved in 1867, Read was able to lobby directly in London for British intervention in the Malay states, proposing as a model the state of Johore, where the British controlled a westernized and tractable ruler. British merchants found excuses for intervention in the civil wars in Selangor, Chinese society rivalries in Perak, and race riots elsewhere. The crucial argument was a petition for intervention signed by 250 Chinese merchants of the British colonies, a document that Read probably instigated. The merchants made the need for action seem urgent by passing on rumors that the Germans would intervene—a completely imaginary threat.

In 1873 Britain opened the door to intervention with a declaration that the government had "no desire to interfere in the internal affairs of the Malay States. But . . . find it incumbent upon them to employ such influence as they possess with the native princes to rescue, if possible, these fertile and productive countries from the ruin which must befall them if the present disorders continue unchecked." A new governor of the Straits Settlements, Sir Andrew Clarke, came out from London with apparent support in interpreting these instructions very broadly. Clarke used the British navy to intervene in the wars in Perak, and on January 20, 1874, signed with the local chiefs the famous Pangkor Agreement which marks the beginning of British government in Malaya. This treaty established the pattern of British rule until 1941, by providing the Sultan with a British adviser who became in reality the governor of the state.

Later in that year Clarke intervened in the state of Selangor on the pretext of piracy on the coast. There and in the state of Sungai Ujong (a part of Negri Sembilan) the British forced the acceptance of a British adviser. Within a short four months in 1874 the British had established control over the principal tin mining areas of Malaya. The Malays did not accept these interventions without resistance. In 1875 uprisings broke out simultaneously in the three states. In Perak, where many chiefs had refused to sign the Pangkor Agreement, the Malays murdered the first British adviser, who had alienated many by his arrogance and hypocrisy. In Selangor insurgents actually captured two important towns before they were put down by British forces. The chief of the state of Negri Sembilan led the attack against British encroachments on the state of Sungai Ujong; his forces were not overcome for three years. The Malays were ultimately defeated because their efforts were uncoordinated in contrast to the British who could apply their naval power selectively to cut off food and supplies.

After checking Malay resistance, the British gradually extended their rule over the rest of Malaysia during the last quarter of the nineteenth century. Britain did not directly annex the states of Malaysia, but enlarged the system of "indirect rule" through British resident advisers. The "fiction," as Resident Hugh Low of Perak called it, was that the sultan ruled with the resident's advice, but actually it was the other way around. The Pangkor Agreement, the nearest thing to a constitution for the residential system, left Malay religion and customs to the sultans and gave the British charge of finances.

Much of the success of the system of indirect rule was due to the capable officials chosen by the British as residents. Hugh Low, a botanist with long experience with administration in Borneo, set a tactful example by permitting the sultan of Perak to preside over the state council, while he in fact ruled. Low also set important patterns for the modern economic development of Malaysia. Outside his house in Kuala Kangsar in 1877 he planted the first rubber seedlings, and in the same year introduced the major technical innovation in tin mining, a portable steam-driven pump. Low began improving transportation, first by clearing rivers, then by building roads, and finally by opening up the first railroad in Malaya from Taiping to the docks at Port Weld.

A firm financial base for development was established when Low adopted the Malayan custom of taxing tin exports for government revenue; this remains Malaysia's largest source of revenue today. The first European-designed tin smelter went into operation in 1884. Tin production rose so rapidly that by 1883 Malaya was the largest producer in the world, a position it has held ever since. Western democratic institutions were introduced under the residential system. In the state of Selangor, in 1877, Resident Bloomfield Douglas called a state council which included four Malays as well as the first Chinese given representation in the government, the prominent merchant Yap Ah Loy.

The resident system was extended to the big west coast state of Pahang in 1884, and in effect to the whole of Negri Sembilan two years later. Thus by 1886 the British had complete control of the four core states. In the other Malaysian states they took over the government less obviously, by assuming responsibility for defense and foreign affairs in Johore in 1885 and in Sarawak, North Borneo, and Brunei three years later.

With the completion of British takeover of the native states, the idea of unification of Malaysia began to appear. In 1887 Lord Brassey, director of the North Borneo Company, proposed the formation of one large colony to include Malaya and Borneo. The British government would not go this far, but in the following year Malaysia was given its first political unity when the governor of the Straits Settlements colonies was also made high commissioner for Borneo. In 1896 a federation was formed of the four core states which had British residents: Negri Sembilan, Pahang, Perak, and Selangor. This unit, styled the Federated Malay States, was headed by a British resident-general. The capital chosen was the present capital of Malaysia, Kuala Lumpur, where the Victorian Moorish style capitol building stands as a symbol of the nation.

The British still sought control of the Malay-speaking areas of southern Thailand, the four states of Kedah, Kelantan, Perlis, and Trengganu. These Thailand yielded in 1909. One by one the rulers of these states accepted British protection and advisers, Kedah holding out the longest, until 1923. With the cession of the four Thai states in 1909 Malaysia had achieved its present boundaries and was under British control.

For the next thirty-three years the British ruled Malaysia through a hodgepodge of eighteen administrative units based upon historical accidents. We can clarify the situation if we describe the units in five basic categories: (1) the colony of the Straits, (2) the Federated Malay States, (3) the unfederated Malay states (and Brunei), (4) the chartered Company of North Borneo, and (5) Sarawak. The first of these was the central unit, a crown colony known as the Straits Settlements, or "Straits" for short. This included the three free ports of Singapore, Penang, and Labuan and the three strips of Malaya's west coast called Province Wellesley, the Dindings, and Malacca. The colony was ruled autocratically by a governor who took the advice of an executive council composed mainly of British officials but with a minority of civilians, including one Chinese. The separate legislative council was hardly representative, but did provide a place where interest groups could be heard and did give a tiny minority of seats to natives: three for the Chinese and one each for the Malays and Indians, which corresponded roughly to their ratio of the population (Chinese, 60 percent; Malays, 25 percent; and Indians, 12).

The four Federated Malay States were governed indirectly by the British high commissioner, who was at the same time governor of the Straits. The real power remained in the hands of the British residents of each state, ostensibly advisers to the sultans. The loss of the sultans' powers was made palatable by granting special privileges to the Malays, such as exclusion of Chinese from the civil service or the ownership of arable land. This expedient set a precedent of discrimination that is still plaguing the country today.

The five unfederated Malay states, Johore and the four states taken from Thailand, and Brunei were administered much the same. Their sultans had more autonomy than those of the Federated Malay States, but foreign affairs and defense were supervised by the British, and real power was held by the British adviser.

North Borneo was unique in form of government, but was run much like the unfederated states. The British North Borneo Company was the theoretical sovereign of Sabah, but the British government was responsible for defense and foreign affairs, and administration was closely linked to the rest of Malaysia. The governor, often a British civil servant, ruled autocratically in consultation with an advisory council and a legislative council on which two Chinese were the only local appointees.

Sarawak continued to be ruled by the enlightened despotism of the Brooke family with the assistance of many British officials. The founding rajah was succeeded by his nephew Charles Brooke, ruling from 1868 to 1917. Charles was a better administrator than his uncle, but suffered from an unwillingness to delegate authority. Aware of the approaching end of colonialism, Charles permitted some local participation in his government. He invited Malay chiefs to his supreme council and every four years called together the local chiefs in a Council Negri to discuss his decisions. Charles was followed by the third and last rajah, his son Charles Vyner Brooke, who ruled from 1917 to 1946. Although he was neither a very effective administrator nor a strong democrat, he did make a small beginning in representative government by permitting the Ibans to elect village councils.

This description makes clear that despite the local variations of names and form in the sixteen political units of British Malaysia, there was much basic similarity which makes integration easier today. Local government everywhere was administered by district officers through regional administrators: a secretary who headed the civil service, British technical service heads, and a British governor or resident. The high commissioner cum governor supervised the whole from Singapore. All of Malaysia was protected by the Royal Navy and supporting troops based at Singapore, and efficient British police standards applied throughout. There was an all-Malaysia currency based on the Straits dollar. Shipping and banking was centered in the entrepôt of Singapore. Malay was the lingua franca, and English the language of government. Thus there were many unifying factors. But the British did not encourage loyalty to any figure other than their king. To have done so would have defeated their purposes.

At the very peak of British power Asian nationalism began to stir. Loyalty was directed toward race rather than to the broader concept of Malaysia, however. The Chinese were the first to develop effective nationalism. The growing turmoil in China in the late nineteenth and early twentieth centuries caused the flood of refugees to swell, bringing with them the strong feelings of Chinese nationalism and anti-imperialism. The Chinese reformer K'ang Yu-wei came to Malaysia to raise funds from the rich merchants and to open modern Chinese schools. Sun Yat-sen followed, winning much support for the nationalist cause. By the time of the 1911 Revolution, the Chinese schools in Malaysia had begun to bridge the gaps between dialect groups whose languages were mutually unintelligible. A sense of identity with China was created. Teachers, texts, and ideas came from the rejuvenated fatherland, and the schools were supervised by Chinese inspectors. The Republican government took a direct interest in the Overseas Chinese, treating them as Chinese citizens and recruiting them into the Nationalist Party, the Kuomintang. When that party split in 1927 the Malaysian Chinese were pulled in two directions, toward the right with Chiang and to the left with the Communists. The Communists' ideas fitted well with the old anti-imperialism of the Malaysian Chinese, and they offered effective organization of the Chinese schools and labor unions.

Malay nationalism developed more slowly than the Chinese, but it, too, began about 1900. It received stimulus from three regions: Indonesia, the Middle East, and Japan. Malaysia had always shared intellectual currents with Indonesia. In recent times it felt the force of Dutch imperialism through Malay refugees, particularly from the Riau Sultanate. The second influence on Malay nationalism was the growth of Pan-Islamic sentiments which reached Malaysia through the students in the Middle East. Thirdly, the example of Japan in successfully defeating a Western power in the Russo-Japanese War in 1905 gave courage to Asian nationalists.

Malay nationalism from the start was a moderate movement. The first leader was Mohammed Eunos of Singapore, the founder of the first Malay newspaper, *Utusan Melayu* (1907), and the first Malay political party, Kesatuan Melayu Singapura (1924), both moderate organizations. He was the first Malay appointed to the

Straits legislative council (1924). His party gradually spread from Singapore to Malaya, and was able to hold its first national congress just before World War II. Future Malay national leaders were brought together unintentionally by the British when they established a Malay language teachers' college at Tanjong Malim in 1922.

Asian nationalism also gave encouragement to various tribal groups in Borneo, who had put up resistance to each of the British forward movements. Serious revolts broke out among the Dayaks, the Muruts, and the Kadazans about 1900, but these uncoordinated efforts were eventually defeated, leaving no permanent organizations such as were formed by both the Chinese and Malays.

Separate national movements only accentuated the divisions between the cultures of Malaysia, creating a plural society. This remains Malaysia's biggest problem today. The only political movement in the prewar period that ran counter to the growing tendency toward racial distinctions was the Straits Chinese Association, dedicated to a nonracial Malayan nationalism. The leader was Tan Cheng Lock, who came from an old Chinese family of Malacca, where the Chinese had intermarried with the Malays and adopted many of their customs. As a member of the Straits legislative council from 1923 to 1934, Tan was the first person to advocate a Malayan nationalism that would unite all the races. He was willing to work within the framework of the British colonial system, and he set the tone for the nationalism that characterizes Malaysia today, moderate and racially tolerant.

While this plural society was developing, a plural economy was also emerging under British rule. Modern mining and plantations soon formed a separate economy geared to the industrial growth of the West. This rapidly left behind the old Malay economy of rice growing, fishing, and barter trade. In this development the United States had a large share, mainly as the major purchaser of tin and rubber, but also as an investor in the economic development of the modern sector.

Tin production was the first to be modernized. With the industrialization of the United States, its demand for tin rose rapidly. Malaysia quickly became dependent on the American price, so that booms and recessions had immediate repercussions in Malaysia. American technology contributed directly to increasing tin production. Hydraulic nozzles to wash the tin ore out of the earth were introduced from the United States in 1892; this new method gave the Europeans their first edge over Chinese miners, who later adopted it and still favor it. The Europeans found an even more efficient mining device in the American gold dredge which was first successfully introduced in 1912. Dredging is the principal European method of mining today. Besides supplying the dredges, Americans supplied capital, as in the Yukon Gold Mining Company, one of the first firms to use electricity for dredging. Its successor, Pacific Tin Consolidated, is still one of the largest tin-mining companies in Malaya. Americans would have put money into smelting of tin ore but were excluded by the British government in the interest of protecting the monopoly of British capital.

Large-scale plantation of rubber, too, was largely in response to American industrial growth, especially the expansion of automobile production after 1900. Rubber trees had been grown in Malaya since 1876, but the first big planting was in 1896 by the Chinese Tan Chay Yan in Malacca. This was soon followed by British efforts, and in 1905 American capital was invested in the Malacca Rubber Plantations, which became the largest producer in Malaya by 1911. A wholly American-owned plantation was opened in Johore in 1906 by Fred Waterhouse, who later developed other plantations in Pahang and Johore. After the First World War the United States Rubber Company laid out two 10,000-acre estates in Kedah, where the company became the leader in the application of modern technology to rubber production—in mechanization, botanical research, and shipping rubber in liquid form.

The demand for workers on the rubber plantations caused the immigration of the third racial group that makes up Malaysian society today, the Indians. The British found that Tamils from south India were far more tractable workers than the Chinese and more industrious than the Malays. By the end of the nineteenth century they were bringing in about 20,000 Indians a year as indentured laborers on coffee and gambier plantations. The rubber boom brought the number of immigrants up to 50,000 a year in the first decade of the twentieth century. After the indenture system was abolished, nearly 100,000 a year came over voluntarily. Though the British government assured better working conditions for the new arrivals than had been available to the Chinese, no effort was made to integrate the Indians into Malaysian society. Many returned to India, and those who remained thought of India as their home and were eventually deeply influenced by Indian nationalism. Thus, a third centrifugal element was introduced into Malaysian society.

The interdependence of the American and Malaysian economies was demonstrated during the period between the two world wars. By the end of the first war the United States was consuming three quarters of the world's rubber and was the largest user of tin. This brought great prosperity to Malaysia, but overextended production. When America had its big recession after the first war, prices fell and many Malaysian rubber companies were ruined. In 1922 rubber growers banded together in the Stevenson Rubber Scheme in an effort to raise prices by limiting production, but the plan failed because of the lack of participation of producers in Indonesia and the small growers in Malaysia itself. American recovery and increased auto production had more to do with raising the rubber price than the Stevenson scheme, which was abolished just before the Great Depression. Again in the early thirties rubber prices plunged, but much farther, with disastrous effects on Malaysia. In 1934 all the rubber-producing countries agreed upon a restriction scheme. Tin prices had also fallen so far that in 1931 tin-producing countries joined to limit their production for the first time. Again, restored prosperity can be credited more to the recovery of American prices than to the restriction, which actually prevented the United States and its allies from getting enough rubber and tin to meet the needs of World War II.

In addition to tin and rubber, American enterprise was active in a number of other developments of the Malaysian economy. American oil companies led in the distribution of kerosine which revolutionized home cooking and lighting in Malaysia in the nineteenth century. When Americans were permitted to search for petroleum in Malaysia, they carried out the first systematic geological exploration of isolated regions, such as Sabah in 1912. After 1900 direct shipping to the United States was resumed by American firms, particularly the Dollar Line, which still operates as the American President Line. American banks took part in investment, starting with the National City Bank of New York, which is remembered for pioneering in the employment and training of Asians. Singer Sewing Machine Company stimulated local entrepreneurship by using local agents, a policy followed by other American manufacturers and insurance companies. The biggest contribution to the diversification and industrialization of Malaysia was the building of the Ford Motor Company assembly plant in Singapore in 1941.

Japanese Invasion and Occupation

Japanese imperialists long had designs on Southeast Asia. They promised the benefits of a Co-Prosperity Sphere in which Japanese manufactures would be exchanged for raw materials like oil, tin, and rubber, which the Japanese economy needed. But when the Japanese occupied China, the Chinese boycotted their goods in Malaysia. The British and Americans also stood in the way of Japanese hegemony over Southeast Asia, and in 1940 denied Japan access to critical war materials by peaceful trade. This forced Japan to resort to military conquest.

On the day following the attack on Pearl Harbor the Japanese struck at Malaysia with landings on the East Coast and air raids on Singapore. American help was rushed in, but with little effect, for the British were not really prepared to defend the area. In two major stages the British had retreated from East Asia, first in 1902 when they recognized Japanese predominance in northeast Asia, then at the Washington Naval Conference in 1923 when they agreed not to fortify Borneo. Britain fell back upon its supposedly impregnable naval base at Singapore. This fortress was completed in 1938, but the war in Europe had prevented Britain from sending the forces necessary for its defense.

All of Malaysia was conquered in a swift campaign of ten weeks. The battleships *Prince of Wales* and *Repulse,* sent out by Churchill at the last minute, were sunk off Pahang on the third day. The Japanese seized the important oilfields at Seria and Miri on undefended Borneo, and then occupied the rest of British Borneo within seven weeks. Meanwhile another Japanese force pushed down from the north of Malaya to Singapore's back door, many of the troops pedalling bicycles down the fine highways unopposed. With complete control of air and sea, and holding Singapore's water supply from Johore, Japan compelled the surrender of the great fortress of Singapore. There, at the Ford plant on February 15, 1942, the British signed the surrender, ending a century of British rule and marking the start of the new era of Asian nationalism. Over 165,000 British troops were killed or captured. British officials and civilians were sent to prisons or to work brigades on the "Railway of Death" made famous by *The Bridge over the River Kwai.* The psychological impact of the defeat and humiliation of the seemingly invincible forces of Britain cannot be overestimated.

The Japanese had three years to prove that their rule was better than the Europeans'; they only proved that Asian rule was possible. One of the worst aspects of the Japanese occupation was that it had the economic effect of repeating the Great Depression. Malaysia was cut off from its normal markets in the United States and Europe, and the smaller portion of production that could be absorbed by Japan was greatly reduced by Allied attacks on Japanese shipping. Great unemployment resulted, particularly in the Malaysian cities, even though the Japanese tried to shift the surplus population to the countryside to grow food. Health suffered from lack of medicines and medical services. The shortage of all goods caused a wild inflation, and excessive taxation and extortion further burdened the business community.

In politics the Japanese record is somewhat mixed. They stimulated the nationalism of each of the three races, but in different ways. Their attitude toward the Chinese was negative, while they encouraged the Malays and Indians, thus accentuating communal differences. The Japanese tried to turn the government over to the Malays, and thus prepared them for independence.

They released Malay nationalist leaders who had been interned by the British and permitted them to form a Malay military force. To maintain order the occupiers used Malay police, who often incurred the hatred of the Chinese whom the Japanese oppressed. Malay collaboration with the occupying forces was widely condemned by the Chinese and British, but was tolerated by the Malay community as long as it served their goal of full independence. This aim was encouraged by the Japanese who established the first elective councils and urged formation of a political party, KRIS, which envisaged independence of Malaya and union with Indonesia. They took a practical step toward such a union in linking Malaya and Sumatra in a political unit like the old Johore Empire. On the other hand, Borneo was separately administered, and the northern Malay states returned to Thailand.

The Indians of Malaysia were also favored by the Japanese. The invaders' interest in occupying India coincided with the patriotic desire of most Indians to see their homeland freed of British rule. The Japanese first encouraged the formation in Malaysia of an Indian National Army and an Indian Independence League. The First Indian Division actually invaded Indian territory and the Second reached Burma. Indian collaboration with the Japanese, like the Malays', is hard for Westerners to understand unless one knows that most Indians were suspicious of the Japanese and gave them only as much support as served their own ends of independence, and that many joined in active resistance to the occupation. The occupation was an important event for the Indian community; for the first time it had a sense of identity and importance.

In contrast with the favor which they showed to the Malays and Indians, the Japanese treated the Chinese with brutality. This policy stemmed from the support the Chinese had given to the government of China and their continued resistance to Japanese rule. Japanese killings of Chinese who might become opposition leaders only increased resistance, as shown in the Double Ten Revolt in Sabah in 1943 when the Chinese killed the Japanese garrison in Jesselton. Reprisals only brought more resistance, and the Japanese retaliated with mass executions. A sixth of the population of Sabah died during the occupation.

Opposition to the Japanese was encouraged by the United States. American forces based in the southern Philippines helped the Sabah resistance movement. In support of anti-Japanese activity in Sarawak former British officials were parachuted into "The Great Within" of Borneo. In Malaya the most effective resistance was carried on by the Malayan People's Anti-Japanese Army, to which the Americans gave support. A country that had been so easy for the Japanese to conquer in a blitzkrieg campaign against a distracted enemy turned out to be harder to hold against a determined alliance with the power of the United States behind it.

American forces were the first to reconquer Malaysian territory. They swept up from New Guinea along the north rim of Indonesia. Their primary target was the same as the Japanese had in 1941, the strategic oil fields of Borneo. The first landings were made from the American Seventh Fleet at Muara in Brunei and at Labuan on June 10, 1945. From there Miri and southern Sabah were liberated while the main towns of northern Borneo were pounded by Allied air raids. Brunei, Jesselton, Miri, and Sandakan were virtually destroyed. American troops then moved on to Japan; the rest of Malaysia remained under Japanese rule until British liberation in September 1945. The final months of waiting were horrible. Imports of food were cut off completely and government authority broke down. Lawless elements armed themselves and settled old grudges. Chinese guerrillas took into their hands the punishment of collaborators, and soon there were race riots.

The effects of three years of Japanese occupation were generally negative. The occupation was a time of privation and severe malnutrition as well as great property loss from confiscation, bombing, and scorched-earth tactics. Education halted with the closing of schools; all public services deteriorated badly. In order to survive, many Malaysians resorted to bribery and payment of blackmail; public morality and respect for government sharply declined. Worst of all, the races were set against each other.

On the positive side, all groups became more politically conscious. The Malays realized their ability to govern and saw the vision of independence. The Indians achieved a sense of self-identity and experience of political organization. Many Chinese had been set into violent opposition to government and found that they could wield effective guerrilla force.

For the British, Malaysia would never be the same. While the British were welcomed back, often affectionately, they were returning to a new postwar world. To their everlasting credit, the British knew it, and did not try to resist the new nationalism.

Postwar Rehabilitation

The peace and order achieved by the British administration after the war gave Malaysia a breathing period for rehabilitation that was denied to Indonesia and Indochina. The British Military Administration which arrived in September 1945 restored order and put an end to race riots. The guerrilla forces were disarmed and Allied prisoners of war and political detainees were released. Economic reconstruction was accomplished in a very short time. American relief supplies were contributed through the United Nations. Rebuilding of towns, particularly those destroyed by air raids, was begun. The basic economic wealth of Malaysia, the tin mines and rubber plantations were largely undamaged, but required a great deal of investment in new machinery.

British political policy was considerably different after the war, for they were now ready to prepare colonies for self-government. In contrast, their moves toward unification were rather hesitant. The British were not ready to unite Malaysia or entrust it to an international organization such as the United Nations, as Americans proposed during the war. Nor were the British prepared for integration with Indonesia, an idea the Japanese had encouraged. In a pragmatic way they began by tidying up the tangle of holdings. In Borneo it was widely recognized that economic rehabilitation would be impossible under prewar protected state governments, so both Sabah and Sarawak were taken over directly as British crown colonies. The North Borneo Company sold its rights to the British government, and Sabah passed peacefully to direct British rule in July 1946. In Sarawak, however, the transfer occurred only after considerable resistance from the old-time

British and from Malays whom the Brookes had favored. The murder of the British governor, Duncan Stewart, in December 1949 finally awoke people to the folly of opposition.

With Sarawak and North Borneo under direct rule, Britain now made some modest steps toward the integration of Malaysia. The governor-general was in charge of the entire area as before the war, but he was now given responsibility for foreign affairs. The first person appointed to this office, Malcolm MacDonald, was a popular choice.

The effort to unify the Malayan peninsula resulted in great discontent. The first step was to bring all of the Malay states into a Malayan Union, excluding Singapore. The separation of Singapore from Malaya on April 1, 1946, was a day of mourning for many. The reasons for dividing the two were a combination of the desire to retain the imperial naval base, a concession to Singapore traders who wanted to maintain the free port status, and consideration of the Malays who feared being outnumbered by the Singapore Chinese.

The Malayan Union met serious opposition from the Malays. The Malay sultans had agreed to the union, but only, as one of them said, after he had been given a "verbal ultimatum" which hinted that he might be deposed for his wartime collaboration. Protests were directed largely against the British proposal to grant common citizenship to all races. This would have given the Chinese about a third of the votes against a half for the Malays. Malay opposition was encouraged by old-time British officials. Malay nationalism suddenly became a major political force, centering around the first Malay political party formed by Dato Onn bin Ja'afar, Chief Minister of Johore, in March 1946. This party, called the United Malays Nationalist Organization (UMNO), is still the governing party of Malaysia today. When UMNO boycotted the installation of the British governor and showed its strength by rallying both the Malay people and the sultans, the British agreed to compromise.

The British satisfied the demands of the Malay nationalists by denying the Chinese equal citizenship. This solution permitted the union to be carried out in effect, though the name was changed to the Federation of Malaya. The form given to this new federation in 1948 still exists in the government of Malaya today. The states retained theoretical sovereignty and were given authority over relatively minor matters such as local government, health, land and agriculture. The federal government exercised the real power, for budget and finance were handled in Kuala Lumpur by the British high commissioner. A legislative council was created, to which a majority of Malaysians was appointed. But the racial balance was reflected in the appointment of twice as many Malays as Chinese. The practical effect of the federal constitution was to make Malaya a Malay country under British rule, which satisfied the Malays temporarily.

Now that Malay nationalism had been satisfied, it was the turn of the non-Malays to protest. The Indian community was dissatisfied at not having been consulted about the federation, but gave no strong opposition. The Chinese, however, were indignant. Led by the moderate Tan Cheng Lock, they organized a multiracial council which presented three demands: (1) reunion of Singapore, (2) elected legislature in Malaya, and (3) equal rights for all races. The council called a general strike in October 1947, and support from a wide spectrum of Chinese brought business in Singapore to a halt. But neither the British nor the Malays were moved, and on February 1, 1948, the federation was put into effect. The moderate Chinese, following Tan, gave in gracefully, but other Chinese went into open rebellion.

The separation of Singapore was not reconsidered or remedied, but formalized in the 1948 agreement. The city colony moved in the direction of a separate country as the British gave Singapore its first representative government and elections.

The Emergency: Defeat of Communist Guerrillas

It is tempting to seek evidence of foreign conspiracy to explain the origins of the Communist insurrection, or Emergency, as the British called it. It did draw inspiration from the worldwide communist movement, and there is some circumstantial evidence that it began after the Asia Youth Conference in Calcutta in February 1948, whose call for revolution seems to have been followed in Indonesia, India, and the Philippines. There is no evidence, however, that the Malayan Communist Party was ordered to revolt. The success of the Chinese Revolution in 1948 may have inspired confidence in the success of arms. But the basic causes of the Emergency lay in domestic discontent, and the experts generally agree that these would have caused the revolt without outside stimuli.

The sources of discontent can be traced to the Chinese community, to which communism appealed almost exclusively. The greatest attraction was the promise of welfare and unity because the Chinese were deeply disaffected with their inferior political status under British rule. Discrimination in favor of the Malays in the civil service, education, land ownership, citizenship, and suffrage was directed against the Chinese. The poor living conditions after the war only accentuated the political problem. To young Chinese who were uprooted from the old society and seeking a new way of life the communist cause offered adventure, comradeship, advancement, and identification with an organization like the traditional secret societies.

The British had trained guerrillas who were largely Chinese and already communist influenced during World War II. During the postwar vacuum the ex-guerrillas had a brief taste of power, but were disillusioned when their arms were taken away and they got little recognition for their wartime resistance. Initially the Communist Party was content to work peacefully, particularly in organizing labor unions among the urban people. But, as the postwar economic situation began to improve, the base for their support began to slip away. The temptation to give in to the violent element in the party increased. The turning point came in March 1948 when a new leader, the twenty-six-year-old Chin Peng, took over from a discredited older leader. The party turned to active terrorism.

In reply, the British declared a State of Emergency in June 1948. The Communists were driven into the mountains of Malaya, using the 425,000 Chinese farmers as a base of support. At the most the Communists had 14,500 troops, against which the British arrayed thirty times the manpower. If one counts only the 3,250 Communist guerrillas against the 40,000 British regular soldiers, the ratio was twelve to one. In the initial four years of the Emergency the British strategy was basically military, to create security for vital installations and for Chinese villages. A key device was the creation of "New Villages" where 650,000 Chinese were reconcentrated into fortified towns. This draconian policy might have alienated the Chinese further, but the British won their loyalty by important psychological measures, such as giving social services (particularly schools), land from the Malay reserves, and some participation in government.

The United States government gave the British full support in its battle, regarding the Emergency as part of an international conspiracy, without understanding the complex social and political roots of the problem. In 1948 the United States sent small arms to Malaya that it had denied the French in Indochina and the Dutch in Indonesia. Later it sent out 10,000 carbines for the police and ten helicopters for jungle operations.

For all the favorable factors, after four years British efforts seemed to make little progress. The Emergency reached a nadir in 1951 when the Communists killed the high commissioner, Sir Henry Gurney. The British faced a cruel dilemma familiar to Americans in Vietnam: security was necessary to make economic and social progress, but military measures would impede such progress. When British Colonial Secretary Lyttelton announced in 1951 that "Law and order must be restored before there is further political progress," he was met by a storm of protest from Malaysia.

Lyttelton's retraction was the turning point in the Emergency. He challenged the Malays and Chinese to unite and prove that they should be given the political freedom they demanded; this gave a strong impetus to Malay-Chinese cooperation. The British sent out a new high commissioner, General Sir Gerald Templer, with the promise that Malaya would become self-governing. Templer's primary task was to restore law and order. He used both the carrot and the stick. Most Malaysians and many British seriously doubt the value of the stick measures, such as cutting down the rice ration of the town of Tanjung Malim and burning a village in Province Wellesley. Templer himself repeated: "The answer lies not in pouring more troops into the jungle, but in the hearts and minds of the people." The decisive British policy, according to Prime Minister Abdul Rahman, was to make clear that they really intended to give Malaya independence. Three key measures were taken: holding local elections; letting Malayans take over government departments; and relaxing citizenship requirements for Chinese. These produced a change in the psychological climate in 1952, and a turning point in the warfare. The Emergency was not officially ended until 1960, twelve years after its declaration, and in 1969 there were still some 400 Communist guerrillas operating on the Thai-Malayan border.

Like all historical events, the Communist defeat cannot be attributed to a single cause. Communist weakness was a factor; their leaders lacked popular appeal, they were poorly organized, their logistics and communications were weak, and they rigidly followed the Chinese strategy of building on a rural base, which the British removed. The revolt never got beyond the terrorist phase, for, as the party confessed, it had cut itself off from the masses. It alienated too many by terrorism; it never did appeal to Malays and Indians, and too few Chinese joined. In addition to Communist weaknesses and British advantages, there were two fortuitous factors in the defeat of the revolt. The economic recovery of Malaya was greatly boosted by the Korean War boom, when American demand for rubber gave employment for resettled Chinese, profits for smallholders and merchants, and revenues for government services. The second chance factor, the growth of a free trade union movement as an alternative to Communist organization, was a result partly of the growing prosperity and partly of government encouragement, to which the United States lent its help. But in the end, the critical element in the victory was the psychological one: by giving concrete evidence that they really intended to get out the British took away the Communists' chief grievance.

Preparing Malaya for Independence

The British scheme of training for self-government is particularly interesting because of its success in Malaya. Basically, the same theme, with variations, was used in the other parts of Malaysia. It involved gradual replacement of British officials with local people, first in the legislature and then in the executive branch of government. In the first stages, local persons were appointed and later elected. Gradually the proportion of Malaysians was increased, first to a majority of the legislature, and finally to the whole. At last the people elected the whole legislature, and from this the majority party leaders formed a government. This was the last step before independence.

The initial tentative steps were taken in the nineteenth century, with unofficial nominees to councils. In the interwar period Malaysians got their first appointed representatives, but without elections. In the postwar era the British permitted elections in Singapore, though not in Malaya, where racial antagonism presented obstacles. United Malays National Organization chairman Dato Onn called a meeting in 1948 to study ways to eliminate racial friction so that a united Malayan nation could be created. As a result, the moderate Chinese led by Tan Cheng Lock decided to form a Chinese party, similar to the Malays' UMNO, to promote the welfare of its own racial community through cooperation with other races. Thus was founded the Malayan Chinese Association (MCA) which is still the major partner of UMNO in Malaysian politics. In his enthusiasm for interracial cooperation, Dato Onn pushed the UMNO farther than the conservative Malay elements would permit and was forced to step down from leadership in 1951. Since then the party has been led by Tunku (Prince) Abdul Rahman, who has had to walk a tightrope of defending Malay communal interests while increasing cooperation with the Chinese.

The unwritten understanding between UMNO and MCA to pursue moderate tactics and seek racial harmony in the interest of independence was gradually formalized into what is today the governing party of Malaysia, the Alliance. The modest beginning came during the first elections in Malaya, held in Kuala Lumpur in February 1952, when UMNO and MCA leaders agreed informally to enter UMNO candidates in Malay wards. This was such a success that the tactic was repeated in other town elections in 1952. Having proved the value of the coalition by winning 94 out of 124 seats, the Alliance set forth its own national program in 1953. It not only requested general elections, a natural move, but demanded that the British give them the second step, an elected majority. That the British granted this unusual request is a tribute both to the moderation of the Alliance leaders and to British foresight in realizing that this was the critical concession which would persuade the Malaysians that they really intended to withdraw. Their confidence was fully vindicated by the elections of 1955, for the Alliance won in a landslide of 51 out of 52 seats.

The British then permitted the majority to form a government under its leader, Tunku Abdul Rahman. As Malaya's first Prime Minister, he formed a multiracial cabinet of five Malays, three Chinese, and one Indian, which reflected the racial representation won by the Alliance in parliament: 34 Malays, 15 Chinese, and one Indian and one Ceylonese (members of the Malayan Indian Congress, which joined the Alliance before the election). With remarkable speed and grace the British granted independence to the Tunku's government after only two years of self-government. Thus, on August 31, 1957, Malaya became the first area in Malaysia to achieve independence.

Meanwhile, the British were preparing the other parts of Malaysia for self-government under the same process of training. Singapore was the most politically advanced, having had its first city elections in 1948. The British allowed it to elect twice the number of seats in the second elections in 1951. By 1955 the colonial power granted the same privileges it had given to Malaya: a wholly elected legislature with a prime minister and cabinet selected from the majority. Singapore actually got this four months before Malaya, with David Marshall of the Labour Front becoming the first elected prime minister of the first fully elected legislature anywhere in Malaysia, in April 1955.

When Malaya gained its independence, Singapore lost its earlier lead in political development, held back by British strategic interests. Prime Minister Marshall resigned after finding that the British would not give up control over internal security, which they felt necessary to protect their naval base. His successor, Lim

Yew Hock, obtained self-government short of independence in 1959 only by conceding British control of foreign affairs and security. As a self-governing state, Singapore set up a parliamentary democracy on the English model. The first elections (Singapore's fourth) gave a clear majority to the People's Action Party and made its leader Lee Kuan Yew prime minister, a position he has held ever since.

East Malaysia, with less economic and educational development, moved far more slowly. In Sarawak, the local governments introduced in 1948 were gradually given multiracial representation. Sabah did not get a legislature at all until 1950, and then with only a few members who were not colonial officials. The first local elections in Sabah were not held until 1952, and in Sarawak in 1956. The people had no experience with general elections before 1959.

Only in the late fifties did the Borneo states make rapid advances toward self-government. A new constitution of Sarawak in 1957 gave a majority of elected members to the legislature, and the first elections in 1959 stimulated the formation of the first political party in all of British Borneo, the Sarawak United People's Party. Brunei too made its first steps toward representative government with a new constitution of 1959. The state held its first elections for the newly created legislative council in 1962. All contested seats were won by the Parti Ra'ayat led by A. M. Azahari, who advocated independence and a Borneo federation under the Sultan of Brunei. North Borneo lagged behind in political development, not getting a majority of nonofficials on its legislature until 1960. Before independence the state had no experience with general elections, and hence little impetus to formation of political parties.

Toward Unification of Malaysia

While rapid progress in the direction of self-government was being made in most of the territories of Malaysia, the British took steps to bring the separate units together. Malcolm MacDonald's proposals in the forties for the formation of a single unit received little public attention or interest in Malaysia. The British began to take several practical steps in the fifties. They created a single currency for all the territories in 1952, held the first interterritorial conference the next year, and arranged to have the colonies represented in the United Nations by a joint delegation. On the other hand, their creation of a separate airline, supreme court, and survey department for Borneo seemed to work in the direction of a separate Borneo state, for which there was much sentiment among local British citizens. British government preferences were never clear, and probably shifted from time to time.

Western Malaysia provided the main initiative for union. As early as 1954 the present Permanent Secretary of the Malaysian Foreign Office, Ghazali bin Shafie, publicly proposed merger. In 1956 Lee Kuan Yew also advocated it; his proposal reflected the long-standing desire in Singapore for reunion with Malaya. By 1958 Tunku Abdul Rahman had endorsed a British suggestion of merger, but favored joining only Borneo with Malaya, leaving out Singapore since it raised Malays' fears of Chinese predominance. The British refused to release Borneo without the inclusion of Singapore.

The Tunku signaled the shift in Malayan policy by his historic address in Singapore in May 1961 calling for merger of all units. The change was precipitated by the victory in a Singapore election of a left-wing candidate over a People's Action Party man who favored merger. This opened the prospect that Singapore would shift even farther left toward a "little China" that would become increasingly chauvinistic and even Communist. The Tunku's proposal naturally delighted the government of Singapore, which had always favored merger, and it worked hard to allay Malay fears. It gave in on the touchy issue of Malay privileges to get autonomy in education, finance, labor, and civil service. The British government gave hearty approval to the idea of merger, but made it conditional on the findings of a royal commission headed by the governor of the Bank of England, Lord Cobbold, on feelings of the Borneo inhabitants. The commission reported in April 1962 that two thirds of the people favored merger. Half of these asked certain safeguards, which were met by granting Borneo states autonomy in education and immigration.

Popular support for the merger was sought and obtained in a series of elections. In the Singapore referendum of September 1962 three quarters of the voters opted for merger on the terms of autonomy worked out by Lee Kuan Yew. Sabah's first elections, held in December 1962, brought victory to a multiracial coalition which favored merger, as did those held in Sarawak in early 1963. Elections were not held prior to unification in Malaya, but those held in 1964 confirmed the widespread enthusiasm for union.

Just when sentiment seemed to be sweeping Malaysia along toward successful merger, scheduled for August 31, 1963, opposition unexpectedly appeared from three sources: Brunei, Indonesia, and the Philippines. Brunei had long been lukewarm toward the idea. Although it had cooperated in many ways with Malaya, popular sentiment seemed to favor re-creation of a greater Brunei state, a solution that would be strongly opposed in Sarawak. The Sultan had approved joining Malaysia in principle, but the elected majority of the Brunei legislature opposed it, and, in apparent frustration, led a revolt on December 7, 1962. This revolt, though suppressed, was one of the factors in the Sultan's not joining Malaysia. Others were the reluctance to have Brunei's oil revenues used for Malaysian development and the unwillingness of the Sultan to wait his turn to become Malaysian chief of state.

The Brunei Revolt gave an indication of internal dissatisfaction with the merger, and precipitated foreign opposition to the formation of Malaysia. Although the Philippines and Indonesia had given their blessings to the idea, they went into opposition for very complex reasons which will be discussed later. Here let us pursue the course of unification, saying that foreign objections were temporarily resolved at a summit meeting at Manila in August 1963. That meeting requested the United Nations to send a representative to ascertain Borneo public opinion about merger. U Thant promptly sent Lawrence Michelmore, an American-born international servant whose commission found that the British elections in Sabah and Sarawak genuinely reflected the view of the people. When it was apparent that the report would be favorable, the Tunku, under strong pressure from Lee Kwan Yew (himself hard-pressed by the left wing), was unwilling to delay independence any longer and anticipated the United Nations report by announcing that Malaysia would be formed on September 16, 1963. Jumping the gun gave Sukarno an excuse to oppose the union by military action, which he called Confrontation. Nevertheless on September 16 Malaysia became a reality, incorporating with Malaya the former British colonies of Singapore, Sarawak, and North Borneo, but excluding Brunei.

In less than a century of effective rule the British had made more impact upon Malaysia than any other invader. Physically, Malaysia had been transformed. Where there had been fishing villages, there were now great wharves and oil tanks with giant steamers lying along side. Where there had been tangled jungle now rose gleaming skyscrapers. Much of the landscape of Malaya was a scarred desert of old tin mine tailings of white sand. Hills that were once clad with virgin forest were now planted in neat contours of rubber trees. Lumber roads spread like tentacles through the vast forests of Sabah. Only the remotest mountains were still untouched by the marks of modern Western enterprise.

Fishermen and rice farmers were now in the minority; far more people lived by trade and by working in factories, mines, and rubber plantations. The majority of Malaysians enjoyed a higher standard of living than before. Each year more people could afford better clothing, a more varied diet, and luxuries like wrist watches, bicycles, and even automobiles.

Under British rule there had been a great advance in public services. In almost every small town in Malaysia one could drink water from the tap and turn on an electric light. Modern medical services were available in most rural areas and fine city hospitals provided advanced surgery and care. Health campaigns had virtually wiped out the terrible scourges of cholera, smallpox, and yaws, and made a strong attack on other diseases like malaria. One sobering result of this medical care was the sudden growth of population, at the rate of over 3 percent a year.

Despite the outward manifestations of Western culture, seen in architecture, literature, art, and music, one cannot measure the depth of the influence of British education. The English school system had been adopted but how much had it altered Malaysian patterns of thought? Ancient superstitions were now questioned; a scientific attitude was now widely observed, at least among the educated. Malaysian students studied the classics of Western culture and absorbed much of that humanistic tradition inherited from Greece and Rome and developed through the Renaissance. But the Malaysian had observed the ambivalent example of European colonialism.

The greatest legacy of the British was their system of government. They bequeathed efficient enforcement methods of the army, navy, customs service, police, and secret service. More important, they left forms of parliamentary democracy based upon free elections, with a responsible executive; the example of an honest and hard-working bureaucracy; and an impartial court system based upon justice and respect for human rights. There is evidence that they also transmitted the spirit behind these forms. Finally, the British gave reality to the concept of Malaysian unity. Whether this form of government would last would depend upon Malaysian culture and its ability to create and maintain a spirit of national harmony. It is to this problem that we now turn.

4
Government and Politics

Some of the best governments in Asia—democratic, efficient, and progressive—can be found in the Malaysian area. Both Singapore and Malaysia have regimes that are democratic in form and practice. Each has conducted several free elections without violence or corruption. Their constitutions are carefully observed and civil liberties are protected. Their leaders are responsible to the people and legislature, where genuine opposition is permitted.

These governments are truly popular in that they have won the loyalty of the overwhelming majority of the people. A nondogmatic approach to economic policy permits free enterprise to develop the economy while the government provides a wide range of social benefits. Administration is not only efficient, but honest.

The biggest problem of government in Malaysia is the creation of a nation out of a multiracial society in which communalism and local interests are far stronger than the sense of nationalism. The effort to build a nation is complicated by the twin specters of economic depression and foreign aggression. The great virtue of these governments is that the problems are faced squarely.

Presently there are three separate governments in the area: The Federation of Malaysia, formed in 1963; the Sultanate of Brunei, which chose not to join this unit, but remained a British protectorate; and the Republic of Singapore, which separated from Malaysia to become an independent state on August 9, 1965. We shall begin by describing the largest of these states, Malaysia.

The Government of Malaysia

The chief of state of Malaysia is the Yang di-Pertuan Agong, called by many the King. As in the British system, the ruler is meant to be mainly a figurehead, a rallying point for national loyalty. The nine hereditary rulers of the Malay states of Johore, Kedah, Kelantan, Negri Sembilan, Pahang, Perak, Perlis, Selangor, and Trengganu elect one of themselves to the post, which has a five-year term. In general, the ruler who has reigned the longest is chosen. Aside from the ceremonial functions that are expected of the British king, the Malaysian chief of state has the authority to safeguard the special position of the Malays. The Constitution (Article 153) specifically permits him to make quotas for scholarships, licenses, and government offices for Malays.

The prime minister. The real power of the Malaysian government is in the hands of the cabinet and its leader the prime minister. Tunku Abdul Rahman has been national leader since 1955. "The Tunku" (Prince), as he is known, was born in 1903 of royal blood, one of forty-five children of Sultan Abdul Hamid of Kedah.

The Tunku speaks proudly of his mixed background: "You know, I am half Thai," he will say, explaining that his mother was the daughter of a Thai official whose family had come from the Shan States of Burma. He was actually born under Thai sovereignty, for in 1903 Kedah was still dependent on Thailand. It remained so until he was six when his father's extravagances (such as a million dollar wedding for the crown prince, including thirty cases of champagne a day for three months) brought British intervention.

The Tunku's education was cosmopolitan. He began the study of English with an Indian teacher. At ten he spent a year at school in Bangkok where he learned some Thai. Then he attended the Penang Free School, perhaps the best secondary school in Malaya, run on strict British lines. From there he went to Cambridge University, where he received his bachelor's degree in 1925, just barely passing his examinations. He then began the study of law; this lasted a quarter of a century with interruptions and distractions.

These years were not entirely lost, for he was deeply involved in the early Malay national movement. He was cofounder of the Malay Society in 1927.

Making little progress on his study of law, Rahman returned home in 1931 to join the Kedah civil service, an important training ground for future administrators. In an organization noted for resistance to British intrusion, he became known as "the stormy petrel" for quietly withstanding orders and opposing the British proposals for centralization. As district officer he established a reputation for interest in the people, as a result of his attempts to improve the welfare of Thai villages. At this time, too, he married a part-Thai daughter of a Chinese merchant.

During the Japanese occupation the Tunku continued in the Kedah government service, which was transferred to Thailand. He did much to help people suffering from Japanese rule and maintained contact with the resistance movement. He was a founder of the Saberkas (Unity) movement which advocated democracy, socialism, and independence. In the postwar chaos he distinguished himself by making peace between Malays and Chinese. After the war he returned to England to complete his law degree. He credits his deputy premier, Tun Razak, with coaching him through the law examinations and keeping him away from distractions.

Returning to Malaya in 1949, he served in the Kedah government first as public prosecutor and later as judge in Kuala Lumpur. In 1951 he was chosen to head UMNO after Dato Onn had lost Malay support by advocating a noncommunal policy. The idea of the Alliance of two explicitly communal parties, the UMNO and MCA, was not his, but he was the person most responsible for making it work; this ingenious solution to racial politics is still the basis of Malaysian government.

The Tunku's greatest contribution was obtaining independence without bloodshed or bitterness. Since independence was granted in 1957, the Tunku has continued to show his genius as a peacemaker with proposals for Southeast Asian regional cooperation, his sincere attempts to solve the Dutch-Indonesian dispute over New Guinea, his generous response to the United Nations request for troops and funds for the Congo, and his leadership of the Malaysian merger.

The natural question is, "Who will succeed the Tunku?" No one, including the logical successors, is willing to discuss the question because the Tunku has been so successful in holding the country together in peace.

The cabinet: future leaders. Likely successors are among the present cabinet ministers. The deputy prime minister is Tun Razak bin Hussein, who holds three key ministries: defense, home affairs, and national and rural development. Razak is the workhorse of the government and administration. He takes over during the Tunku's absences, which are becoming more frequent, and became prime minister for four months when the Tunku went out to campaign during the 1959 elections. He is nearly twenty years younger than the Tunku, and thus the logical successor as premier.

Razak gives a soberness to the administration that balances the Tunku's light touch. Though friendly, he is more reserved than the Prime Minister. The government radio used to play a song praising him: "Even though you seldom laugh, you are appreciated by all."

While the Tunku comes from the heavily populated farm state of Kedah, Razak is from the Texas-like giant frontier state of Pahang. He was born in Pekan, where his father was a key adviser to the Sultan of Pahang. He was educated in the traditional pattern. He attended the Malay College at Kuala Kampar, an English-language preparatory school which the British had established to train sons of the minor aristocracy for administration, and Raffles College in Singapore, the predecessor of the University of Malaya.

In 1947 he went to England to study law at Lincoln's Inn, and passed his examinations in eighteen months instead of the usual three years. It was then that he helped the Tunku pass his examinations and teamed up with him in the revived Malay Society, which determined to avoid the bloodshed of communal riots like those they observed at India's independence. Razak also joined the Fabian Society and was strongly influenced by democratic socialism and state planning.

Returning to the Pahang civil service in 1950, Razak rapidly rose to become the youngest chief minister of Pahang at the age of thirty-three. Five years earlier the UMNO had tried to get him to take over its chairmanship, but he had declined with true modesty, saying he was too young. He did take on the deputy chairmanship under the Tunku and has remained the number two man in national politics since 1951.

Razak became the youngest member of Rahman's first cabinet. Given the crucial portfolio of education, Razak produced in 1956 a report, which bears his name, outlining a system of national education. The report declared that the key to unity and economic progress was education. Cultural differences could be preserved by permitting Chinese, Tamil, English, and Malay schools to continue, but a national language must be taught in all. The report recommended that resources be poured into education, into both school buildings and teacher training; more money was to be spent on this than any other item in the budget. To modernize and progress, the educational system had to emphasize science and technology.

With the implementation of the Razak Report in 1957, its author was moved up to deputy premier and defense minister. In this position, he directed the final operations against the Communist guerrillas from his now famous Operations Room. When the Emergency ended, this room became the center for Malaya's economic development program for which Razak was given responsibility in 1959. Razak has directed the Five-Year plans and kept track of their progress by weekly reports of his subordinates which he checked personally by visits to the field.

When Indonesian Confrontation began in 1964 much of Razak's efforts were diverted from development to defense. He also took an increasing role in foreign affairs as chairman of the Malaysian delegation to the United Nations and on tours of the African states.

Much of the efficiency, hard work, and honesty of the Malaysian government stems from the example of the Deputy Prime Minister. Yet there is much caution about accepting his succession to the Tunku. Razak has an undeserved reputation for not being sympathetic to the Chinese. Some of this is merely in contrast to the Tunku's cosmopolitanism. There is no evidence of any kind of racial prejudice in Razak.

Next to the top is a kind of inner cabinet of five men who make most of the decisions. Two non-Malays represent that racial and political balance of the party and the country: Tan Siew Sin and V. T. Sambanthan. The choice of portfolios is interesting. Tan, representing the economic interests of the Chinese, is minister of finance. Sambanthan, an Indian, is minister of works, posts, and telecommunications, areas that have always had many Indian administrators, laborers, and unions.

Tan Siew Sin is national chairman of the Malayan Chinese Association, a post in which he follows his father, Tan Cheng Lock, the founder of MCA and promoter of interracial cooperation. The Tan family is an old Straits Chinese one from Malacca, wealthy from rubber investments, but traditionally devoted to public service. Tan has established a reputation for impartiality and honesty. In appearance he is every bit the tough banker peering from his steel-rimmed glasses.

Sambanthan, a gregarious giant of a man, is president of the Malayan Indian Congress (MIC), the third member of the Alliance. He was educated in one of the best secondary schools in Malaya and graduated from an Indian university. One of his pet ideas is the establishment of rubber plantations cooperatively owned and operated by the workers.

Neither Tan nor Sambanthan can hope to become premier as long as UMNO is the major partner in the Alliance. They have shown no ambition for this, but continue to be indispensable representatives of the multiracial balance.

One of three top Malays in the inner cabinet has the best chance of becoming premier. The minister of education, Mohamed Khir bin Johari, is the kind of person who could duplicate the national interracial mediator image of the Tunku. Though a very outgoing and genial person, he has a reputation for being a tough administrator and party leader. Khir Johari is from the same town in Kedah as the Tunku, though twenty years younger. He got his start in politics during the war with the Tunku, running the welfare organization for destitute workers who returned from the "Railway of Death," and working in the nationalist Saberkas party.

His vote-getting ability was proven in the first elections in 1955 when he won the largest majority of any of the fifty-two candidates. He was then thirty-two, and started in the government as assistant minister for economics. In 1957 he took over the Ministry of Education from Razak and successfully implemented the national education program. He was a highly successful minister of commerce and agriculture, and when a national scandal affected the minister of education he restored the reputation of that ministry. An astute politician, long a key party official, Johari resumed the job of secretary-general of UMNO after Syed Ja'afar resigned over the expulsion of Singapore in 1965. He travels everywhere with a photographer and clearly knows the art of public relations. Above all, Khir Johari has made it absolutely clear that he believes in interracial harmony; like the Tunku he is a supporter of Malay rights but is practical enough to feel and to say that he sees no point in submerging the other cultures.

Senu bin Abdul Rahman is another promising politician. After graduating from the Malay-language teachers' college at Tanjong Malim, he went to sea. He jumped ship in Los Angeles, where he worked as a waiter to support himself while studying at the University of California. He earned a bachelor's degree in political science. Like Johari, Senu was an early trainee of the Tunku and succeeded Johari in Saberkas and UMNO. After diplomatic training by the government of Australia, he held the critical post of ambassador to Indonesia; he later served as ambassador to West Germany. He is now minister of information and culture.

Sardon bin Haji Jubir has had less variety of government jobs, remaining minister of transport continuously since 1959. He attended Singapore's best secondary school, Raffles Institution; he went to England to study law, and was admitted to the bar from the Inner Temple. Returning to Malaya just before the occupation, Sardon got administrative experience under the British and Japanese. He was one of the founders of UMNO. One of the first Malays to run for elected office, he was elected to the first Singapore legislative assembly in 1948 from a racially mixed constituency. He has been re-elected repeatedly from predominantly Chinese districts in Johore state. In 1951 he became leader of UMNO youth, a job he still holds, though he is close to fifty.

There are five other Malays in the cabinet who are possible successors, but two are of the Tunku's generation, and the others hold relatively minor posts. There are five Chinese in the cabinet, but no non-Malay is likely to become prime minister. The junior Chinese and Indian ministers are merely in line to succeed as leaders of the MCA and MIC.

Civil service. A major reason for the strength of Malaysian government is the remarkable quality of its bureaucracy which numbers about 100,000, less than 1 percent of the population, which is low by any standards.

Malaysian public servants have a reputation for honesty; high salaries are undoubtedly in part responsible for this. At the lower levels, the standard of pay is high enough that officials do not need to supplement their salaries with outside income as they do in so many Asian countries.

The bureaucracy appears to be efficient and increasingly competent. Educational standards are high, in part because of the quality of Malaysian education itself. There is, of course, a shortage of technically trained persons, and the attractions of industry and the professions have been great. Yet the prestige of public service is considerable, so that many of the best university graduates do go into government.

The most frequent complaint concerns the quota system in the elite Malayan civil service. The British reserved it entirely to Malays until 1953, when they established a quota of one non-Malay to five Malays. Later the quota was reduced to the present one to four for the civil service and one to three for the foreign service. The quota itself does not reveal the whole situation, for, as administered, the government will recruit the four Malays before it fills the non-Malay position. It is not surprising that university students find this situation frustrating.

Lack of promotions and salary discrepancies are also problems of the colonial legacy. The large number of promotions into the Malayan civil service to fill vacancies left by the British caused a bunching of a certain age group. This now limits promotions for lower officers, and will cause some frustration until the older group retires in ten to twenty years. The great disparity in salaries between the top and middle levels of the civil service is a carry-over from the colonial era when extra compensation had to be given to the British for living abroad and to keep them from going into private employment.

Another serious problem is the long delay in replacing British officials in Borneo. The tendency was to keep them until Borneans could be trained rather than bringing in Malayan civil servants. This policy became a political issue between Kuala Lumpur and Borneo, although actually there were few Malayans who were eager to go to East Malaysia. Some sent initially were not success-ful, in part because of traditional Borneo resentment of Malay bureaucracy, a legacy of Brunei rule. The unhappiness of the Malay officials, who had often left their families behind, and the attempt of some British officials to retain their own jobs may have aggravated the problem. Whatever the balance of causes, the Malayan civil servants were withdrawn and were sent only for special projects. This failure to integrate administratively is one of the main hinderances to Malaysian unity.

Parliament and the People

A democratically elected parliament controls the government which we have just described. The legislature consists of two houses, the Senate and House of Representatives. The Senate is much like the British House of Lords. In practice it has tended to act as a rubber stamp since its approval of legislation is not neces-sary and it cannot originate financial bills. It does provide a forum where the views of states and various interest groups can be aired.

The House of Representatives works much like the British House of Commons. Members are elected for five years unless the House is dissolved sooner. Although all 159 members will be elected directly by universal adult suffrage in the next election, the first Malaysian parliament was made up of representatives variously chosen by the four components of the 1963 merger. Malaya's members were directly elected in 1964; the Borneo states' members were chosen by indirect elections in 1962–1963. As a result of these separate elections, Parliament contains over twenty parties representing a wide range of political views.

Government parties. The government is run by the Malaysian Alliance, a group of regional coalitions which bring together communal parties. The result is not as unstable as might be expected, for there is a solid majority controlled by the Malaya Alliance Party which in turn has the strong United Malays National Organization (UMNO) at its core. The Alliance has no common membership or national conventions, but is in principle governed by a national council and executive committee. In fact, however, party decisions are made by the inner cabinet members, such as the Tunku, Razak, and Johari working with the MCA and MIC chairmen Tan Siew Sin and Dato Sambanthan.

The Alliance claims to have no ideology, but certain basic ideas can be detected. Above all, it upholds the principle of cooperation and preservation of the individuality of the races. It acknowledges that the Malays will have to be protected politically as long as the Chinese have economic preponderance. In economic policy the Alliance emphasizes national development within a free enterprise framework, which admits to a kind of mild socialism.

The Alliance is composed of the three communal parties: the Malays' UMNO, the Chinese MCA, and the Indian-Ceylonese MIC. The dominant member of the trio is the UMNO. It has always appealed exclusively to Malays, but its position on the communal issue is moderate. While it defends Malay privileges, it also emphasizes racial harmony and cooperation. This, in any event, is the majority viewpoint; UMNO contains a wide spectrum of opinion ranging from rabid ultra-nationalism and racism to fairly liberal views. The pull to the right has always been strong, but since 1965 the Ultras of the right have clearly lost influence. In that year Secretary Syed Ja'afar, whom many considered responsible for the extreme statements that contributed to the separation of Singapore, resigned from party leadership. Another rightist party leader, Syed Nasir, resigned in 1967 over government moderation on the national language issue. The moderate views held by the Tunku and the Malay cabinet ministers seem genuinely representative of the bulk of party members.

UMNO's economic policy is progressive, favoring both private enterprise and welfare socialism, with an emphasis upon rural development and improvement of the rural Malays' standard of living. UMNO is strongly anti-Communist as a result of its experience in the Emergency, but it has resisted the idea of joining a Western alliance. There is a definite anti-imperialist element within UMNO that sympathizes with the Afro-Asian bloc, particularly on such issues as Arab opposition to Israel. Since the party is predominately Muslim, it favors Malaysian cooperation with Islamic nations. Because of Malay cultural ties with Indonesia the party is strongly attracted to friendship with that country.

The Malayan Chinese Association (MCA) is the major partner of UMNO in the Malayan Alliance. More than UMNO, MCA represents the conservative social and economic interests of its community, but it does support social welfare programs. The MCA is strongly anti-Communist; indeed, it originated as a reaction to the Communist insurrection. It would certainly oppose any kind of nationalization. As we have seen, MCA has been interested in interracial cooperation from the beginning and has encouraged the formation of the Alliance and of Malaysia. Like the UMNO, the party has its periodic disciplinary problems. The most troublesome issues have been the lack of speed with which Chinese are given equality, especially in electoral representation, and the use of the Chinese language.

Very much the junior partner of the Alliance is the Malayan Indian Congress (MIC)—whose initials some Indians jokingly say stand for "May I come into the Alliance?" The party supposedly represents a wide range of Indians, businessmen and moneylenders as well as railway and estate laborers, and linguistic and religious groups ranging from Muslim Pakistanis to Ceylonese Hindus. There is some doubt that the MIC fully represents the Indian community. Its present leadership is mainly from the business class, though the Alliance has won the support of the predominantly Indian labor movement, particularly the National Union of Plantation Workers.

The Alliance won nearly 60 percent of the vote in Malaya's election of 1964, compared with 51 percent in 1959. The victory can be credited to the leadership of the Tunku who emphasized the party slogan: "Safeguard Your Independence—Onward toward Prosperity." The campaign coupled economic development with the special issue of war with Indonesia, which had broken out in 1964.

Opposition parties. The opposition in Malaya covers a wide spectrum, from religious conservatives who demand a state run according to the law of God to persons who have been accused of being godless Communists. On the right we find the Pan Malayan Islamic Party (PMIP), a strictly racial party appealing to Malay chauvinism. It is openly anti-Chinese and favors more restrictive immigration and citizenship laws. It advocates greater protection of the Malays and criticizes UMNO for giving in too much to the Chinese. Among the parties it alone makes a direct religious appeal, favoring an Islamic theocratic state. It is thus strongest in the conservative Malay rural areas of the East Coast. Despite this conservatism on social issues, PMIP has a strong appeal to the left. Although it is quite firmly anti-Communist it advocates socialism. Its international outlook is anti-imperialist and pro-Indonesian. It actively promoted union with Indonesia and opposed the Malaysia merger. Both ideas were considered unpatriotic during Confrontation, and, at the height of tensions in 1965, Dr. Burhanuddin and other PMIP leaders were arrested on charges of conspiracy to set up a Malaysian government in exile in Karachi.

PMIP is still the main opposition party and could easily regain strength if there were race riots or crises on the domestic or international scene. UMNO must watch the party carefully because of the appeal of its stress on Malay rights and religion. To be truly representative of the views of rural Malays, and to keep them loyal, the UMNO is pulled strongly in a conservative direction.

The opposition on the left is far more important than appears from the six seats in Parliament scattered among four different parties. These parties won a quarter of the popular votes in 1964, over half a million. About a sixth of the vote was won by the Malayan People's Socialist Front, a coalition of three left-wing parties: the Labour Party, the Party Rakyat, and the National Convention Party. The oldest member of the Front is the Labour Party which talks about socialist economics rather than race, though it appeals most strongly to Chinese. The Party Rakyat, the Party of the People, has an ideology that sounds much like Sukarno's. These two parties formed a Socialist Front which was joined by a third, the National Convention Party, with a program of democracy, anti-colonialism, and cooperatives.

The Front fought the 1964 elections on a platform advocating complete socialism and opposition to foreign colonialism, which included the Malaysia merger. The Alliance picked up the merger issue and tried to prove that the Front was unpatriotically pro-Indonesia. Though the Front won few seats, its third of a million popular votes showed considerable support from the urban masses. Further evidence of support came in 1965 when the Front staged mass demonstrations in the national capital. Since then the Front has broken up and various efforts have been made to form a coalition of all of the parties of the left.

Left-wing opposition is likely to continue to appeal to the masses in the cities, largely Chinese, on the platform of equal rights, greater social benefits, a more independent foreign policy, and reunion with Singapore. If Malaysia's prosperity continues and the Alliance undertakes more urban development and keeps the racial situation calm, the opposition will not gain in future elections.

Singapore Parties and Politics

Singapore has been an independent republic since 1965 with a democratic parliamentary system very much like Malaysia's. There are the same standards of honesty and efficiency and understanding of the democratic process. The main difference in government structure is its single-chambered Parliament; this small area does not require a two-house legislature.

The dominant party in Singapore is the People's Action Party (PAP). It appeals to the electorate with a democratic socialist program which provides big public housing programs and honest government. It is anti-Communist, but inclined to neutralism in foreign policy. Although multiracial, PAP has not been able to escape some identification with the Chinese who constitute a majority in the city and in the party hierarchy.

Lee Kuan Yew has been the leader of the PAP since its founding in 1954 and chief minister since 1959. Lee is the son of a Chinese immigrant who was an employee of the Shell Oil Company. He was an outstanding scholar at the Raffles Institution and at Raffles College. Lee was nineteen when his education was interrupted by the Japanese occupation. He says of its effect on him: "My colleagues and I are of that generation of young men who went through the Second World War and the Japanese Occupation and emerged determined that no one—neither the Japanese nor the British—had the right to push and kick us around. We determined that we could govern ourselves."[1]

After the war Lee went to Cambridge where he won a "double first," that is, top grades, in two examinations (in law), an unusual distinction. In England he also read Marx, and like the Malayan leaders was influenced by the Labour Party, then establishing Britain's postwar socialist government. In 1950 Lee returned to Singapore to practice law and took on labor union defense. He says of his work, "We extracted every ounce of political and material advantage out of the dispute with the colonial government and got the maximum benefits." As a socialist and labor defender he became acquainted with Communist leaders in Singapore and worked with them for independence. In the process he got to know Communist tactics and finally broke with the Communists in 1961. This partnership made Lee suspect in the eyes of the many who determine guilt by association, but it is clear

[1] *The Battle for Merger* (Singapore: Government Printing Office, 1961), pp. 110–111.

that Lee was never a Communist. His subsequent career has amply substantiated this.

He has established an effective political style of grassroots campaigning that appeals to all the races of Singapore. His open white shirt, a contrast with the coat and tie of the old regime, has become the uniform of Singapore's civil servants. This is not just for show; Lee's example for hard work has spread throughout the government. Lee is impatient, and it is this that led to so many conflicts with the more deliberate Malaysian leaders. He has a quick mind, and a tongue that is quicker, which often gets him into trouble. But Lee's efforts on behalf of the working men and all the racial groups of Singapore have been so selfless that few people question his sincerity. He will never be loved like the Tunku, but he is sure to be remembered as the founder of Singapore's independence and the man who defeated the Communists and established a welfare state for the benefit of all the people of Singapore.

Singapore elections in 1963 were held only five days after the formation of Malaysia. Lee Kuan Yew successfully reversed the trend to the left, and the PAP won a solid majority. Much of the success was due to the highly effective personal campaign by the PAP leaders. Lee talked to his audiences in four languages: Mandarin, Hokkien, Malay, and English. Although the issue of merger with Malaysia had been decided in the referendum of 1962, the PAP campaigned for its successful implementation, pointing out how critical this was for Singapore's economic prosperity. The PAP's socialist economic program which had produced such spectacular public benefits as low-cost housing were also emphasized. In addition to personal appearances, the PAP effectively used the government-controlled radio and television. Another important factor in the campaign was the "detention" of the major opposition leaders.

The PAP won a clear majority. Nearly half of the Singapore electorate voted for the PAP in a 93-percent turnout (voting is compulsory in Singapore). The only real opposition was the left-wing Barisan. Though its leaders were jailed, it was permitted to campaign and retained its thirteen seats. The Barisan Socialis is a pro-Communist party which broke away from the PAP in 1961. The split developed shortly after the Tunku's Malaysia proposal in June of that year. Ostensibly the cause of the split was the union leaders' demands for the release of left-wing detainees and more rapid progress toward self-government. But increasingly the issue which divided the PAP and the Barisan was merger. The final split liberated the PAP from its inhibitions about communism and the party went out of its way to prove that the Barisan was pro-Communist and pro-Indonesia.

In the 1963 elections the Barisan attracted a third of the popular vote. It proved strongest in the rural areas of Singapore, except for two districts in the downtown area. After the elections the Barisan members resigned piecemeal from their seats in the legislature. The largest desertion was the resignation of nine in October 1966 in protest against Lee's "fascist" government. In subsequent elections to fill vacancies, the PAP won every contest until the Barisan disappeared as an overt political force. However, underground the Barisan remains a potential source of Communist agitation in Singapore. The greatest protection against this is the removal of the popular grievances which they might exploit through an effective social welfare and industrialization program such as the PAP is providing.

The PAP again proved its popularity by winning all seats in the 1968 general elections, which gives Lee Kuan Yew another five years in power.

Elections in East Malaysia

The elections in the Borneo states of Sabah and Sarawak took on international significance when attention focused on them to gauge the degree of support for merger with Malaysia. The delegates from these states to the Malaysian Parliament were chosen by indirect voting. A United Nations team investigated these elections and certified that they were free and democratic.

The first elections in Sabah's history were extended over a period of five months because of the remoteness of some localities. Voting began in December 1962 for district councils. When these positions were filled, in May 1963, the councils sent representatives to electoral colleges in each of the four residencies of Sabah. In July the four electoral colleges chose eighteen assemblymen. Finally, the state Assembly (which included three nonelected members) chose the fourteen representatives to the Malaysian Parliament.

At both the state and national levels a coalition called the Sabah Alliance won all the seats. Though this was modeled on the national Alliance, it does not have the same cohesiveness. It has contained four or five communal parties headed by rival leaders. The United Kadazan Organization (UNKO) is the oldest member as well as the oldest party in Sabah. It was founded in 1961 by Donald Stephens, a newspaper publisher who has been the leading politician of Sabah. His party appealed mainly to the Kadazans of the coastal area. A rival party, representing the Kadazans of the interior, was founded by the Murut chief G. S. Sundang. Only after the elections did these two Kadazan parties combine to form the United Pasokmomogun Kadazan Organization (UPKO).

The Kadazan party's main competitor in the Sabah Alliance is the United Sabah National Organization (USNO), which claims the support of about 100,000 Muslims, mainly Malays and Bajaus. The leader is the Bajau chieftain, Datu Mustapha bin Datu Harun, Donald Stephens' chief rival in Sabah politics. The Sabah Alliance also includes Chinese and Indian parties, but they are weaker than in Malaya.

In the 1963 elections in Sabah popular interest was high; 80 percent of the voters cast ballots. The polling went quietly, although the outbreak of the Brunei Revolt caused the detention of a few voters and delay of balloting in a couple of places. The United Nations declared that "The elections were freely and impartially conducted" with almost no voter complaints.

Following the elections the Alliance formed a state government that was theoretically unified, but which was in reality a rivalry of the competing Muslim and Kadazan parties. The second elections in Sabah, held in April 1967, did little to resolve this rivalry. The Kadazan party bested the USNO by only two seats. Nevertheless, by allying with the Sabah Chinese Association (SCA) and other Alliance candidates, Datu Mustapha was able to form a state government without Stephens' party. When UPKO voted to leave the Sabah Alliance, the Federal government persuaded them to remain for the moment in the name of unity. Although it is unfortunate that this opposition has developed along religious lines, it is encouraging that Sabah has developed a two-party system.

The Indonesians, who had the greatest doubts about the popular support for Malaysia in 1963, observed the 1967 elections and declared themselves satisfied that they were "peaceful, orderly and smooth."[2]

Sarawak's politics have followed somewhat the same pattern as Sabah's: early opposition to Malaysia; then support by a proliferation of parties which coalesced into a loose Alliance for the 1963 elections; and a breakup of the Alliance when the state chief minister moved into opposition. The main difference is that Sarawak's politics have been made more exciting by the open opposition of a strong left-wing party, the Sarawak United People's Party (SUPP). This was founded in 1959 on a platform of independence, democratic socialism, and interracial harmony. Despite efforts to appeal to other races, it is predominantly Chinese. There is much uncertainty about the extent to which the People's Party is controlled by the Communists. Certainly its top leaders, Ong Kee Hui, a wealthy banker, and Stephen Yong, a British-trained lawyer, are not. However, the governments of Britain and Malaysia have both published substantial evidence to show that the party was infiltrated by Communist agents who use it as a front for eventual takeover.

The dominant party in Sarawak has been the Sarawak Alliance. The senior member was the Sarawak National Party (SNAP), led by Stephen Kalong Ningkan, an Iban of the Second Division, where the party is strongest. As in Sabah, the main tribal group is split politically; the Temenggong Jugah, the paramount chief of the Ibans of the Third Division, represents a more conservative

2 *Straits Budget*, June 7, 1967, p. 14.

and federalist faction, analogous to the position of Mustapha in Sabah. Jugah's Party Pesaka Anak Sarawak (PAPAS) was the leading member of the Alliance, supported by a Malay party, Barjasa, and a Chinese party.

As in Sabah, the British held the first Sarawak state elections at four levels, first for district councils, next in the five divisions, then to the state council, and finally to the national Parliament. The Sarawak Alliance won an absolute majority of the state and national seats in 1963, though winning only a third of the total vote, which represented three quarters of the electorate. The United Nations mission heard many complaints from the People's Party that there had been coercion, but concluded that the elections were "conducted smoothly, fairly and efficiently." As in Sabah, the United Nations did not feel that the detention of persons during the Brunei Revolt materially affected the election. It found that the major issue was merger with Malaysia, which 60 percent of the population favored.

Since the elections the Sarawak Alliance has split somewhat along the same lines as in Sabah, but more deeply. After much jockeying the first chief minister, Ningkan, took his National Party out of the Alliance in 1966, creating a crisis. Since Ningkan did not have a majority he was unable to retain the state premiership; he was replaced by Kuala Lumpur. Ningkan successfully challenged the constitutionality of this action in the courts (on the grounds that there had been no vote of confidence), so the federal government amended the Malaysia Constitution to permit removal of the premier by the state council. When this amendment was voted in late 1966 Ningkan denounced the move as "Kuala Lumpur's brand of guided democracy."[3] The National Party then campaigned for the coming elections as an opposition party with a platform of anticommunism, multiracialism, dedication to defense of the Sarawak constitutional democracy, independence of the civil service and its Borneanization more gradually than Kuala Lumpur urged.

The whole Ningkan crisis upset the schedule for the elections

[3] *Straits Budget,* September 28, 1966, p. 19.

in Sarawak, which were to have been held at the same time as Sabah's in 1967. As in Sabah, Sarawak developed effective opposition which is not entirely encouraging because of its tribal orientation.

Communism in Malaysia

The communist movement is forbidden in all parts of Malaysia, Singapore, and Brunei, but still is an underlying threat to the country. In Malaya the danger is the least, since the Emergency effectively defeated and discredited the movement. The threat there really ended by 1958 when the guerrillas were driven into the wilds of the Thai-Malaya border. Under the leadership of Chin Peng, about four hundred Communist guerrillas still operated in 1969, mostly on the Thai side. The Malaysian government cooperates with Thailand in military and intelligence operations to get rid of this menace; the United States has encouraged this.

In the big cities of Malaya and in Singapore the Communists can exploit the grievances of non-Malays and the lower classes. The governments keep a close watch over the movements of leaders and periodically arrest them under the emergency laws. The strongest weapon against the Communists, however, is political and economic progress.

The communist movement is more threatening in Eastern Malaysia. It started with the anti-Japanese activities of the Chinese during World War II, but did not form any real base until about 1951 when the Overseas Chinese Democratic Youth League was founded. Although the party was suppressed by the British it gained strength during the 1950's by following a characteristic anti-colonial line. Independence robbed them of this appeal, but they still exploit Sarawak regionalism by talking about the new imperialism of the Malays. They also capitalize on the old grievances of Chinese inferiority and economic poverty, especially among the Chinese farmers. In Sarawak politics the party is believed by some to operate through the People's Party, whose ideas often coincide with those of the Communists.

The covert activities of the Communists in Sarawak were lumped together by the British under the name Clandestine Communist Organization (CCO). At the start of the Confrontation the Communists sent several thousand young Sarawak Chinese across the border to Indonesian Kalimantan for training as guerrillas. Some of the young agents were captured when they recrossed the border, but the boundary area is so rugged that many escaped detection. The total of hard-core CCO members was estimated at about two thousand, and they might have been able to rally from ten to twenty-five thousand sympathizers in the Chinese villages in widely spread parts of Sarawak. During Confrontation it was the constant fear of the government that the CCO might lead a popular insurrection to coincide with an Indonesian invasion. It is not clear why the Communists did not revolt when they had the support of Indonesia, but it is probable that the CCO leaders felt that they were not yet prepared for successful action.

The most serious threat came in June 1965 when a Sarawak police post was attacked and the brother of Chief Minister Ningkan killed. The post was only eighteen miles from the state capital of Kuching in a heavily patrolled military zone which the raiders penetrated after crossing the rugged border without detection. What was most perturbing was the apparent cooperation or acquiescence of the local population. The British, who were in charge of local security, reacted with severity, hoping that this would prevent any future risings. Their "Operation Hammer" put the Chinese residents of the area under twenty-four-hour curfew and reconcentrated them into secure locations modeled on the New Villages of Malaya.

Following the end of Confrontation in 1966, Indonesia stopped its guerrilla training and most of the guerrillas were rounded up. But the CCO threat is still there as long as there is local Chinese discontent to feed upon. The real test of the Malaysian government will be whether it will rely solely upon suppression of the movement or whether it can identify the sources of dissatisfaction and remedy them and thus win the people back to its side.

Problems of Malaysian Democracy

There are some limitations on Malaysian democracy; the most important concern citizenship restrictions and civil liberties. These are the areas where the most progress can be made toward a freer society.

Citizenship restriction affects voting and freedom of movement. British laws operated to favor the "indigenous" peoples over the Chinese. A person of Malayo-Indonesian race, even if born outside of Malaysia, had no difficulty in becoming a citizen, but if a person or his parents were born in China, citizenship was limited. In recent years the tendency has been to relax citizenship requirements so that the right extends to all persons born in the country, but this is being done at a different pace in each of the states. The laws are so complex that a summary only approximates the legal situation.

Singapore, with its predominantly Chinese population, is the most generous, and hence a model to which Chinese elsewhere aspire. Everyone born in Singapore is automatically a citizen. All foreign-born, perhaps as many as a quarter of a million, are excluded from voting until they have lived in Singapore for a decade. The Borneo states are more restrictive. Birth does not automatically confer citizenship except to Borneo peoples. Thus, many Chinese are excluded, even though they may be second-generation residents. The number affected is not known, but is less than 15 percent of adults. In Malaya in general, Malays and Indonesians had no problem becoming citizens, but Chinese and Indians found it more difficult. As a result, at the time of merger there were nearly a million unenfranchised adults, a quarter of the whole. This number is shrinking rapidly, for all Chinese can become citizens after ten years' residence if they have no police records and learn a little Malay. In Singapore, Borneo, and Malaya more and more Chinese are becoming elegible for citizenship.

The greatest limitation on Malaysian democracy lies in the emergency powers which the government can exercise in time of crisis. Even in normal times freedom of movement, speech, and assembly and protection against arbitrary arrest can be waived for the public good. Freedom of the press is restricted by licensing, import controls, and prohibitions against inciting violence and racial hatred. Free speech is limited to the extent that it is forbidden to spread subversive rumors. The right of assembly can be limited if it is considered dangerous. The right of association is controlled by official registration.

These restrictions are potentially serious. So far, however, they have been exercised with moderation and care. The insecurity of the times, produced by the Emergency up to 1960, and Confrontation from 1963 to 1966, explain the necessity for limitations in the minds of Malaysians, even if it does not entirely justify them. Most of the restrictions are directed against Communists, who have made clear their desire to overthrow the state by violence. The continuing threat of violence, especially from the CCO in Sarawak and the Communists in Singapore and northern Malaya, may justify continuing security measures.

For the ordinary citizen there is little restriction of freedom. In contrast to the surrounding countries of Asia where arbitrary acts of government and restraints of liberty have become commonplace, Malaysia's limitations are not very great. There is no overt censorship, and the press says some surprisingly critical things about officials. Meetings are held about almost every subject. Most people accept the restrictions of movement as a means of keeping the Chinese from overwhelming the local populations. The most unpopular limitation is the inequality of Malay privileges. Most Malaysians consider this part of the bargain on which the country is founded, and all except the Malay ultranationalists hope that protection of the Malays can be removed as quickly as the Malays can be brought into a more competitive economic position.

Certainly the elections held in Malaya, Singapore, Sabah, and Sarawak have been free and democratic. There has been virtually no violence at the polls. The voters turned out in large numbers and seem to have understood the issues. What criticism there has been about freedom of elections in Borneo has been resolved by the United Nations and international observers. The only real doubt about any of the election processes is the detention of opposition leaders in Malaya, Singapore, and Borneo under emergency powers—to date with restraint.

The biggest question for the future is whether the governments of Singapore and Malaysia will continue to use their emergency powers with restraint. The most serious recent application in Malaysia, deposing of the chief minister of Sarawak in October 1966, was widely criticized. There is always the danger, of course, that emergency powers can be used to maintain a government in power when it is threatened by peaceful opposition.

5
Creating a Malaysian Nation

Unity is the fundamental political question of the Malaysian area. It is important to know if the breakup that began with Brunei's refusal to enter the federation in 1963 and was continued by Singapore's secession two years later portends the further disintegration of Malaysia. Will Borneo remain within the federation? Is there real hope that Singapore and Brunei will eventually join Malaysia to form a united nation? We shall try to answer these questions by analyzing the forces that work toward disunity or unity.[1]

Perhaps the most important integrating factor in any federation is a common way of life. Our historical survey has already showed that there are basic similarities in the culture of the whole Malaysian area. There is the underlying Malay society with its community cooperation, a subsistence rice economy, and village council decision-making. Among all the Malay-related peoples there is a prevalent core of beliefs, particularly the belief in the existence of spirit in all objects, which has been overlaid by Hinduistic religious influences. There is moreover a similarity of native social practices linked by customary law. The Malaysian cultures are linked by closely related languages, one of which, Malay, is the lingua franca.

But side by side with this traditional Malay culture is another,

[1] This analysis of integrative factors reflects the ideas of Karl W. Deutsch, *Nation Building* (New York: Atherton, 1963), and *Political Community and the North Atlantic Area* (Princeton: Princeton University, 1957) and intervening works.

the Chinese immigrant society. The coexistence of these funda-
mentally different societies is an important cultural feature.
Throughout the area one finds a symbiosis of the Chinese and
Malays: the most obvious sign is the row of Chinese shops along
a road or stream, from which the Chinese supply and purchase
the goods of the surrounding Malays. In a sense Singapore is a
tremendous expansion of this phenomenon. This Chinese city is
not some isolated foreign implantation, but an integral part of
the economy of the area, even more dependent on the surrounding area than the reverse.

The symbiosis of Malay and Chinese cultures is neither complete nor harmonious. The great question is whether the things
which divide them are greater than those which bring them
together. Their ways of life—religious, cultural, artistic, linguistic, and even economic—seem so far apart that one wonders
whether they can ever understand each other. Yet there are
numerous examples of the integration of the Chinese with other
peoples: the Baba Chinese of Malacca whose Chinese customs and
language have become Malayanized; the Sino-Kadazans of Sabah;
the complete disappearance by peaceful assimilation of the Chinese in rural Trengganu; or the Chinese and Malays living side
by side in the modern city of Singapore, happily adopting each
others' children, learning the National Language (Malay) in a
predominantly Chinese city. This process of integration has been
going on for centuries, and continues today more strongly since
the Chinese are separated from their mother country. If one
focuses solely on the traditional cultures, they seem far apart, but
if one looks at the whole picture of relatively peaceful symbiosis,
one can speak of a Malaysian culture.

The Indians, in all their variety, add another different culture,
some of it familiar in the great Hindu tradition of Malaysia, or
to the Chinese through Buddhism. This third culture was also
modified by the Malaysian environment and accepted into it quite
peacefully.

British rule, as short as it was, gave some uniformity to Malaysian culture. The English language became the second lingua
franca of the area; not everyone speaks it, but this common vocab-

ulary and stock of ideas has a tremendous binding force. The English education system is a strong integrative factor, especially among the elite. The values instilled by English education have been reinforced by a common government system. One cannot be sure how deeply ingrained English ideas are, but they are certain to influence to some degree the evolving Malaysian political system.

There is, then, a base for a common way of life that is stronger than the separate cultures of China, India, and Indonesia.

Communications and mobility of persons are another important factor in creating an integrated community. Between Singapore and Malaya there is a great traffic of people over the Johore Causeway, which carries a railway, road, and footpath. Thousands of autos cross this link daily and there are regular bus trips. Customs formalities are not great, but there is control of immigration; still this does not keep thousands from commuting daily between Johore and Singapore.

On the other hand, the flow of people between Malaya and Borneo is quite small. The distance between the two parts is a serious obstacle to contact. People do travel by weekly steamer between Borneo and Singapore; a couple of hundred are transported weekly by steerage, and about fifty passengers in second and third classes. Businessmen and officials find it cheaper and faster to travel by Malaysia Singapore Airways, which has a couple of flights a day, taking about a hundred people. There are also small trading craft moving back and forth. Though the total traffic does not amount to a very large exchange of people, it does represent the influential elite of businessmen, officials, and professionals and artists.

Economic links between the parts of Malaysia are surprisingly strong. Singapore is the hub of the area; like New York it cannot live without its hinterland, and it is not easy to imagine Malaysia completely cut off from Singapore. The island processes much of the produce of the outer areas, cleaning Sarawak pepper, sawing Sabah timber, and milling Johore rubber. Singapore is the storekeeper to the whole area, furnishing oil products from the big bunkering stations, cigarettes for the smuggling trade, and bulldozers for the Sabah forests. Of course, Singapore's economic links with the mainland of Malaya are the strongest; they include such necessities of life as the water that is piped across the Causeway from Johore.

Singapore is also the banker for all of Malaysia, its insurance agent, and its shipping center. It is the hub of the jointly owned Malaysian Singapore Airways. The Singapore-operated Straits Steamship Company provides the main freight and passenger link, not only between Singapore and Eastern Malaysia, but between Brunei, Sarawak, and Sabah themselves. There has always been a common currency for the area. After the decline of the international currency of the Spanish dollar, the British introduced the Straits dollar, which was common currency until 1967; the currencies continue to have the same value and name. The post offices of Singapore, Brunei, and Malaysia are closely linked by a common British system. The bulk of external postal traffic before merger was among the Malaysian states. Other communications are also regional. There is a radio-telephone from Singapore to Kuching and from there to northern Borneo. The completion of the SEACOM cable from Singapore to Kota Kinabalu tied Sabah into Western Malaysia with an excellent telephone service. It is possible to telephone from one end of the region to the other (say, from Tawau to Langkawi), though reception is not very good.

National newspapers circulate quite widely, particularly the *Straits Times,* published in Kuala Lumpur, which has more circulation in Singapore than any other paper and is flown daily to the major towns of East Malaysia and Brunei. The *Times* is one of the most important sources of political and economic news and is influential among the elite of the country. The weekly *Borneo Bulletin,* published in Brunei, circulates widely in all three Borneo states.

Brunei is an important hub of communications for northern Borneo. Practically all the traffic by air, sea, and land into Sarawak's Fifth Division comes through Brunei. The island of Labuan, in Sabah, is closely tied to Brunei by ship, boat, air, and military traffic. In the other direction Brunei is closely tied into the Miri area of Sarawak by Shell Oil operations. Brunei oil is piped across the border to the oil refinery at Lutong in Sarawak, and from there sent all over Malaysia. There is still a great deal of traffic across all the artificial borders created by the Brookes.

It would be interesting to quantify all the contacts between various parts of Malaysia, but that would not tell us much about their qualitative impact. How much mutual knowledge is created between the parts of the area by all these contacts? The people of Borneo seem to know more about what is going on in Singapore than they do about any other place in the world; Sarawak people certainly know less about their neighbor Indonesia than about Malaysia, even without the barrier of hostilities created by Confrontation. Sabah is more cosmopolitan, and there is almost as much knowledge about Hongkong, the Philippines, and Celebes as there is about the rest of Malaysia and Singapore. On the other side of the China Sea, Malayans tend to know more about Singapore than any other place, but little about Borneo. There is a corresponding ignorance of Borneans about Malaya.

Frequently a school child will know more about England than about his home. William the Conqueror is more likely to be familiar than Parmeswara, Shakespeare better known than Malay writers. On the other hand this in itself is a unifying factor among the English-educated elite. Textbooks are rapidly filling this gap by offering more geography and history of Asia, and particularly about Malaysia. Already elementary school children know more about their country's history and economy than their parents.

The rapid growth of modern mass communications between the parts of Malaysia is also remedying the information gap at a tremendous rate. One cannot underestimate the importance of the national radio to integration. Radio Malaysia broadcasts to all parts of the region, giving the same news about mutual concerns. The voice of Malaysia is picked up in remotest parts of the area by the inexpensive transistor radios that almost everyone can afford. It also broadcasts in local languages and gives local news, but at the same time gives lessons in the National Language. Television now reaches most of West Malaysia and links Singapore and Malaya; soon it will be available to East Malaysia.

Television first reaches the remote villages when installed in the community centers and coffee shops. Inexpensive Japanese sets, though, are coming more within the budget of the average person.

Frequent exchanges of political leaders are also important in fostering political cohesion. The Malaysia Solidarity Consultative Committee, formed on the initiative of Borneo in 1961, was an early beginning of cooperation among leaders. The provision for twice as many Borneo delegates in the Malaysian Parliament as their proportion of the population called for (40 delegates out of 159, over a quarter, compared to 13 percent of the population) showed Malayan willingness to widen the political base of the country. Two cabinet posts out of fourteen were given to Borneo leaders, though not major ones. Further participation in the Malayan political system was encouraged by the extension of the Alliance system to Borneo in 1963, with the formation of the Grand Alliance Party. This, however, tended to perpetuate the weakness of the Malayan Alliance's coalition rather than create a cohesive party.

In Malaysia as elsewhere the success of a union is inevitably affected by each of the merging state's expectations of benefit from the new political arrangement. From the beginning, the state most eager for merger was Singapore, which had always regarded itself as part of Malaya and felt deprived by the British separation in 1948. Consequently, every government of Singapore made merger a primary goal. The governing People's Action Party from the day of its inception in 1954 accepted Lee Kuan Yew's objective to "establish an independent national state of Malaya" of which Singapore was a part. Two benefits were envisioned: freedom from Britain and economic union with Malaya. Economic considerations were important, for Malaya, Singapore's main market, was beginning to build its own industries and ports in competition with Singapore's. But union had been rejected by Malaya because of the city's overwhelming number of Chinese. Singapore also had to find some way of reassuring the British about the security of the British base.

By 1961 fear of communism was stimulating Malaya's interest in merger. The continuing shift of Singapore toward the radical left caused Malayan officials to fear that the island might become a communist base, "another Cuba," as they put it. Malaya overcame its scruples about the large number of Chinese in Singapore when they saw the prospect that the Malay-related people of Borneo might counterbalance the Chinese. Thus, Borneo was brought in to serve Malayan interests and fears.

What did Borneo hope to gain? Independence within a wider federation was not a strong attraction. Borneans had known considerable autonomy under the British, and in the 1950's colonial officials had teased them with the prospect of an independent Borneo federation. On the other hand, Malaya's financial capital and effective government administration could bring rapid economic development to Borneo. At the time of merger, the fine record of the Federation of Malaya in effective government and its excellent record of economic growth were very promising features.

Borneo also hoped for security against Communist internal threats, which the Malayan government had handled so effectively. The danger of communism in Borneo was increasing, and it seemed to many Borneans that it could be contained best within a larger community. An independent Borneo, the major alternative to Malaysia, seemed less secure amid the turmoil of Southeast Asia in 1963, when war in Vietnam was escalating, when there was chaos in Laos and increasing Communist influence in Indonesia. Few Borneans wanted to become part of Sukarno's guided democracy. A third attraction of the Malaysia idea on the part of some non-Chinese was the hope of special protection against Chinese economic power such as the Malays possessed in Malaya.

Brunei, of all the three Borneo states, expected the least from merger, because it was wealthy, autonomous, and relatively free of the threat of communism. It was the first to desert the idea of merger.

In addition to the main factors of common way of life, shared values, close communications, mutual expectations, and administrative effectiveness, there were some lesser integrating factors. The Malaysian states share a common regional history, and have had in modern times a common experience: British colonial rule;

their sufferings under the Japanese and the exhiliration of dis-covery that Asians could rule themselves; and the postwar experi-ences of recuperation, economic development, population pres-sures, and Communist threats. Insofar as this history has created a common outlook and value system, it is important, but common experiences are not necessarily integrative.

Nor should we put too much weight upon geographic factors. Proximity such as that of Singapore and Malaya does not neces-sarily produce common interests. The thousand miles separating Kota Kinabalu and Kuala Lumpur tell us nothing of the shared interests. Such natural factors as common Malaysian flora, fauna, and climate hardly bring men together.

In balance, if we take the factors that are most important to integration, Malaysia has a great many things favoring success. But there are many troubling questions. Is communalism stronger than racial cooperation? Are traditional values more important than those learned in school? Can the abysmal lack of knowledge of one group about another affect the groups' expectations of each other? Can ignorance and social gaps be bridged? Can Malaysia respond effectively to the needs of people newly brought into the federation? Analyzing the causes of the separation of Brunei and Singapore will suggest answers to these questions.

The Loss of Brunei, 1963

The first break in the impetus toward complete integration of the Malaysian area came with the refusal of Brunei to join in June 1963. Basically, this reflects the operation of parochial inter-ests. Brunei did not want to be submerged in a larger unit to which it would have to make contributions without tangible gains.

The first signs of such parochial interests came in 1956, with the formation of Borneo's first political party, Parti Ra'ayat of Brunei, which advocated a Borneo federation under Brunei leadership. This party was founded by Sheikh A. M. Azahari, who had studied in Indonesia during World War II, and remained afterwards to fight in the Indonesian army. Conditioned by the anticolonial struggle of Indonesia, Azahari represented a far more revolutionary kind of politics than usually found in Malaysia. He advocated nationalization of the oil industry and a democratic government.

Although Azahari's party claimed the support of 16,000 to 19,000 members out of a total population of 65,000, its advocacy of a Greater Brunei was rejected by Sultan Omar in 1958. Rather, the sultan moved in the direction of cooperation with Malaya. As a beginning, oil-rich Brunei lent Malaya $33.3 million (U.S. dollars). In return, it accepted the services of Malayan civil service officers: ten high-ranking administrators, forty-two teachers, and some police. Also Brunei police were trained in Malaya. This experiment in cooperation was not successful, for Malayan officials sent to Brunei encountered hostility, culminating in a violent attack on one Malayan officer by three Parti Ra'ayat members. Brunei persons alleged that the Malayan officials had been arrogant. The Malayans felt threatened and unwanted; they were deterred from resigning only by the personal appeal of the Tunku.

Shortly after the Tunku's Malaysia proposal in 1961, Azahari joined with the other political leaders in Borneo to pronounce the idea of merger "totally unacceptable." Sarawak's Ong and Sabah's Stephens at least went on to investigate the idea; Stephens was converted, but Ong and Azahari continued their opposition. With the leader of a manifestly popular Brunei party opposing the idea, Sultan Omar held off declaring in favor of Malaysia until 1962. The sultan did appoint a commission to inquire into the Malaysia idea; Azahari was one of the two Malay members, joined by a Chinese and an Iban. The fact that the report of this commission has never been published leads one to suspect it indicated that the majority of the Brunei people preferred Azahari's solution of a Borneo federation. However, the Legislative Council of Brunei was informed in July 1962 that the few people who had been consulted "conveyed the impression that they agreed in principle to the concept of Malaysia." On this rather hesitant note, the council approved going ahead with negotiations on Malaysia.

Brunei's first, and long-postponed, elections, held on August 30, 1962, seemed to confirm that the people opposed immediate merger. A landslide victory was won by the Parti Ra'ayat, which opposed union and advocated creation of a three-state Borneo headed by the sultan. Abolition of internal security measures, defense of Malay privileges, mass education including vocational training, rural development, and elimination of the evils of corruption, favoritism, and "family privilege" were campaign appeals unrelated to the Malaysia issue. Parti Ra'ayat won fifty-four of the fifty-five district council seats in Brunei; the other winner joined the party right after the election. The party's victory entitled it to all sixteen elective seats in the Brunei Legislative Council. However, it was blocked from controlling the legislature because the sultan retained the right to appoint a majority of seventeen seats. It was under such conditions of frustration of the popular will that the Brunei Revolt broke out in December 8, 1962.

Azahari was at the head of about 3500 rebels who seized the vital Shell Oil installations in Seria, as well as several administrative centers in neighboring Sarawak and Sabah. Despite this striking success, which took the British by surprise, the rebels failed to capture the crucial government posts in Brunei itself, particularly the police station and the palace of the sultan, whom Azahari claimed to be supporting. The British flew in reinforcements from Malaya. They put down the revolt in a few days and jailed some 3000 suspects. The Brunei Revolt cost sixty-seven lives and several hundred wounded.

The causes of the revolt are complex and not entirely attributable to the proposal for union. The best explanation is that a new generation of politicians led by Azahari were eager to take political power from the feudal aristocracy that surrounded the sultan. They wished control over and participation in the profits of the rich oil companies. Azahari, an ambitious man, found a great deal of ideological kinship in Indonesia, and got support from Sukarno. Though the promised 100,000 Indonesian volunteers never materialized, some of the Azahari supporters received military training in Indonesian Kalimantan.

This foreign support for the revolt tempted many persons in the heat of Confrontation to overlook the domestic discontent in Brunei, on which Azahari capitalized. Among these was the un-happiness of the Kedayan minority, who were reported to have felt treated as second-class citizens by the Brunei government. The revolt also played upon popular dissatisfaction with what Willard Hanna describes as "an ineffectual and corrupt government which showed little concern for their interests," a government "domi-nated by incompetent, conspiratorial, and increasingly corrupt feudal courtiers."[2]

All of this may seem surprising in view of the massive develop-ment program in which the "Shellfare state" provided extensive social welfare programs that were the envy of the poor in Sarawak and Sabah. But, as in other countries, the beginning of develop-ment is the leaven of society which raises expectations and shows the contrasts between the progress of a few and those who have not yet benefited. In Brunei the lot of the rural people had still changed little.

The Revolt made both Brunei and Malaya reconsider the desirability of merger. Rather than force the issue, the Tunku publicly stated that Brunei was not essential to Malaysia. Perhaps this was a tactical error. Having defeated the anti-Malaysia rebels, the sultan was in a strong position to go through with merger. An effort at this time to affirm the importance of Brunei to Malaysian union probably would have had positive results. In-stead of this the Tunku said that his interest in Borneo was in counterbalancing Singapore, and for that Brunei was not essen-tial. Nor should merger be delayed, he said, having in mind, undoubtedly, the Communist threat in Singapore. This would seem a case where a short-term interest worked against the long-term integration.

Despite the lukewarm attitude of Malaya, the Brunei Alliance Party, newly formed of government supporters, came out in favor of Malaysia, and the sultan reaffirmed his interest in merger by reopening negotiations. These proceeded so satisfactorily that by

[2] Willard A. Hanna, *Formation of Malaysia* (New York: A.U.F.S., 1964), pp. 142, 149.

February 1963 the Brunei government announced that it was in favor of joining Malaysia provided agreeable terms could be arranged. It turned out that the two critical issues were money and prestige, and on these negotiations foundered. On the question of financial assets, Brunei did not wish to turn over its entire three hundred million U.S. dollars in reserves to Malaysia, but did agree to contribute $13.3 million a year to the Malaysian treasury. This offer was rejected. Malaya insisted on control of the Brunei oil revenues within ten years and collection of other taxes and duties before that. The final position of the parties on this financial question has not been revealed. It is possible that the Malayan negotiators yielded on this point when an alternate source of development funds came from a Singapore offer of a loan of fifty million dollars to the Borneo territories. Malaya, at least, officially stated that "it was possible to find a solution" to the financial problem.

The more serious question was the rank of the Sultan Omar of Brunei in becoming chief of state of Malaysia. If placed at the bottom of the list of rulers, as a newcomer, he would probably never become chief of state. If he were placed like the others, according to the date of his accession (1950), he would be fourth in line and his chances to succeed would be excellent since the first on the list had been passed over several times. The Tunku agreed to refer the issue to the Council of Rulers, whose prerogative it was constitutionally. It was reported that the sultan of Brunei rejected this, perhaps knowing that the other sultans would not let him be placed ahead. The Malaysian government said the refusal was regrettable, but made a virtue out of defeat by saying that it showed that no state was forced to join Malaysia.

Negotiations with Brunei were broken off. The other states signed the Malaysia Agreement in July 1963, and in September formed Malaysia without Brunei. Thus, the British were left with one last colonial remnant in Southeast Asia, which they still said they hoped would join Malaysia. However, the strongest inducement to get Brunei to do so, the military one, was not very persuasive. The British had said that their military defense of Brunei was in no way assured if it did not join Malaysia, but they were bound by a defense agreement of 1959, and they responded in strength to the threats of both the Brunei Revolt and Confrontation. Brunei became an important base for British operations in Borneo from 1963 to 1966.

Brunei's decision not to join Malaysia is a triumph of parochial interests. Unlike the other Borneo states, Brunei had no need to join Malaysia to get funds for development; Brunei was lending money to Malaya, and had been asked for more. Brunei was already profiting from the benefits of Malayan administrators, but the arrangement had caused friction. So Brunei was inclined to turn to British expatriate officials for help. The sultan's prestige was greater as the ruler of a self-governing protectorate than as a member of the Malaysian rulers' council with few government responsibilities. Nor was there any realistic way that Brunei could recover its lost territories in Borneo, unless it were under Sukarno's tutelage, clearly a risky gamble that no sultan would take.

From the Malaysian side, there was apparently not enough to gain from Brunei membership to justify great concessions. In Sarawak, there was a great deal of talk about Brunei "imperialism." Malaya had not profited from the experiment in helping Brunei; in fact, it had caused bad feeling between Malay cousins. The racial balance of Malaysia could be maintained without the addition of Brunei Malays. Best of all, Brunei's refusal was used to refute the accusation of neocolonialism by showing that any state could reject merger without coercion.

What are the prospects for the future political development of Brunei? The major alternatives are: (1) integration with Malaysia, (2) independence, (3) continued British protection, or (4) affiliation with some other local nation, like Indonesia. The least likely possibility is some association with Indonesia. Such a proposal would bring at least as many problems as integration with Malaysia. The lack of a common frontier would make communications difficult. There would be as much resistance to spending oil revenues for the support of the nearly bankrupt Indonesian economy. It would be difficult to satisfy Brunei hopes for lost territory in Borneo. And the sultan would feel even more uncomfortable within a state that had experienced its social revolution against the feudal classes in 1946–1949 than he would among his fellow Malay sultans.

The Revolt was a warning to the government of Brunei that if it did not progress toward more popular government, unrest might recur, and the Parti Ra'ayat would be in a position to assume leadership. After the Revolt, the British nudged the sultan to give up some of his autocratic powers, which he shared with a conservative aristocracy, and to move toward more representative government. The Constitution and the legislature, which were suspended during the Revolt, were restored in 1964 and the sultan promised to move toward a ministerial system. Security had been restored to the point that elections could be held in March 1965. These were Brunei's second elections, but the first direct ones for the legislative council. The large turnout (80 percent) was surprising because emergency regulations checked the opposition. About a hundred of the hard-core leaders of the Revolt were still detained despite recantation and their avowal of loyalty to the sultan. (These British colonial regulations permit continued detention without trial or specific charges.) The election to the legislative council was only a cautious step toward democracy, for the ten elected members were outnumbered by the six officials, including two British, plus the five nominated members, which included two Chinese.

The beginning of the ministerial system in Brunei in 1965 was even more cautious. The ministers of the major government departments had not stood for election. Four members of the legislative council were admitted to the council of ministers as assistant ministers; two of these were nominated men representing the minority groups. Thus only two junior ministers had stood for election, Pengiran Haji Yussof and Pengiran Damit. Following the normal pattern of development in British colonies, after the popularly elected leaders gain experience in administration, they will move up in the ministries. By 1965 Brunei Malays held only four ministries, that of chief minister, deputy minister, state secretary, and religion.

There have been reports of dissatisfaction with the number of British expatriates who hold important positions in Brunei, and there are no doubt many Brunei citizens who are capable of handling greater responsibility. While there is obvious reluctance on the part of the British expatriates to give up pleasant and well-paid jobs, some of the resistance to responsible government stems from the conservative aristocracy which was supported by the sultan.

In 1967 Sultan Omar abdicated in favor of his twenty-one-year-old son Bolkiah. Though the father has retained much of his influence, the new ruler may bring more rapid development of representative government. The next step is to give more legislators ministerial posts and to have an elected majority in the legislature. At the present leisurely pace these developments do not seem imminent, but eventually some popularly elected person must assume the chief ministry over an all-Malaysian cabinet. He will have to accept a possible opposition of the Parti Ra'ayat leaders like Zaini and other young men who have been educated abroad and will keep up the pressure for more representative government. The development of a constructive opposition will be a healthy thing.

The development of Brunei toward self-government is important because the indefinite continuation of the British protectorate is unlikely. The pressures of the United Nations and of Asian neighbors for decolonization are great, and the British are not apt to hold on to Brunei for mere sentimental reasons as their last colony in Southeast Asia, as the Dutch did New Guinea. By 1967 the British had decided to relinquish all their military commitments east of Suez. Some sort of Commonwealth defense obligation might be assumed by Australia and New Zealand, perhaps in association with SEATO or ANZUS. This might permit Brunei to achieve independence.

It may seem absurd to speak of independence for such a microstate of only 2200 square miles; yet Singapore achieved that status with a tenth the territory. The population of Brunei is a mere 100,000; but the British gave independence to smaller populations in the Indian Ocean and the Caribbean. Clearly such a small state would continue to be dependent upon the goodwill and defense of other countries. One possibility would be for Brunei to find protection within a larger international organization, either regional or the United Nations itself.

Even as an independent state, Brunei would continue to have the closest associations with Malaysia. At the time of Brunei's rejection of union, it was officially stated that Brunei "certainly maintains strong relationship and friendly ties with the Federation."[3] The question of Brunei's joining Malaysia arose again following the Singapore split in August 1965. Chief Minister Marsal rejected the idea, saying that the sultan had not changed his mind, though Brunei still sought friendship with both Malaysia and Singapore. The London *Times* reported that money was not the problem, but rather the fear that "sudden immersion in a relatively democratic entity would mean the precipitous collapse of the feudal structure" which was still "in the grip of the country aristocracy."[4] Assuming a continued development of representative government in Brunei, the barriers to affiliation should become less. With the loss of Singapore's loans for Borneo development, Malaysia has greater interest in further financial assistance from Brunei. Certainly the Malays have much to gain by the addition of the Brunei Malays now that they have found that all Malaysians do not regard them as brothers. The royal precedence problem is now less important with the new sultan who might accept being at the bottom of the list, yet stand good chance of eventually becoming chief of state.

Working against integration of Brunei into Malaysia is the continued resistance of the Borneo states, Sarawak in particular. Trying to accommodate Brunei to the federation might be the straw that would break the patience of East Malaysia. One step away from integration was taken in 1967 when the separation of the currency systems of Singapore and Malaysia brought about Brunei's creation of a separate currency. Brunei's economy remains closely tied to Malaysia's, however.

The most likely prospect for the future of Brunei is that after it achieves independence it will be welcomed by Malaysia and Singapore as a sister state, and helped to join regional and international organizations. The achievement of independence will

3 State of Brunei, *Annual Report* (Kuala Belait: Brunei Press, 1965), p. 14.
4 August 27, 1965, p. 6.

make it harder to integrate into Malaysia, since national pride
becomes involved and the prerogatives of freedom are hard to
give up. After some years of living together, the differences that
separate Brunei and Malaysia may gradually become less, and the
two states may increasingly recognize that what they have in common in their history, culture, multiracial society, and underlying
values and way of life are far more important than the things that
separated them in 1963.

The Separation of Singapore, 1965

The second state to break away from the original Malaysia plan
was Singapore. Basically, Singapore and Malaya had more in
common than any other units: a common way of life and values;
the habits of racial cooperation; frequent and large interchange
of people, goods, and ideas; a shared historical experience; and
geographical proximity. The merger broke down on the fundamental issue of communal rivalry between Malay and Chinese.

This began at the party level where the People's Action Party
challenged the Malayan Chinese Association for leadership of the
Chinese. The rivalry spread to the national level, where Singapore
challenged Malayan leaders on Chinese equality with the slogan
"Malaysian Malaysia." The appearance of these issues showed
that a serious difference of value systems in Singapore and Malaya
had been obscured at the time of the merger.

The older of the conflicts was the rivalry of the two Chinese-
dominated parties, the PAP and MCA. This had begun to show
in the final bargaining over the terms of merger, from February
to July 1963, which involved touchy questions particularly affecting the Chinese community: taxes and tariffs. The share of Singapore revenues to go to the federation and protection of Malayan
industries versus Singapore free trade were both issues that were
fought with some bitterness between the two tough finance ministers, Goh Keng Swee and Tan Siew Sin, who are cousins but arch-
rivals.

During the final negotiations the Malayan Chinese Association
began to challenge Singapore's People's Action Party politically
on its home grounds. These activities evoked PAP leader Lee

Kuan Yew's sarcastic comment that the "merchant adventurers" had come to loot Singapore's wealth. Both the MCA and the Alliance entered the Singapore elections immediately after merger, in September 1963. They won no seats. The PAP returned the challenge by entering the Malayan elections. The Tunku stated that this was "quite contrary to what we agreed" at the time of merger. PAP's conscience seems to have been assuaged by the fact that it did not challenge the Alliance directly, and in fact openly praised the Malay leaders and the Malaysia idea. But it said the MCA could not win "the loyalty of the sophisticated urban population," emphasizing the differences in philosophy between the conservative MCA and the socialist PAP. Even more challenging was Lee's public identification of his party as a possible partner of UMNO, so that PAP would oust MCA. This was regarded as an affront to the MCA. The Alliance took it as a challenge to its own integrity.

Malaysian fear of Lee's ambitions was a major factor in the deterioration of relations. This problem was not at all helped by Lee's frequent ventures into foreign policy. Conflicts had arisen before merger over Lee's trip to Moscow, his meeting with the Indonesian foreign minister, and his tours of Afro-Asian states. Wherever Lee went there appeared newspaper editorials that seemed to reflect his criticism of the Malaysian government. For instance, one editorial during Lee's visit to London referred to "mounting racial distrust" which could only be remedied by the Tunku, who was compared to the Rhodesian racist Roy Welensky.

For the first year of merger the conflict between Lee and the government appeared to be bearable. It was still confined to party rivalry and Lee's apparent bids for national leadership. The racial issue became more important after mid-1964, as the PAP and UMNO got into a contest for the affections of the Singapore Malays that was to culminate in terrible race riots. The race problem arose in part from the fact that merger had led some Singapore Malays to expect the same special privileges that they had in Malaya, though this was excluded by the merger agreement. Instead of legal protection of Malays, the PAP offered a whole different approach to the problem of underdevelopment; it offered benefits to all groups. In fulfillment of its election promises, the PAP was building fine apartments to replace the slum housing. This ran up against the Malay preference for individual houses. When Lee offered to meet protesting Malay community leaders, the UMNO pre-empted him by holding a convention. At this Syed Ja'afar Albar and other UMNO organizers came into Singapore and made a direct communal appeal to the Malays by talking about Malay privileges and the "traitors" who had voted for PAP.

Bloody riots broke out in Singapore in the summer of 1964. On the day before the important Muslim holiday celebrating Mohammad's birthday, highly inflammatory leaflets were passed out to Malays raising the fear that the Chinese planned to kill the Malays and saying "Before Malay blood flows in Singapore, it is best to flood the state with Chinese blood." The Muslim procession the next day would have gone through the Geylang district as quietly as usual but for the tension in the crowd. No one knows how the riots began. Perhaps it was nothing more than a little incident like a Chinese audibly clearing his throat and spitting into the drain (a frequent occurrence), and a Malay taking this as an insult to his religion. Perhaps the throng bumped into one of the Chinese sidewalk food stands, which crowd the narrow streets of Singapore, and the Chinese vendor shouted some curse. A bottle was thrown, shouting and fighting started, and people began defending themselves with anything on hand. Vigilantes roamed the streets and twenty-two people were killed and four hundred and fifty injured before the riots were stopped four days later, after the imposition of an all-day curfew and 1,700 arrests.

The greatest damage of the riots was to the confidence between the races. This was the first race riot in Singapore's long history, though there had been many riots among the Chinese or against the government. Further riots broke out on September 3, probably started with ease by Indonesian provocateurs. (The first riots, however, were probably not started by Indonesians but by racial tensions.) There is no way to assess immediate blame for this tragedy except to politicians who excite racial hatreds.

To its credit, the Malaysian government put a lid on extremist talk and arranged an informal truce with the PAP on "sensitive issues." The terms were poorly understood, for the truce lasted hardly a month, when a political remark by a cabinet official reopened the debate. Khir Johari said that the Alliance could beat the PAP in the next elections and take over the government in Singapore. In reply, the PAP went into complete opposition to the government and to the Alliance in parliament in late 1964.

The issue chosen by the PAP was the final blow to Singapore's participation in Malaysia. This was the slogan "Malaysian Malaysia." On the surface this slogan would seem to emphasize racial harmony; a Malaysia for all races. But as criticism of government policy, it implied clearly that in a Malay Malaysia the Chinese were disadvantaged. By pointing, ever so subtly, to Malay privileges, the PAP was making a communal appeal to the Chinese and the Indians, and reopening the whole racial issue. Lee seemed fully aware that he was taking a great risk in using this slogan, and appeared to be forcing a showdown on the whole racial issue on the assumption that he could thus get rid of the Malay extremists.

It was at the time the Malaysian Malaysia issue was raised, in January 1965, that Lee first suggested the idea of separation, perhaps not seriously since he may have believed the fear of breakup would force the government to repudiate the Malay racists. The Tunku called talk of separation foolish, harmful, and dangerous, but within nine months he had changed his mind.

One of the final straws was another of Lee's highly publicized foreign jaunts. His visit to the United States in February 1965 was the occasion for some American editorial criticism of the Malaysian government. The same sort of incident in Australia and New Zealand the next month roused the Malaysian government to expel Lee's press secretary, the British journalist Alex Josey. When the Malay ultras demanded that Lee himself be seized, the government declared that it "would never make a martyr" of him. It now seemed likely that there might be a repetition of the race riots of 1964. In the summer of 1965 the Tunku was away from Malaysia for two months. At the Commonwealth meeting in London he came down with shingles, which some people described as allergy to Lee. As he lay in his hospital bed, the Tunku concluded from reports from Malaysia that he could not control the situation to prevent riots. The only alternative now seemed to be separation.

Upon his return from Europe on August 5, the Tunku met with Lee and informed him of his decision. In great secrecy an agreement was signed between the inner cabinets of Singapore and Malaysia (August 7). Even the British were not informed, presumably because they would object strongly to the breakup of the federation. The announcement of separation came like a bombshell on August 9. Lee went on television and, with tears in his eyes, announced the decision to the people of Singapore. A popular comment likened the separation to a Malay divorce: say "I divorce you" three times and it is done. The Tunku had taken the initiative and expelled Singapore from the house. Perhaps Malaya had not been the perfect husband. But Singapore had wooed Malaya and then had made its life miserable. Borneo, the infant child of this marriage, neither Malay nor Chinese, could stay with father, but for how long no one dared to predict.

In two years of merger many of the original common interests and expectations of the partners had been lost or disappointed. Malaysia had always been reluctant to take Singapore in because of its fears of Chinese radicalism. Now these fears had been confirmed. Lee challenged the whole basis on which racial and political harmony was established, the intercommunal party and protection of the Malays. A political challenge was tolerable, but bloodshed was not. The biggest mutual interest that had brought the parties together in 1961 was their fear of communism. This threat had been removed almost immediately after merger when the People's Action Party (not Malaysia or the Alliance) so roundly defeated the Barisan and stopped the leftward trend of politics. Malaya had little interest in merger left.

From the Singapore standpoint, too, the inducements had lessened. The independence which the British would not give in 1963 without merger was available in 1965. Other Singapore expectations of 1963 were stymied: the common market negotiations, for which Singapore had bargained so hard, had made no real progress, and Malaya seemed determined to go ahead with its own industrialization and hold back Singapore's progress. In fact, there was relatively little that merger offered Singapore. Rather, it encountered annoyances on fairly important things, such as the increased taxes proposed in November 1964, the government control over radio and television, and the closure of the Bank of China. No federation can be free of such problems, and their solution may strengthen the union. In Singapore's case, though, little had been gained to offset the disadvantages.

Singapore was not permitted a leading part in the affairs of government. The number of seats in the House was far below Singapore's proportion of population and wealth; this was the price it had paid for autonomy in budget, citizenship, education, labor, and civil service. PAP had been denied a seat in the cabinet by the fact that it was in opposition. Its attempt to take a place in the Alliance was rejected indignantly. Its intrusion into peninsular politics was deeply resented. When it took the only role left, that of a critical opposition, it was suspected of being disloyal and even subversive.

In summary, then, the factors working against integration of Singapore into Malaysia were stronger than the apparent common interests. In rough order of importance, these were: (1) a difference of outlook on the all-important question of racial equality, epitomized by the slogan "Malaysian Malaysia"; (2) a difference of social values, reflected in the openly socialist appeal of PAP contrasted with MCA's conservatism; (3) the declining expectations of gain—independence and the defeat of the Barisan having been achieved easily, there was only the uncertain common market; (4) the partial admission of Singapore into federation politics; (5) the lack of evidence of mutual benefits in a joint government; (6) some unexpected behavior which surprised the other partner: Singapore's challenge to the Malay supremacy and entry into the 1964 elections, and Malaya's tossing the merger out on such short notice; (7) the inability to control the appeals to race hatred.

At the time of separation Lee sincerely expressed the hope that Singapore would rejoin the federation. Not all government ties were severed in 1965. Malaysia undertook to train Singapore's foreign service. Since the Singapore military bases are important to defense of both, continued use by Malaysia was guaranteed under the Separation Agreement. Cooperation on national security is achieved through a joint defense council. Singapore currency continued to be the Malayan dollar until June 1967, controlled by the joint commissioners of currency. Postal arrangements were not fully separated until 1967. Malaysian Airways, the national airline, renamed Malaysian Singapore Airways, continues to be jointly owned, though it operates out of Singapore. Singapore continues to get its water and much of its produce from Johore, and is still heavily dependent upon Malaysia as its economic hinterland and market. Singapore's immigration service and police were separated from Malaysia's in 1965, but cooperation continues to the obvious benefit of both governments.

There are thus very close ties between Malaya and Singapore, and the underlying factors favoring integration are still strong. As Lee stated after separation, "Geographically, historically, and economically we are still one." But the tendency following separation has been for the two countries to draw farther apart. Almost immediately there was a tariff war, with each side setting up measures to protect its infant industries. What progress had been made to achieving a common market stopped. The very achievement of independence made any future integration more difficult if only because it will be hard for Singapore to give up the prerogatives of an independent foreign policy, to say nothing of the same old compromises that will have to be made in domestic policy. Some optimists initially hoped that independence would relieve the tensions that had been building up between the PAP and the Alliance. But clearly the result has been to the contrary. Independence released some of the inhibitions that both sides tried to observe in order to hold the merger together, and some of the postindependence invective is more poisonous than ever. It would be pleasant to think that all this is brotherly fun, but it will be difficult for the current generation of politicians to forget some of the insults that have been exchanged.

The prospects for remerger of Singapore into Malaysia do not seem very bright. What could bring it about? Probably only a complete replacement of the present leadership with new persons who could make a fresh start by putting more emphasis upon the common interests than upon past differences. This will take statesmanship, but Malaysia and Singapore have shown it in the past and might surprise all the skeptics.

Integration of East Malaysia

It might have been expected that the separation of Singapore in August 1965 would have caused Malaysia to fall completely apart. Actually, although everyone was surprised and disappointed by Singapore's departure, the decision was received quite calmly in East Malaysia. The opposition Sarawak United People's Party did call for a referendum on the continuation of merger. But there was no strong pressure for separation. Despite the surface calm, there was a great deal of uneasiness about the future, and there have been two serious crises in Sabah and Sarawak when secession was openly talked about.

The Borneo states had been given a very favorable position within Malaysia. All of the major demands the local population made to the Cobbold Commission and to the Inter-Governmental Commission had been met by generous concessions. The concessions were in six major areas: (1) To meet the widespread desire that British expatriate officers be retained until there were Borneans available, state Public Service Commissions were set up with the right to retain foreigners. (2) In answer to the fear that Malay would become the national language in 1967, the Borneo states were given ten years (until 1973), or longer if the state legislatures desired, for English to continue as the official language. (3) Since language was tied to education, the Borneo states were permitted to retain their own school systems with autonomy of policy until the states wanted to change. (4) The objection to Islam being the state religion of Malaysia was met by the concession that there would be no state religion in Borneo and that when grants were made to Muslim schools, proportionate grants would be given to Borneo—where there is a low proportion of Muslims—for social welfare. (5) The specter of being flooded by Chinese immigrants was laid by giving the states control over immigration. (6) To protect the native people, the privileges given to Malays were extended to Borneans.

In addition, the Borneo states, like the original eleven Malayan states, retained control over Muslim law, land, agriculture, forests, local government, and inland fisheries. The Borneo states were also given special privileges, such as the disproportionately large representation in Parliament. Sabah and Sarawak had control of their own citizenship, the Borneo High Court, museums and archaeology; Sabah kept its own state railway. To all these concessions were added special development grants.

Thus, the federal government tried to make the Borneo states welcome. In fact, it could be argued that the government had given up several matters which would be of critical importance to national integration, such as education, the national language, civil service, and free movement of persons among the territories. Yet there was no way the federation could have been created unless these powers were conceded, for the Borneo states probably would have preferred to remain British colonies than to give them up. Here is the nub of the problem of Malaysia's federal-state relationships. The federal government understandably wished to promote national integration, but by so doing it risked causing disintegration by arousing local resistance.

Often in the center of the state-federal conflict in the first few years of merger was the issue of British expatriates. The shortage of qualified Borneans for government positions meant that if the foreigners were not retained the posts would be empty or filled by Malayans. Thus, some Borneans wished to retain the expatriates to defend local rights, while the Malayans wished to see them depart as quickly and peacefully as they had from Malaya. A strange inversion of the anticolonial situation emerged. The central government's representative in Borneo, the federal secretary, was sometimes regarded as a foreign intruder, while the British were seen as defenders of local rights. While Kuala Lumpur filled this spot, it was careful to choose not a Malay, who might be accused of imposing Malay domination, but the highest ranking Chinese, Yeap Kee Aik. There were, of course, no Borneans in the Malayan civil service.

Postmerger conflicts over states' rights tended to focus on the critical power positions of the state secretary, an old colonial position at the peak of the civil service pyramid, or the key posts of financial secretary and education officer. In Sabah and Sarawak these positions initially were held by highly competent British civil servants. But the fact that such officials had previously served in Malaya, where they may have left some hard feelings, and resented having been terminated in Malaya, made the situation no easier. Federal officers sometimes felt that they were being obstructed by expatriates who were trying to retain their jobs. When the federal officeholders criticized the British, the Borneans saw evidence of desire to expand federal powers. The situation called for the greatest tact and discretion, and the participants, being human, did not always rise to the occasion.

Sabah turned its expatriates away more rapidly than Sarawak, which was slowed by a popular view of the British rajahs as defenders of native rights, by the tradition of an independent Sarawak civil service, and by a stronger feeling of Sarawak identity. By 1965 the major policy posts in Sabah had been taken over by Malaysians, except for education, which was finally filled in 1966 by a top Malayan education officer.

The separation of Singapore in 1965 aroused complaints that the Borneo states had not been consulted, not even through their cabinet representatives. But then, no one else had been consulted, including higher ministers, the UMNO, or the British. There was a brief flurry of talk about secession when Sabah's Donald Stephens resigned his cabinet post in 1965. Again, in 1966, in connection with the Ningkan crisis there were hints of secession in Sarawak, which have died down.

What are the reasons for the breakdown of integration between East and West Malaysia? The ties between Borneo and Malaya are even weaker than those between Malaya and Singapore. There are basic differences between Borneo and Malaya, such as tribal traditions, Muslim religion, and language. There are some real differences in their material condition, too. Borneo has a relatively undeveloped economy, education system, and political structure compared to sophisticated Malaya. This creates some differences in values, though they share the same basic value system. Attitudes toward Borneanization is a good example, but one could add a number of others like the importance of English language, of the sultans, or the Muslim religion.

There is no question that the great distance between East and West Malaysia has contributed to the difficulties of communication. There are fewer contacts between Borneo and Malaya at all levels than there should be. The federal prime minister and cabinet officers went over to Borneo less than once a year in the first years of merger. When they went, they occasionally made the situation worse by their comments on sensitive issues, or by unintentionally slighting minority groups. This merely reflected a poor understanding of the nuances of the local situation. Moreover, Malayans generally are more sophisticated than the bulk of the Borneo peoples; they are better acquainted with modern industrial ways. More frequent contacts between the peoples have been restrained by immigration restrictions and the high cost of transportation.

It has been remarked that merger was oversold to Borneo, particularly the independence aspect. Some people were unintentionally led to believe that the slogan "Independence through Malaysia" promised full autonomy. Borneo's right to protect its customs, language, civil service, and education system was guaranteed by the Constitution. Yet all these things seemed to be threatened by federal pressures to open up land, to get rid of the expatriates, to widen the educational base, and to use Malay as the national language. Instead of achieving security, Borneo was plunged into the Brunei Revolt, then Confrontation and the Communist threat. Sarawak took the brunt of the fighting in Confrontation. Although it suffered little physically, the danger was greatest there and restrictions the most severe. And it was obvious to everyone that the British not Malaysia provided the protection. While the few Malayan troops involved in Borneo were well-behaved, they did not win any distinction in fighting nor many friends among the local people.

On the other side, although Malayan expectations from Borneo had not been very great, they were probably mistaken. The main motivation for merger had been to counterbalance Singapore, which was ejected. Furthermore, the hope that the Borneo people would regard themselves as Malays turned out to be illusory. In practice, Borneo has been more of a burden than an asset to Malaya. Certainly from the security standpoint, merger has added new problems. It added the new internal threat of the Clandestine Communist Organization. Malaya might not have been involved in the war with Indonesia if it had not been for merger, and friendship with the Philippines and its regional cooperation would not have been stopped short. Confrontation increased the financial burdens of Malaya by diverting funds from its own development and also from Borneo.

Premerger Malaya had been able to demonstrate to the Borneo peoples its capacity to push economic development rapidly. And Borneo has achieved economic growth since 1963, but it is not apparent that this was a result of merger. For instance, the Sabah timber trade went on booming as it had before. At the other end of the scale, the plight of the Sarawak pepper farmer did not seem very much better. What had happened to the federal projects for Borneo? They took time to plan and implement. They were held up by unforeseen problems like scarcity of local technical data, land titles, too little labor, lack of skilled managers, competition of funds for defense, shortage of administrators' time that could be devoted to the solution of problems. It is too early to say that the federal government failed in the development of Borneo. The government certainly has made clear its intention to help by devoting $133 million to Borneo under the first Malaysia Five-Year Plan. But it lost the initial psychological push.

Kuala Lumpur does not seem to have taken advantage of the

opportunity to give the Borneans a share in the government. One Borneo Malay was made assistant minister and later raised to cabinet rank. Men from Sabah and Sarawak were given cabinet posts corresponding to their states, but without departmental responsibilities until 1965, when Stephens was given the smallest and most unimportant department of civil defense. That these regional leaders were not consulted on the issue of the separation of Singapore seems indicative of their lack of importance in the national structure.

The same problem arose within the governing party mechanism. Because of the looseness of the Alliance coalition, it was difficult to bring in the Borneo alliances, which were even more uncohesive than the Malayan model. A Grand Alliance was created, but it is doubtful that it operates effectively at a national level, or that the Borneo parties have a voice in policy.

At the lower level, a large number of Borneo officials have visited Malaya for the first time and received training, but few were given any opportunity to serve in the federal government or to share responsibility for national decisions. While serving apprenticeship, the Borneans might have found a sense of partnership in Malaysia.

Looked at as a whole, merger multiplied the political burdens of the country rather than simplifying things. The problem of creating a multiracial society in Malaya was big enough without adding the disparate and mutually hostile groups of Borneo, which were on generally low levels of political sophistication. Thus, the federation that had started so hopefully in 1963 seemed an almost intolerable burden by 1966.

The Political Future

What are the alternatives to the continued federation of Borneo and Malaya? The most improbable is affiliation of Borneo with some neighbor. Association with the Philippines has not been mentioned in Borneo because of the lack of contact and common interests except in eastern Sabah. Such a union is only a faint possibility even if Sabah had to go it alone, for the differences in political experience are greater with the Philippines than with Malaysia.

Association with Indonesia has been proposed by the Azahari faction, but it does not have much appeal in north Borneo. While there are many cultural ties between the peoples of the interior of Borneo on both sides of the border, the coastal traditions have been too different. Only if Indonesia were to break up would a Borneo federation seem at all possible, but even then there would be major obstacles. Present-day Indonesian economic problems and political uncertainty do not make union at all attractive to East Malaysia.

Borneo's association with Singapore was seriously suggested at the time of Singapore's breakaway. Trading interests are strong, but fear of Chinese dominance would probably keep Borneo away; only the counterbalance of Malaya can make association with Singapore acceptable. Nor would Singapore be eager to assume the burdens of the CCO threat or the financial responsibilities for Borneo development.

Integration with Brunei seems improbable under the present circumstances. There is too much fear of Brunei imperialism. Even a more liberal government which was willing to share its oil wealth would be looked upon with suspicion. This is not an impossible alternative, however, if a government of Brunei saw advantages in the investment of its capital in Borneo in return for the business which would flow through the city. Such a regime would have to be highly sensitive to Borneo opinion to avoid charges of buying influence or of trying to dominate local politics or imposing its Muslim or Malay way of life.

More likely than all these is some independent status for the Borneo states. Sabah and Sarawak could each become independent, but each would be relatively poor and weak, and certainly would consider combining before they struck off on their own. The combination is the major alternative to union with Malaya at the present. This would create a state of about a million and a half people and over 75,000 square miles, quite respectable by present United Nations standards.

Integration of Sabah and Sarawak would be difficult. There are differences in the way of life between the two and among the individual tribes. There are few overlaps of tribes between the two states; Kadazans and Bajaus are more strange to Land Dayaks than are Malays. Each state would bring its own problems to the merger. For example, the Communist threat in Sarawak—which Sabah can now ignore as a Malaysian problem—would become Sabah's concern.

The Cobbold Commission remarked how few contacts there were between the two states. There is virtually no traffic of any kind across the rugged land boundary. Along the coast the traffic is largely through Brunei and by means which the two states now share with Malaysia: Straits Steamship Company and Malaysia Singapore Airways. Probably Sabahans and Sarawakians know less of each other than they do of Malaya.

The two states could hardly expect to gain much from each other that they would not gain from the federation of Malaysia. It is hard to imagine what they would gain by joint administration; each has a desperate shortage of skills and would have to continue to rely upon expatriates. Sabah's income from timber puts it on a sounder financial basis than Sarawak, but it has nothing to spare above its own development needs. There might be economic growth in union, but each faces similar problems of extreme reliance on primary commodities. The development of industries in Borneo is a long way off, and both states must continue to rely upon the outside world, Singapore in particular, for manufactured goods. Huge sums must still be spent on basic social services like education and clinics, and the money would be hard to find.

One can imagine Sabah and Sarawak setting up a joint administration in some place in the middle, like Labuan, Limbang, or Miri. This would seem artificial, and like a satellite of Brunei. After the unit is put together and paid for, is it likely that the politicians would have any fewer differences than they have now? The basic problem of all the Malaysian states would still be there: how to create cooperation among the different communities. There would still be the problems of Muslim and non-Muslim, chauvinism in the Chinese schools, and Communist dissidents. To this would be added the burdens of handling foreign relations with new neighbors and the expense of sending delegations to the big powers and to the United Nations, all worthwhile in terms of national pride, but expensive. Borneo is already short of educated people to run the state governments and to teach in schools. There would be the problem of defense. Although the British responded well during Confrontation, they are reducing their military commitment in the Far East. No other non-Asian power is going to rush in to assume the unpopular task.

These are just a few of the more important problems that can be anticipated for an independent Borneo. They are the same ones that face Malaysia, but federation offers the resources and experience of Malaya to help.

6
Livelihood of the People

Malaysia's governments have brought prosperity to their peoples. Today they enjoy the highest incomes in Southeast Asia, and second only to Japan in the Far East. Oil rich Brunei has a per capita income of $1190 a year, Singapore $450, and Malaysia $300. Malaysia's economy is the only one of the three growing at a rate faster than its population so that there is real growth of prosperity.

"If the U.S.A. sneezes, Malaya will still catch influenza," said a Malaysian economist, pointing to the fundamental fact that their prosperity is dependent upon the United States more than any other country.[1] The prices that Americans pay for rubber and tin are absolutely critical to Malaysian prosperity and well-being. The great cloud that hangs over this economic relationship is the fear of another depression. If the United States permitted a repetition of that disaster, with its plunge of prices, Malaysia would be ruined. On the other hand, good prices can mean a "great leap forward" in economic development, as happened during the Korean War. This period brought prosperity to producers of rubber and tin and to exporters; the prosperity, in turn, brought the Malaysian government money for economic development. We have seen that the government's ability to integrate the states of the new federation and to weld the various racial communities into a cooperative society depends heavily on economic prosperity and proof of progress. If prices were to go down drastically, radical

[1] Lim Chong Yah, "Malaya," in Cranley Onslow, ed., *Asian Economic Development* (London: Weidenfeld & Nicolson, 1965), p. 109.

elements would be quick to blame the government and the United States. It is, therefore, very important that more Americans be aware of the dependency of Malaysia upon the American economy and know what can be done about it.

The Rubber Industry

The two main supports of the Malaysian economy are rubber and tin. Rubber is the giant of the two—a million tons of it exported in 1966 made up over a third of Malaysia's export earnings. The industry brought in nearly a half a billion U.S. dollars and gave jobs to 600,000 people. Rubber is also the leading export crop of Brunei; $400,000 worth of annual exports provides the main livelihood for the rural people. Singapore is the largest rubber market of the world. Much of the rubber of Brunei, Malaysia, and of Sumatra goes through Singapore, where it is refined and manufactured into a variety of goods ranging from tires to sandals. These operations provide employment for much of the city's population. Thus, the prosperity of each of the Malaysian political units is very much tied to the fickle price of rubber.

About a third of the cultivated land of Malaysia is laid out in rubber gardens which produce about 40 percent of the world's natural rubber. Malaysia is not only the world's greatest producer, but the most efficient one. There are big plantations known as estates, mostly on the west coast of Malaya, owned largely by Europeans and Americans, but also by Chinese. Smaller rubber plots, known as smallholdings, can be found in almost any part of the area, including Singapore and Brunei. These plots are always owned by Asians, especially by the Malays and other Malaysian peoples; well over half of the rubber is produced on them. Their methods of production are usually less efficient than that of the estates; the trees yield less and the quality of the rubber is not as pure. As a result Asians do not earn as much as European producers and are hardest hit by price drops.

Modern estates like those of the United States Rubber Company can afford the machinery and the quality control to produce latex, which earns a fifth more than the ordinary rubber. This represents the difference between the modern world of technology and the backwoods approach to rubber production. Since synthetic rubber is becoming more and more competitive, there is increasing pressure to improve the quality of natural rubber. The smallholder must replant his land with high-yielding trees and use more care in keeping dirt out of his pans in order to stay in competition.

An important factor in the relations between the United States and Malaysia has been the price American buyers are willing to pay for rubber. In boom years, such as the start of the Korean War, they paid the high price of over fifty cents a pound. This price jump resulted in a 60-percent growth in the economy of Malaya in one year; the government was able to spend money on economic development at the same time that it fought the Communists, and it put aside funds for the future.

Prices rose during the war not only because of American war needs, but also because the government was adding rubber to its strategic stockpile. This reserve is the object of more Malaysian complaints than any other single thing; they are never pleased by American stockpile disposals, that have the effect of depressing prices. The Korean armistice provides an instance. After the war the United States government found itself with huge stockpiles. Since rubber cannot be kept indefinitely without deteriorating, the government eventually had to sell the stored rubber, usually at a price considerably lower than that at which it was bought. When the General Services Administration sells the reserve, it becomes a supplier competing with Malaysia and lowers the price as it sells its stocks.

The price of rubber has been going down gradually ever since the Korean War, except for a couple of years (1955–56 and 1959–60). In the sixties the price has gone down every year. In 1966 it hit the lowest price since the war. The decline of a cent and a half a pound that year meant a drop of about 7 percent in the income of the thousands of producers, but hit hardest the poorer ones. It caused a loss of about forty million dollars in government revenue needed for development. A major reason for this price fall was the decision of the United States government in 1966 to sell

50,000 tons more than the 120,000 tons it normally released. These 50,000 tons represented 10 percent of the quota normally imported by the United States annually. The Malaysian press was indignant, and the Malaysian government made a strong protest to Washington, which responded by going back to its original release quota. But every bit of the remaining huge stockpile that is released will continue to push the price of rubber down. The price is also being pressed down by the competition of synthetic rubber, of which the United States is the major producer, and by the more efficient estates which have improved their yields.

The way out of this dilemma is difficult to see at first. Restricting production was tried in the 1920's. This attempt to keep prices up failed because some producing countries, notably the Netherlands, did not join, and the United States merely bought more rubber from the Dutch East Indies than from Malaysia. A more comprehensive scheme of the 1930's was successful, but resulted in rubber prices fixed artificially high at the expense of the consumers, Malaysian and American. (The Malaysian bicycle owner is more affected than the American car owner since more of his total expenditure will go into tires than the American's.)

A completely free-market mechanism will not protect the consumer and the producer. Unregulated, rubber prices go too high during inflations—especially during wartime—and in recessions they plummet. A minimum price is needed to guarantee a living wage to the producer and a steady revenue to his government; a maximum price is needed to protect the customer and to keep buyers from turning to substitute products. Clearly, regulation of rubber prices to any degree must take into consideration stockpiling practices. Thus regulation would have to represent a joint effort of producing and consuming countries. A beginning in international control, which may provide a model for rubber, has been made with Malaysia's second major commodity, tin.

The Tin Industry

The Federation of Malaysia is fortunate not to be dependent on a single export for its livelihood. Tin, too, is a major commodity. Unfortunately the price of tin also is tied to American demand, which tends to reach peaks and lows in the same periods as demands for rubber. Like rubber, tin reached a high during the Korean War (over $1.50 a pound), and fell after the war to about seventy-five cents a pound. But whereas the long-range trend of rubber prices has been downward, since 1954 the price of tin has been gradually rising. There has been a worldwide shortage of tin, and though American industry has found ways of saving by putting thinner coats of tin onto steel plate—the biggest industrial use—and has developed all kinds of substitutes for the old tin can, such as plastic coating, glass containers, cardboard and aluminum packages, the worldwide demand for tin has gone up faster than the increase of production.

Malaysia is the world's greatest producer of tin as well as natural rubber, its share of each being just over 40 percent. Although tin is not quite as important to the economy of Malaysia as rubber, it does provide 20 percent of Malaysia's export earnings and jobs for about 50,000 people. Tin is far more localized in production than rubber. There is none in East Malaysia, and most of that found in West Malaysia is concentrated in the west coast states of Perak, Selangor, and Negri Sembilan. Half of the tin that has been mined has come from the greatest field in the world, the Kinta Valley around Ipoh.

Malaysia sets the world's standards for purity of the metal. Its famous Straits tin, 99.9 percent pure, is refined at two big plants on opposite sides of Penang harbor. The tin is produced at lower cost than anywhere in the world, in part because of the rich fields, but also because of modern methods. There are great contrasts, however, between the modern European and American dredges, like those of Pacific Tin Consolidated, and the poorest method pursued by little old women panning tin like the forty-niners. About half of Malaysia's tin is still produced by nineteenth century techniques, and much in mines so marginal that a slight drop of price will put them out of business.

There is constant concern that Malaysia will run out of tin. Unlike rubber—where yields are growing and there are great areas on which it can be planted—tin, like other minerals, is a limited asset. Yet, in 1966, with high prices, the production was 68,886 tons, a postwar record, and an increase of 8 percent over the previous year. Professional geologists are confident that tin mining will continue to be important for many years. The most immediate prospects for expansion are opening up new lands, using more efficient methods, and reworking old deposits. Perak has recently opened up some promising new areas, and there are Malay reservations in other states that may be opened later. Two new giant dredges started work in 1966, and such dredges and better jigs will recover a great deal of ore from fields that were less efficiently mined in the past. For the future there are sources of tin that are inaccessible to present methods: deep deposits near the main range of the mountains, and ore that has been washed out to sea over the centuries. Deposits at sea on the continental shelf of Indonesia have been mined with dredges for years, and in 1967 the first prospecting began in the sea off Malaysia.

More important than the supply of tin is its price. The United States has a greater direct effect on tin prices than on rubber because it consumes a larger proportion of the total world supply. In 1966 it paid directly to Malaysia nearly twice as much for tin imports as for rubber (nearly 100 million dollars against 56 million for rubber). The tin price is particularly important to the government because tin export duties have always formed a large part of its revenue.

Though tin prices have been gradually rising since 1954, sales of the American stockpile threaten to depress them. This is a major irritant to Malaysian-American relations. Pressure to release the stored tin has come from two sources. The world's demand for tin exceeds the supply so that there would be a real shortage if there were no stockpile releases. The second impetus to dispose of tin has come from the fact that the United States needs the money derived from tin sales, especially for the Vietnam War and to ease the balance of payments problem by saving foreign exchange. In 1962 the United States announced that it would sell over a period of years about 150,000 tons of its 350,000-ton stockpile, worth several billion dollars. This raised a storm of protest in Malaysia. Each year the American government's announcement of the annual release has caused bad feelings and recriminations. The United States shares the blame with curious company. Each year Communist China releases about the same amount of tin as the United States, ten to twenty thousand tons, just enough to keep prices from going up. At the beginning of 1967 only 67,000 tons remained to be disposed under current American targets; at the annual rate of about 22,000 tons, it will be sold off by 1970. That will still leave a stockpile of 200,000 tons, which Malaysians fear the United States will want to sell for its current value of two and a half billion dollars.

The remedy to this constant irritant to Malaysian-American relations is like that of rubber: cooperation. With neither commodity has the United States yet joined an international scheme for control of prices, but it has been close to cooperation on tin. The control schemes before World War II, the Bandoeng Pool of the 1920's and the Tin Producers' Association of the 1930's were primarily producing country restrictions. The United States did not even have an observer at the latter until 1937. Postwar tin conferences, on the other hand, have taken consumer interests into account, and the United States has participated in them and even encouraged discussion of cooperation. Yet in the last resort it did not join the International Tin Agreements of 1953, 1960, or 1966. These international agreements have set the objectives of protecting producer interests in a minimum price, conserving resources, and securing full employment, and have taken into account consumer desires for adequate supplies and stable prices. For this reason, in part, the United States adopted an attitude of "benevolent neutrality" to the first international agreement, and has cooperated with the Tin Council, especially by making releases from its stockpile in a very responsible manner so that it has actually stabilized the market for tin. Malaysia's participation in these agreements is essential because it is the largest producer. It hesitated to join the third Tin Agreement in 1965 because of the prospect of profiting from the highest prices in history, which stood at $4,800 a ton in October 1964. Malaysian hesitation seems to have given the United States an excuse not to join, although when Malaysia made the agreement effective by signing in 1966, the Americans did not follow suit.

A recent example of the effect of United States policies on the price of tin was its announcement in March 1966 of a plan to dispose of 23,000 tons in the following year. At this, the price slipped from $3,920 a ton to $3,360, a drop of nearly 15 percent. The Malaysian press and government made strong protests, and the American administration held back about half of the quota for disposal in 1967. This kind of response is very much appreciated by the Malaysians, but it leaves cooperation on a year-to-year basis, dependent upon the goodwill of a particular administration rather than upon a long-range American commitment to stability.

Economic Development

Malaysia has been so successful in its efforts at economic development that it has become a model for other developing countries. In part this success has been due to the good fortune of having the resources of rubber and tin on which to base its economic growth, but neighboring nations which have identical resources and greater diversity have not made as good use of them. The most important element in Malaysia's economic progress has been rational planning.

In 1954 a careful economic survey of West Malaysia was made by the International Bank. This mission, headed by Sir Louis Chick, with several American members, laid the groundwork for Malaysia's planning by identifying the basic problems and recommending solutions. Most of the commission's recommendations have been implemented within a decade. Among these the most important were: replanting of rubber trees; a program for family planning; creation of a central bank; encouragement of private investment (particularly in industry); government investment in transport, communication, and power; provision of social services (especially in education and health); assistance to agriculture; and centralization of economic planning.

In 1955 Malaya's First Five-Year Plan (1955–1960) was implemented. This followed the main lines of the World Bank's report, and involved government expenditures of U.S. $340 million in five years. Major projects were grants to replace old rubber trees, industrialization through a Pioneer Industries policy (1958), improvement of transportation, and introduction of universal primary education. Malaya had real reason to be proud of its economic progress under the First Five-Year Plan. From World

War II to 1960 its economy grew at the rate of 4.5 percent a year. Since population increased at an annual rate of 2.7 percent, this gave a margin of growth of 1.8 percent per capita. Nevertheless, in 1961 the government recognized that it still faced three big problems: "The high rate of population growth, the depressed condition of the rural areas, and the need for economic diversification."[2]

To solve these problems the Second Five-Year Plan set a goal of doubling public expenditure to $717 million. The plan actually exceeded this goal by more than 100 percent and achieved a higher rate of growth than under the first plan. By 1965 annual growth was 6.4 percent, against the 4.5 percent for the period since the war. Much of the success was due to capable administration of the development program.

Direction of the Second Five-Year Plan was given highest priority in the cabinet. Tun Razak—who had made such a success of the program of universal education—was chosen minister of rural development as well as deputy prime minister in 1959. A development operations room was set up, in imitation of the planning techniques so successfully used to defeat the Communists. In it were visual displays of the development projects; maps showing locations of schemes, grids indicating the monthly progress with red flags for projects that were behind schedule, and the famous Red Book, a collation of all the requests made by the local people, with the status of their approval by local governments and a record of the progress toward fulfillment.

This operations room became renowned as a model for control of development, but much of the success is attributable to the activity and interest of Tun Razak himself. He held regular meetings at which he was briefed by other ministers and department heads, and traveled widely throughout the country to check on projects by talking to the local people and responsible officials. Razak's personal interest inspired an enthusiasm throughout Malaya. It was his role in guiding the country's development that earned him the 1967 Magsaysay Award for community leadership. High tribute was given by two American experts on development

2 Malaya, *Second Five-Year Plan, 1961–1965* (Kuala Lumpur: Government Printer, 1961), para. 50.

administration: "the most dazzling speed with which development has taken place in recent years must be attributed in large measure to the drive, inspiration, and genius of one man."[3]

Malay Poverty

The greatest effort of the Second Five-Year Plan went into raising the standards of living of rural people, particularly the Malays. The economic poverty of the Malays is, of course, at the root of many political problems, such as their defensiveness against the Chinese and the need for protection and special privileges. At the start of the Second Five-Year Plan only 10 percent of the payers of income tax were Malays, though they were half the population. The Malays paid an average of U.S. $110 in income tax, against $275 for non-Malays. The reason was that three quarters of the Malay workers in Malaya were farmers and fishermen whose monthly incomes averaged only $17 a month for farming, and $33 for fishing. Nearly all the rice farmers were Malays, who still used the ancient methods of backbreaking manual labor. Malays composed two thirds of Malaya's fishermen, another depressed occupation using antiquated methods.

Most observers agree that the reason for Malay poverty is low productivity in relation to the size of the rural population, but they dispute about the causes of this; and, therefore, the remedies are contradictory. Professor Ungku Aziz, the Malay who has taken the greatest interest in this subject, places emphasis upon the exploitation of the Malay by the middlemen. The farmer or fisherman usually buys his goods from a single shopkeeper, to whom he becomes indebted, and sells to a single broker. In most cases these middlemen are Chinese. Professor Aziz is very careful not to put his argument in racial terms, but this communal element is often implicit in the complaints of the Malays.

Professor Aziz condemns another form of exploitation which involves Malays alone: tenant farming. Less than half of the rice farms of Malaya are owned by the farmer working the soil; and

[3] John D. Montgomery and Milton J. Esman, *Development Administration in Malaysia* (Kuala Lumpur: Government Printer, 1966), p. 1.

in the "Rice Bowl" (Kedah-Perlis-Wellesley) 70 percent of the
land is operated by tenants. In Kedah a mere two thousand families control 80,000 farms. Throughout Malaya tenancy is increasing.

Tenancy in itself would not be alarming if the farmer were sure
of his livelihood, but insecurity of tenure is a great problem. The
length of tenure is only three to four years on the average in the
Rice Bowl, and only one year in Kelantan. Moreover, rents are
high, and Professor Aziz shows that the rent control law passed in
1955 is not being enforced. Besides, the plots of land are too small
to be economical, 80 percent of them being less than five acres in
size. This is due in large part to the Islamic law of inheritance,
which provides shares for each survivor, and in part to Malay attachment to the land which prevents disposing of a plot even
when consolidation might be more economical. Insecurity of tenure is a major factor in low agricultural productivity. Farmers
who do not own the land have as little incentive to improve it as
absentee landlords. Fertilizers are little used on Malay lands, tools
are still primitive, and there is little interest in improving seeds,
in double cropping, or in amalgamating holdings.

Aziz places much of the blame for this situation on the neglect
of the farmer by both the Malay elite, which has gone away to the
big towns, and the Malay-dominated government. Farm labor has
fewer social security benefits compared to workers on the plantations or in industry. The farmers are unprotected against accidents and unemployment. There is little recourse for the rural
laborer who is involved in a dispute, and the migratory laborer
has no protection against exploitation. It is clear that the government could provide better rural communications and health facilities. But much of the rural illness and high mortality rate is
due to malnutrition caused by limited diet. The problem is circu-
lar because poor health and diet are causes of poor productivity.
Besides improving health, the government could provide more
rural education, particularly in agricultural extension services.

When we get onto the question of rural education we are on
touchy ground, for we are talking about affecting Malay beliefs
and philosophy of life. A Malay colleague of Professor Aziz's ef-

fectively argues that rural Malay attitudes are not conducive to economic development.[4] He cites the Malay's lack of confidence in man's ability to change nature, his belief in magic and animistic practices, and a passive attitude toward life. Others have recognized in Malay resistance to change a major factor in their economic poverty. The Malay's conservatism and his fear of the unfamiliar stems from a natural need for security against the fears of confiscation, the hierarchical society, the teachings of Islam which encourage surrender to God's will, and to Malay child-rearing practices which discount initiative.

The causes of Malay poverty are obviously complex, and one cannot blame only the Chinese, or the Malay himself, or the government. Clearly much can be done to remedy it through legal means, particularly in land reform and rent control. But we have a difficult problem if a major part of the cause lies in the attitudes of the people, whether in the indifference of the urban Malays and landlords or in the cultural attitudes stemming from the Muslim religion or the Malaysian value system. If progress means abandoning the treasured values of Malay culture, it is clear why many Malays resist it. The question remains whether scientific education, community development ideas, and modern agricultural techniques can be extended to the Malays without destroying their traditional culture.

Recognizing that one symptom of the rural problem was land hunger, the Second Five-Year Plan put a major effort into a program of "Land for the Landless." The main agency for this was the Federal Land Development Authority (FLDA), established in 1956. The program planned to open up plots of 4000 acres each, cleared of jungle forest and planted with high-yielding rubber trees, and to settle on each plot about 500 landless persons, who were to be provided with individual houses and modern social services. When the rubber trees came into production seven years after planting, the settler would tap his own eight acres of trees. His yield should earn about $1700 a year, from which he would

[4] Syed Hussein Alatas, "Collective Representations and Economic Development," *Kajian Ekonomi Malaysia*, 2.1 (June 1965): 110–112.

repay the government for the land and investment. During its first years the FLDA opened up 145,000 acres of new farm land and settled 12,000 families on them. The government admitted that this was disappointing since it had hoped to settle twice as many people and open 250,000 acres during the second plan.

The high cost of development by the FLDA is so much above that of estate costs that several Malayan economists have been critical. But it is clear that there are social as well as economic purposes being served by the FLDA. The big problem is that the rate of settlement is making only a bare dent into the numbers of the rural unemployed. Some have feared that the heavy emphasis upon settling Malays would only widen the gulf between races. However, many of the schemes have settled non-Malays as well, and the cooperation between the races has been exemplary.

Of greater concern is the question of whether the paternalism of the schemes would not reinforce Malay attitudes and repeat the British error of protecting the Malays against modern economic competition. It remains to be seen if a real change in attitude toward initiative has been achieved by the FLDA. The very fact that the settler was willing to leave his native village and try a new life does indicate an encouraging receptivity to change. Many people have wondered whether the settler will have the incentive to work efficiently land acquired with such ease, and to stick with it when the going gets rough. Clearly both the problem of attitudes and persistence would be helped by some sort of community development program, but the FLDA has emphasized the physical aspects of production. In this the agency has been influenced in large part by the estate orientation of many of its managers and by the government's own concentration on concrete goals.

Another concern in the FLDA's early years was its almost exclusive emphasis upon rubber. When the price of rubber was declining and the government plan pointed to the excessive dependence of the country on rubber, it seemed dangerous to put more people into rubber production. This problem was not fully acknowledged until 1960 when the first FLDA scheme was planted with oil palm, which yields a crop that earns more and at an earlier time, though it does require a higher investment in factory and transportation and more organization of the harvesting process.

The second agency for rural development was the Rural and Industrial Development Authority (RIDA), now known by its Malay name, Majlis Amanah Ra'ayat (MARA). This was founded in 1951 to encourage enterprise among the rural Malays. Its program has concentrated largely on giving small loans to Malay businessmen, especially for rural bus lines. MARA runs a business college in Kuala Lumpur, which has been helped by faculty from the Peace Corps. There have been efforts to expand Malay handicrafts for the tourist industry and a Malay boatyard in Kuala Trengganu.

Two early efforts to introduce community development into the rural development program (in 1953 and 1957) faded away as the government became increasingly oriented toward concrete projects such as bridges, roads, and schools. The building of this infrastructure was, of course, essential to the future economic development of the country.

Borneo and Singapore Development

While Malaya was progressing on its Second Five-Year Plan the British were trying to implement similar plans in the other states. Sarawak had two plans, in 1947–1956 and 1959–1963. All told it spent $55 million on development, about two thirds on roads, such as the transnational highway, which in 1967 connected Kuching and Sibu. Like early Malayan plans, the spending on concrete projects exceeded goals; while social services received the planned amount, agriculture lagged. The United States Peace Corps made a major contribution to the agricultural extension service in Sarawak by starting up a 4–H Club program among the rural youth. Under its second plan Sarawak's economic growth was 3.4 percent a year, well ahead of the population growth of 2.5 percent. Sarawak's problems were very much like Malaya's, primarily an excessive dependence upon exports, especially rubber.

But there was the additional complication of the decline of revenues from the old oil fields of Miri which, after a half of a century of production, were down to a mere thousand barrels of oil per day. Sarawak's inadequate development of education, transport, industry, and power justified the heavy emphasis upon concrete projects.

North Borneo did not begin a development plan until 1959. It allocated about the same as Sarawak, $53 million for the six-year period until 1964. A large portion was spent on public works, with only 15 percent on social services and 10 percent on agriculture. At the end of the plan period a quarter of Sabah's primary-age children were still not in school, and agriculture production was lagging. The spectacular growth rate of about 7 percent a year (well above the population increase of 2.9 percent) was largely due to the timber trade and the construction boom. But Sabah was too heavily dependent upon timber. While its second largest crop, rubber, was improved by some replanting, the value of exports in both rubber and copra declined. The encouraging side of Sabah's economy was the beginning of the export of palm oil and cocoa which added to the diversification provided by hemp exports.

Two economic problems that are unique to Sabah are a desperate shortage of labor and inflation. The first problem has been met by encouraging a thousand laborers a year to emigrate from West Malaysia to Sabah starting in 1967. The re-establishment of relations with Indonesia and the Philippines reopened the old sources of labor in those countries.

While Sabah and Sarawak struggled with a shortage of funds, Brunei went on its happy way as the "Shellfare state," as one American scholar dubbed the country that could spend as much as it pleased on welfare projects from revenues of the Shell oil fields at Seria. Shell had first discovered oil at Miri in northern Sarawak in 1910 and refined it at Lutong nearby. When the Miri production began to decline in 1930, Shell found oil just across the border in Brunei. It was this discovery that transformed the very poor Malay sultanate into the richest state in the Far East.

The Brunei oil is piped across the border to the refinery at Lutong, now the largest in Malaysia with a capacity of 50,000 barrels
a day.

Brunei began its first development planning in 1961 with the
assistance of International Bank adviser Joseph S. Gould, whom
the United Nations had recruited in the United States. At that
time its population growth had the highest rate in the world, 4
percent. The high per capita income figure of $1190 was meaning-
less since most of the people were still living in the subsistence
economy of the nineteenth century. If oil is subtracted, per capita
income averages out to $234 per person, well under Malaysia's
$300 and about the same as Sabah's. Outside of oil, the main
money earner was rubber which in the early 1960's yielded only a
hundred and fifty pounds per acre against a potential of a thousand. Rice production was three quarters of the average in Malaya. With the decline of oil production each year, Brunei's gross
national product was declining at the same time that the population was going up.

Brunei's National Development Plan, 1962–1966, anticipated
investment of $50 million to achieve an economic growth rate
higher than the anticipated population growth of 3.5 percent.
Brunei, like Malaysia, wanted to diversify to escape dependence
on exports. Its plan included programs to improve farming, fishing, and lumbering; stimulate industries based on the use of oil,
glass, timber, cement, salt, and fish; develop transport, communications, and power; and invest in social improvements such as
schooling, health, and housing.

With revenues of $15 million a year from oil and $10 million
more from its investments in London, valued at $100 million,
Brunei has been able to make impressive progress. Much has gone
into showy projects like the $700,000 national mosque and other
government buildings. But the progress in education and public
services has been great. Free education through university and
graduate study was made available to any qualified student,
though only a hundred had reached the university level by 1965.
Free medical care included "a flying doctor" who arrived in remote villages of Brunei in a helicopter. But actual population

growth was an astounding 11.88 percent in 1965 despite a cholera epidemic, perhaps the last one the state would see. There was little indication of agricultural improvement, for rice yields remain very low, and rubber production is going down as replanting lags.

The most encouraging development was the discovery of a new oil field offshore in 1963. It had been suspected for some time that the Seria field might extend out to the continental shelf. American exploration companies confirmed this by discovering the Ampa field. From Texas towers in the China Sea eight wells in 1968 produced over 26,000 barrels of oil per day. Although this gives Brunei a new lease on life, the economy is still too dependent on one export, and there is little improvement of the rural economy. This disparity between the export-based society and the continued rural poverty has all the makings of social discontent which could lead to a repetition of the Brunei Revolt.

Singapore began its first development plan in 1961, proposing to spend $290 million in government funds in four years. In an interesting contrast to the approach of the Borneo states, the openly socialist People's Action Party government allocated 40 percent of its budget to social services and nearly as much to industrialization. The most remarkable thing is that this city-state was willing to spend more on rural development than Sabah and Sarawak combined. About 20 percent of the budget went into a $50 million public housing program and over 10 percent into education. Singapore's great economic problem is unemployment, so that the major effort of Singapore's plan went into increasing industrial production. Thirty-three million dollars was given to the Economic Development Board, established in 1961. About half of this financed the opening up of a whole new industrial city of Jurong on 9,000 acres on the southwestern side of the island. The government built a new port there connected to the old city by railroad lines and utilities.

Singapore actually spent nearly 10 percent more on development than planned by adding a fifth year (1965). Nearly a hundred new industries were granted permits, and more than half went into operation. Fifty-five million dollars in new foreign capital came to the island; ten million dollars was American investment. This included an oil refinery at Jurong with a capacity of 21,000 barrels and American-owned factories making plywood, fertilizer, paper, and candy. Mobil Oil eventually invested thirteen million dollars in its refinery. Over fifty thousand housing units were built under the plan giving new homes to half a million people, a quarter of the total population. But Singapore was hard-hit by Confrontation, which cut off its trade with Indonesia. In 1964 its annual growth rate of 8.5 percent fell to 2 percent, about the same as its population increase. By 1965 unemployment rose to 76,000 or 10 percent of the work force despite a resumption of economic growth after the end of Confrontation. The closing of the British bases threatened to add 83,000 more unemployed. Singapore still had some way to go down the runway before it could be sure that it was "at the threshold of economic take-off into economic growth" as predicted by some of its economists.[5]

Diversification and Economic Progress

Malaysia has recognized that it must diversify its economy to get away from the dependency upon rubber and tin. Under the Second Five-Year Plan this was undertaken in two ways: by industrialization and by getting more crops. The most promising new crop is the oil palm, which was recommended by the World Bank in 1955 and more recently by the Ford Foundation survey of diversification. The government gave oil palm priority over rubber where the soils were suitable, but it needs much better soil than rubber. Despite all its advantages—it has twice rubber's yield per acre and an early maturity, and is a high exchange earner at a more stable price than rubber—there is considerable uneasiness in Malaysia about too much reliance on palm oil. There are the drawbacks of the heavy capital investment and technical skills which make it less suitable than rubber for smallholders. There is also a general downward trend of prices coupled

5 Ronald Ma, "Singapore—the Economic Challenge of a Growing Population," *Australian Outlook,* 16.1 (1962): 62.

with growing foreign competition. Thus far Malaysia's major competitors—Indonesia, the Congo, and Nigeria—have been upset by civil disturbances; but these crises will not continue indefinitely. Palm oil is subject to the same depressions and price instability as rubber and tin, so some caution is probably justified.

Among the other crops that are promising for agricultural diversification are pineapples, which have long been a major export earner. Cacao has not taken hold because of diseases. Sugar cane has been grown since Balestier started it in Singapore and ought to do well. Local tobacco companies are helping farmers to grow tobacco for Malaysia's cigarette factories and thus save foreign exchange. Manila hemp is grown successfully in Sabah and could be grown elsewhere to get high earnings from export. Nuts like cashews have potential. Citrus, which is native to Malaysia, could be developed to take the place of expensive imports from the Mediterranean. Bananas, papayas, and mangoes could be grown commercially on a larger scale. The traditional spices of the Indies are still neglected except for pepper in Sarawak and cloves in Penang. Valuable medicinal plants and aromatics that were high-export earners in Sumatra before the war could be grown in Malaysia. Coffee used to be a major commercial export before rubber became popular, but because of the world oversupply, it is not promising. Tea is presently grown in the Cameron Highlands, but it, too, is subject to overproduction by the established producers of South Asia.

Other possibilities for expansion of food production are livestock and fishing. The Malaysian government has done much experimentation to improve the breeding of cattle and their feeding. The government has also encouraged the farmers to raise fish in freshwater ponds to provide proteins for the rural diet and extra cash.

Forests of Malaysia already provide 150,000 jobs, and a great deal of the prosperity of Sabah is due to the timber industry boom. Since 1960 Sabah's forest exports have exceeded rubber, and timber production has gone up 700 percent in a decade. Much of the shipments go to Japan from one of the great logging ports of the world, Sandakan. A major contributor to this development has been the American Kennedy Bay Timber Company, which lumbers the area west of Lahad Datu with modern equipment. A striking result of the development of the Sabah timber industry has been the fine network of roads which has made possible the opening of the fertile lands of the interior to settlement. Careful conservation policies must be established so that there is reforestation and soil protection, but there is no reason why the logging boom of Sabah cannot be extended to the large areas of Sarawak and Malaya that are still untouched. The timber industry also provides the natural base of secondary industries such as plywood, paper, and lumber, which will help diversify the economy.

Mineral resources of Malaysia still need exploiting. There has been some export of iron ore to Japan, and there are several fairly rich deposits of ore in Pahang that can be worked. Bauxite, for aluminum, is mined near the southern tip of Johore and exported to Japan. There have been some promising indications of copper in Sabah, and thorough geological surveys of East Malaysia may uncover other commercial deposits of minerals. Foreign capital is usually anxious to help develop such resources under reasonable conditions of national control. American oil companies are being given more of an opportunity under the independent government than they had under Britain. Esso has been exploring for oil in Sabah since 1965, Clark Oil Company started searching for more oil in Brunei in 1966, and Continental Oil began exploration in the continental shelf off the east coast of Malaya in 1967.

Malaysia has put strong hopes on industrialization as a way to diversify and develop its economy. The government gives assistance to "pioneer industries" by providing new industrial sites, relief from income tax for two to five years, tariff protection for "infant industries," free remittance of capital to the sterling area, protection against expropriation, and numerous services such as roads, power, loans, personnel training, and research. American investors have responded enthusiastically to this policy by providing $17,500,000 of new capital. The largest pioneer industry was the $15.5 million Esso refinery at Port Dickson, which had a capacity of 34,000 barrels of crude oil a day, the largest in West Malaysia. Five other American pioneer industries were established in Petaling Jaya, the first industrial suburb of the capital. Beatrice Foods invested $650,000 in a plant making canned milk; Singer Sewing Machines put in $200,000, Carrier Air-conditioning $125,000, Federal Paints $66,500; and Colgate has two plants producing soap and toothpaste. In Johore American pioneer industries were Malayan Batteries ($650,000), Malayan Veneers (making plywood), and South Pacific Textiles, making cotton socks and towels at Batu Pahat.

The Malaysian Common Market

We have seen that historically the Malaysian area has been an economic unit. Singapore succeeded Malacca and Johore as centers for the inter-island trade. Today Singapore is the fifth largest port in the world, partly because of its strategic location at the tip of mainland Asia, but largely because of its role as an entrepôt. At least a quarter of Singapore's income and 70,000 jobs are directly dependent on buying and reselling the goods of the world. Most of Singapore's imports are Indonesian products, especially Sumatran rubber; but copra, spices, palm oil, and rice also come from neighboring Southeast Asia. Much of this Straits produce is cleaned, graded, sorted, and exported to the United States and Europe by Singapore as it has been for over a century. In return, Singapore imports consumer goods, especially cotton textiles which it re-exports to Southeast Asia. Because of its location on the world sea lanes, the city is an important fueling center for ships. European and American oil companies (including Esso, Caltex, and Mobil) maintain bunkering facilities nearby; fuel comes from the American fields in central and south Sumatra and Shell fields in Brunei and Sarawak as well as from the Middle East.

Singapore has always been an important center for the commercial life of the Indo-Malaysian area, housing much of its banking, trading, insurance, and service industries. Extremely important to the economic unity of the area has been the existence of a common currency, the Straits Dollar, which beginning in 1903 served all the British areas including Brunei and which was even more acceptable than Indonesian currency in the neighboring Indonesian trading areas like the Riau Islands. Almost a quarter of the trade of Malaysia before merger was between the various units. A third of Malaya's trade was with Singapore; a fifth of Singapore's with Malaya; about a tenth of Sarawak and Sabah trade was with the rest of Malaysia. Indeed, one of the main arguments for the federation of Malaysia was that this natural economic linkage should be made even tighter. Although Brunei chose in 1963 not to join Malaysia, it was still closely linked economically with the federation.

The possibilities of a common market for the area have been examined by a special mission of the World Bank. The group, headed by Jacques Rueff, reported in July 1963 that such an arrangement would have many advantages. The wider economy would be more stable because it was more diverse. It would give wider scope for use of capital and labor. The domestic market for goods would be expanded. The units could share their technical knowledge. The report concluded that the general result of a customs union would be greater economic growth for the entire area. On the other hand, there would be obstacles to overcome. Malaya and the Borneo states had tariffs protecting new industries and export duties for revenue, while the traditional free ports of the Straits (Singapore, Penang, and Labuan) depended upon free trade to maintain their entrepôt prosperity. The Rueff mission thought it would not be difficult to reconcile these aims and recommended a common market, that is, elimination of internal barriers with common external tariffs to protect goods produced and used within Malaysia.

The first two years of merger produced no real progress toward realization of the common market. Then in 1965 Singapore and Malaysia separated without real consideration of the economic consequences. The tragedy of the separation was not only in the loss of potential benefits of economic union but the disintegration of previous cooperation such as in currency. Almost immediately each side began to raise restrictions of traffic across the Johore Causeway. Each threatened to raise duties on manufactured goods coming from the other in order to stimulate local industry. One result was a slowing down of foreign investment which had been attracted by the anticipation of a common market. Manufacturers were faced with the prospect of having to establish plants in both Singapore and Malaysia. Jurong in particular suffered, for much of its future was predicated upon manufacturing for the whole of Malaysia. Malaysian leaders began to refer to the desire to have all Malaysian trade go through Port Swettenham or Penang rather than Singapore. Not only did this deny the logical economic development of Singapore as the center for trade for Johore and southern East Malaysia, but it threatened to cut off Singapore as the processing center for much more of Malaysia.

These were all steps backward from a common market. But the heaviest blow was the abandonment of the common currency. Unable to agree upon common financial policies, the three states of Malaysia, Brunei, and Singapore began issuing their own currencies on June 12, 1967. Initially these were pegged at the same rate (approximately one U.S. dollar to three local dollars) and made interchangeable, but separate fiscal policies could drive the currencies apart in the future.

Economic Prospects

After the separation of Singapore there were in effect three different countries with different economic policies. Malaysia went ahead with a combined development plan for Malaya, Sabah, and Sarawak in January 1966. This plan had been drawn up in the Economic Planning Unit of the Prime Minister's Department under the initial direction of an American, William Phillips, who turned it over to the brilliant Malaysian economist Thong Yaw Hong.

This First Malaysia Five-Year Plan squarely faces the problems of (1) the excessive dependence on export of rubber and tin, (2) the population growth at a rate of 3 percent a year, adding a million and a half people in five years, (3) a striking difference in the standards of living of the city dwellers and the rural people, and (4) an acute scarcity of trained manpower. The plan set ten objectives for Malaysia: (1) national integration, (2) rising per capita income, (3) rural improvement, (4) more jobs, (5) diversification, (6) education, (7) population control, (8) opening up more land, (9) more public services, and (10) provisions for social welfare. The core objective of the plan was to promote exports, industries, and local food production. It set the long-range targets of $500 per capita income by 1985, 2.4 million jobs by that year, a redistribution of income through agricultural extension programs and education, a high level of social and public services and a reduction of the population increase to 2 percent annually. The government pledged one and a half billion U.S. dollars to achieve these goals.

The first year of operation of the plan was somewhat disappointing. Gross national product rose only 5 percent compared with a nearly 10 percent rise in the previous year, and real income went up only 3 percent, just slightly over the population growth. The main reason for this was the decline of export earnings, especially from rubber. As anticipated, rubber grew in its share of total exports (to 38 percent), but its price declined, in large part because of American stockpile disposals. On the encouraging side was the increased export of palm oil, a hopeful harbinger of diversification.

Under the Five-Year Plan the first steps were taken to relieve the labor shortage in Sabah by encouraging migration from Malaya. In 1966 the family planning campaign was launched. Plans went ahead for the opening of the largest land development scheme yet devised, the Jengka Triangle, three hundred square miles in central Pahang, which was laid out with the assistance of an American engineering firm. Work was begun in 1966 on Malaysia's first complete steel mill at Prai, opposite Penang, financed by the World Bank and Japanese interests. The most interesting aspect of this plant is that its blast furnaces will use charcoal made of overage rubber trees instead of coking coal, of which Malaysia has little. Work was begun on improving agricultural education by contracting with Louisiana State University to revamp the Serdang Agricultural College. Weaknesses in the government's administration of development found by an American mission were remedied by the appointment of a Development Administration Unit.

The government spent less on development than expected in 1966 and allocated less for the next year because of shortage of funds. One cause was the fact that separation of Singapore had delayed presentation of plans to prospective foreign sources of funds. However, by the end of 1966 the United States presidential adviser on Southeast Asian Economic and Social affairs, Eugene Black, had pledged major aid to Malaysia. This included not only assistance through multilateral organizations, but bilateral loans for port development, $13 million for the trans-Malayan highway, and $40 million for new aircraft. American banks also showed their confidence in the economic future by loans like the Chase-Manhattan Bank's $5 million for bridges in Johore.

Whereas the Malaysian Five-Year Plan was merely delayed a few months by the separation of Singapore, the government of Singapore did not publish a plan at all in 1966. It merely announced that it would double expenditures to about U.S. 500 million dollars. Singapore began a slight recovery in 1966 from the depression during Confrontation, but was still plagued by unemployment. A major stimulus to recovery was the extensive American purchasing in Singapore for the Vietnam War; this offset the decline of British military spending. The end of Confrontation also led to the reopening of trade with Indonesia, which had always provided a large part of Singapore's livelihood; but much Indonesian trade may have been permanently diverted from Singapore. Lacking a development plan, Singapore did not make a concerted appeal for foreign aid, either to the United States or international sources. American capital began to show interest cautiously after the loss of the common market.

The economic "takeoff" of both Singapore and Malaysia had been predicted.[6] Malaysia seems to have the greatest momentum, with its wider market, a stable government, efficient administration, and foreign confidence. But there are many troubling ques-

[6] The American economist William T. Phillips predicted Malaysia's in the 1970's; see his "Malaysian Development," *SAIS Review,* 9.2 (Autumn, 1964): 4–8.

tions. The rural situation is still backward; little progress has been made in improving the earnings or productivity of the rice farmer; the FLDA schemes have not really drawn off much of the extra population; urban slums are growing more crowded and depressed; population control has just begun; rubber production is increasing at the same time prices are dropping; oil palm, one alternative to rubber, might not be worked efficiently by small-holders; Malay entrepreneurship has still not appeared except in a few unusual persons; there are still doubts about whether rural Malay attitudes could be changed or whether they should be changed; Borneo has just begun to feel the economic benefits of federation.

The most serious question is whether economic nationalism will drive Singapore and Malaysia farther apart. Clearly both states would profit not only from continuing their existing economic cooperation, but by increasing it; but the will to achieve this seems lacking and old political feuds stand in the way of effective reconciliation.

7
Society and Culture

Population Explosion

Malaysia's population is growing at well over 3 percent a year, which means that it will double from twelve million to twenty-four million in twenty-five years. What has happened to Malaysia is an explosion that has occurred in other parts of the lesser developed world following the improvement of health. Birth rates have been high, for all Malaysians love children. But until recently tropical diseases and poor medical care kept the death rate high, especially among tiny children, so that the population would have remained almost static if it had not been for immigration. There was even a decline of population among some groups, such as the Muruts of Borneo, whose extinction was threatened. Then came the revolution brought by the British medical officer. This first affected the big cities, particularly Singapore, and is just reaching the remote villages of the interior. The British brought the malaria eradication campaign with drainage of swamps and spraying of houses. Medical care was made accessible by opening of communications, especially roads. Roads also brought prosperity and better diets. New methods of maternal and infant care were introduced by rural health clinics. The schools began teaching hygiene. The British also assured a pure water supply, better sewage disposal, and control of food in markets and restaurants.

The improvement of health conditions resulted in two simultaneous pressures for a larger population: families wanted to have more children at the same time that more children were surviving.

This combination of a rise in fertility and lowering of death rate gave postwar Malaysia one of the highest population increases in the world. Singapore first hit the rate of 4 percent growth a year in the decade 1947–1957. Malaya's increase of 3.7 percent by 1955 caused the International Bank Mission strongly to urge family planning. The latest projections for Eastern Malaysia are 3.4 percent for 1970–1980. Brunei has one of the world's highest growth rates: nearly 12 percent in 1965.

Malaysia is not really overcrowded when compared to the rest of Asia. In 1961 it had a population density of only seventy-eight persons per square mile, half of the average of Southeast Asia, which itself was only a third as densely populated as China and India and has a sixth of Japan's density. Sabah and Sarawak are really sparsely populated with only sixteen persons per square mile. Malaya's 140 persons a square mile is about the same as Thailand's, and less than Indonesia's average. But Singapore's population, which is now at two million, packed into 224 square miles, gives it one of the highest national densities in the world, nearly 9,000 persons a square mile. Even this does not tell the story of the congestion of urban Singapore, for the island has large rural areas and uninhabited swamps and water catchment reserves. In the downtown parts of the city density runs 640,000 persons in a square mile, or a thousand per acre. Similar crowding is found in the other large cities where even the east coast town of Kuala Trengganu has densities of 15,000 a square mile, comparable to downtown Penang. The national capital has 100,000 per square mile.

The low population density of the area as a whole is deceiving in another way because Malaysians are moving out of the rural areas into the cities. They are attracted by better job opportunities and more modern social services, especially education. Once in the cities these migrants are likely to stay. It is certainly almost impossible to get highly educated people like doctors and nurses or agricultural workers and government officers to move from the city back to the farm.

Malaysia has been fortunate in having the resources and organization to make its economic growth match the expansion of population. But the huge population increase puts enormous strains on the governments. Consider some of the burdens of adding about 3.5 percent to the population each year. School rooms and teachers must increase at a comparable rate. Already half of the Malaysian population is under twenty-one and demanding universal education. But before children go out on their own, the parents must feed and clothe them—yet there are relatively fewer adults to support them. Where will the school graduates find jobs? What is to be done with the dropouts? Are crime and political radicalism going to increase? Huge amounts of capital will have to be spent by the government for all kinds of social services, not only schools and clinics, but slum clearance and low-cost housing.

The exceptionally high increase of population cannot be maintained, and a decline has already set in in the places it first started. The drop seems to be associated with urbanization, as it was in the West. The proportion of city dwellers in Malaysia was already high. Malaya (including Singapore) was the second most urbanized area in Asia after Japan, and rivaled Japan in its rate of urbanization by moving from 35 percent of its population in cities in 1947 to 50 percent in one decade.

Some of the shift to the cities had been caused by resettlement during the Emergency. A large part of the rural Chinese population, 650,000, was forcibly moved into New Villages along lines of transportation or near large towns. This relocation had an adverse affect on racial integration. In their original rural settings many Chinese had mixed with the Malay population to the extent that they intermarried with it. That the British missed the chance for getting the races to live together in the New Villages is regretted by prominent Malays.

The tendency to create ghettoes for the various races in the big cities was begun with Raffles' policy of racial segregation in Singapore. The same colonial pattern can be seen in a city as new as Kuala Lumpur. The Chinese are mainly in the old downtown business district; the Malays are set apart in Kampong Bahru, a British created reservation of the 1880's; and the Indians are still concentrated near the railroad yards at Brickfields, Bungsar, and

Sentul, where they were housed in barracks when brought from British India. The Europeans and the other members of the upper classes have spacious garden spots in the Kenny Hills and overlooking the golf course. Although the capital's population doubled in the ten years after the war, the prewar segregation persists. New Villages in the suburbs have only added new islands to the cultural mosaic; Aer Panas to the north is entirely Chinese, and Dato Kramat to the west is Malay. This same pattern of racial segregation can be found in the smaller towns of Malaysia and in the emerging cities of Borneo.

Malays leaving the country move first to the small towns which still have a rural atmosphere. Even in the big cities they cling to the rural style of living. It is striking to see the one-story Malay houses shaded by palms against the background of the tall buildings of Singapore's Geylang Serai or Kuala Lumpur's Kampong Bahru.

Urban crowding alone may have much to do with the drop of births in cities. One Malay demographer sees middle-class values setting in. Clothing costs more and so does education, and people want to do better by fewer children. But part of the decline is related to a privately sponsored birth control campaign. In Singapore, the striking decline in the birth rate began in the 1950's following the opening of the first family planning clinic in 1950. By 1958 nearly a tenth of Singapore women of reproductive age were attending such clinics. The Singapore population increase has declined from the high of 4 percent to below 2.5 percent in 1968.

Malayan figures have also begun to drop from the high of 3.5 percent increase in 1957, in part because of the family planning programs. Urban fertility is also falling in the towns of Borneo, even among the prolific Malays of Brunei. The Malaysian government has undertaken a public program of family planning under its First Malaysian Five-Year Plan with the assistance of the Ford Foundation. But if this program is successfully implemented and urbanization continues to depress birth rates, there is still the problem of caring for the people already born, and the two or three children they are likely to have.

Some of the problems of urban growth are already apparent. Unemployment in all cities is high. Joblessness is Singapore's major worry. About 76,000 (10 percent of the work force) are out of work and about 19,000 new jobs a year are needed for the school graduates. West Malaysia's unemployment figure of five percent conceals that 8 percent of the women workers are unemployed, and the situation is worst for ages fifteen to nineteen; 16.5 percent of these young men and 19 percent of the young women have no work. Many youths are high school dropouts who have not been able to meet the rigid standards for advanced education, yet have no technical training. This is a recipe for discontent. Already there is an increase of delinquency and crime in the cities.

Immigrant areas of the cities are also fertile ground for left-wing politics. The Socialist Front is strong in the Indian Sentul district and in the crowded downtown area of Kuala Lumpur. Similar radical politics can be traced to the crowded slums of Ipoh, Penang, Singapore, and Brunei. The shantytowns built by squatters are natural sources of discontent. There are 20,000 such squatter families in the capital city. The conditions of these people are incredibly bad. Although they live in the center of town, their houses have not been connected to the sewerage system, so much of the refuse runs down open ditches and into the river. There are no sidewalks or streets, only wooden planks over the puddles of mud paths which lead to shanties built of packing crates and corrugated tin. Fires start easily from the open charcoal stoves and kerosine lamps and sweep rapidly through the settlements. Yet, within a few days the people can be seen rebuilding with new planks.

Social Services

What are the governments doing about these consequences of rapid urbanization? Singapore was faced with the problem earlier, in greater dimensions, and with more force through Communist agitation, and therefore responded first. Low-cost housing has been one of Singapore's major approaches. The government estimates that it has rehoused a quarter of its population, some half a million people, in 75,000 living units. The first housing development was the immense Queenstown, four miles west of the center of the old city. Within a decade after its founding in 1953 it accommodated 150,000 people in 17,500 apartments. Queenstown's apartment houses rise seven to fourteen stories. A one-bedroom apartment with bath rents for less than seven dollars (U.S.) a month; two bedrooms cost thirteen, and three rooms only seventeen. Queenstown is a self-sufficient unit with its own schools, community center, stores, and health clinic.

One most important aspect of these developments is the mixing of the races. But the Malays are reluctant to give up their tradition of individual housing. The government has responded to this by selling them three-room houses in the Jalan Eunos settlement for only $1,333 and $183 down. Apartment units like Queenstown have been built in other parts of Singapore at the rate of a new apartment every forty-five minutes. The biggest development is yet to come—a satellite town at Toa Payoh, where 40,000 units will eventually take care of 200,000 people.

There are problems in these new communities. The land needed for them is often occupied by squatters who will not move or owners who will not sell. Maintenance is a big problem where the sense of civic pride has not yet developed. At one time there was some fear of political radicalism in the housing areas when many inhabitants were attracted to the Communists, but there have been no race riots in the new projects, and the People's Action Party made effective political capital out of their provision of low-cost housing.

The Malaysian government has not been as active as Singapore in responding to urban problems, partly because the problem is less pressing, but mostly because of its emphasis on rural development for the Malays. The capital city has taken care of about 17,500 people by building 2,825 units, 1,200 of them individual houses for Malays in the Kampong Pandan and Dato Kramat areas east of the city. The largest apartment house, Sungei Besi Flats, has only 336 units. Rents are roughly comparable to Singapore's. There is as yet no indication that the government feels any urgency to meet the need for low-cost housing and slum clearance despite the rapidly growing population of Kuala Lumpur. As the Malay proportion increases by migration from the country there will be more pressure to act.

The most impressive government effort is the satellite town of Petaling Jaya, carved out of old rubber estates to the south of the capital. It is an impressively laid out town of 40,000 on 4,500 acres, complete with neighborhood stores and schools, a central shopping center with a public Olympic-style swimming pool, a public tennis club and fishing pond, a nearby industrial park, two hospitals including the university's teaching hospital, three colleges, and the country's first superhighway leading to the capital, a jet airport, and the harbor. Although there are a few low-cost units, most rents are high. The majority of houses are for the middle class or better who have followed the sultan of Selangor and members of the cabinet to lots on the northern heights.

Penang has built some much needed low-cost housing under the impetus of the Socialist city government, but this has run into federal snags. Seremban has completed a tall skyscraper apartment under government sponsorship. But these are just beginning to meet the problem of rapid urbanization. Problems of urban crowding are going to hit the Borneo cities too. Sandakan and Kota Kinabalu had the lead on others by having to build from scratch after the World War II bombing destroyed the cities, but rents are outrageously high. Brunei has announced a plan to clear out the water town, that picturesque remnant of the past, which poses such a fire hazard with its boardwalks linking the wooden houses, and a health problem with its lack of sewage disposal. The government's plan is to offer houses on plots that are already planted with rubber. It can be predicted that most Malays will not want to leave the comforts of the breezes blowing over the water and the convenience of stepping into the outboard motorboat to get to town.

In social welfare other than housing, all parts of Malaysia have a good start. Before the war a number of voluntary organizations had begun a wide variety of services including orphanages, leprosaria, help for the blind and deaf, youth work, hospitals, and schools. The only major government efforts before World War II were in education (that far from universal) and in health. It was only in 1946 that the British administration undertook social welfare services. These rapidly expanded after independence, and today the Malaysian government operates children's homes, rehabilitation centers for the physically handicapped and for beggars, homes for old persons, and a probation service, and sponsors a national youth organization including a national training center in West Malaysia. The colonial government social services were on a voluntary basis; as a result much still needs to be done in East Malaysia. The first work in social welfare and probation for juveniles in Sabah was started by Peace Corps volunteer Doris Abraham.

Singapore has a highly developed program of social welfare. In addition to services like those in West Malaysia, the city supports creches for infants of working mothers and a program of public relief, on which 25,000 families now draw benefits for old age, disease, physical or mental handicap, unemployment, or for being a widow or orphan.

Politically conservative Brunei has the most advanced social welfare program in Southeast Asia. The government has 5,000 people over sixty on old-age pensions of $6.50 a month and 200 others receiving the same amount for blindness or other disability, or as dependents of mental patients and lepers.

It is the magnificent medical services of Malaysia that the British can be most proud of having founded. The World Bank found that what once "was one of the unhealthiest places in the tropics, today is among the healthiest . . . This is one of the world's outstanding achievements of public health and medicine, a tribute to the British administration and their medical and public health officers."[1] Modern hospitals are supplemented with local clinics, traveling maternity services, and sanitation campaigns.

Since the British departure the American Peace Corps has assisted greatly in filling the gap in medical services. Two Peace

---

1 *Malaysia Official Year Book,* 1963, p. 546.

Corps physicians and a large number of nurses worked in West Malaysia until 1965, when Malaya had trained sufficient staff. For the first time in its history, the Peace Corps had worked itself out of a job, and could turn from the primary medical services to other areas. Need for volunteers has continued in the government leprosarium at Sungei Buloh, the two mental asylums in Johore and Perak, and in tuberculosis eradication. The medical program for Malayan aborigines has been staffed in large part by American volunteers, first by a woman doctor, a helicopter-borne X-ray technician, and nurses of the Peace Corps, and lately by the CARE-Medico Foundation. The outstanding center of the study of tropical medicine at Kuala Lumpur, the Institute for Medical Research, has been heavily assisted since 1947 by a United States Army Medical Unit.

In Sabah, too, the Peace Corps has helped to relieve the shortage of trained medical personnel by providing nurses for remote rural health centers. Volunteer nurses have started a school health program; a team of medical technologists established the first medical laboratory in Sabah at the hospital in Kota Kinabalu; and a volunteer dentist opened one of the first three public dental clinics in the state. In Sarawak the Peace Corps provided nurses, laboratory technicians, and a physician who took his turn of duty at the Kuching hospital. Brunei has three model hospitals, and since 1965 a rural health service. A "flying doctor" arrives in remote villages in a helicopter.

Education for Unity

Education is Malaysia's key to national integration and to modernization and development. It is now recognized that the British administration's educational policy was detrimental to the creation of a sense of national unity and development of a modern society. British education succeeded in accentuating the racial differences and stultifying Malay development. It is easy to attribute this to a policy of divide and rule, which may have been a thought in the minds of a few administrators, but the evidence is that the British blundered into the situation with altruistic motives.

At the heart of British policy was the desire to protect the Malays, whom they regarded as the "original" inhabitants of the country. This feeling was fostered by a deep appreciation of the value of Malay culture on the part of men like Education Officer Richard Winstedt and a fear of the aggressiveness of the "immigrant" races, particularly the Chinese. This policy decision led to giving the Malays alone an education in their own language. Britain's program was some improvement over the traditional religious education, although they merely replaced the rote learning of the Koran with rote learning of Western knowledge. Malaysians now feel that this "was a philistine educational policy which led the Malays down a blind alley. British paternalism towards the Malays was stultifying and a disservice to the race."[2]

The British approach to Malay education was very much conditioned by the ideas of imperial administrators like Frank Swettenham, who argued that the Malays should learn "the habits of industry, punctuality and obedience." This would make them "better citizens and more useful members of the community than if imbued with a smattering of English ideas which they would find could not be realized."[3] Even as late as 1920, when Winstedt was improving Malay education, the government declared that its aim was "to make the son of the fisherman or the peasant a more intelligent fisherman or peasant than his father had been."[4] English education was considered "impractical" in that it would only "make the people litigious and arrogant, to create a class of literary malcontents, useless to their communities and a source of trouble to the Empire."[5] Aside from making Malays tractable peasants and fishermen, a cardinal policy was to train Malays for government administration, but of course they were largely confined to the lower brackets by their lack of knowledge of English. The government did establish the Malay College in 1905 to give

2 Chai Hon-chan, *The Development of British Malaya 1886–1909* (Kuala Lumpur: Oxford, 1964), p. 286.

3 Report from Perak, 1890, in Chai, *Development of British Malaya*, p. 239.

4 F.M.S. Report, 1920, quoted in Ho Seng Ong, *Education for Unity in Malaya* (Penang: Malayan Educator, 1952), p. 86.

5 Report of the Malay scholar and inspector of schools R. J. Wilkinson, 1902, quoted in Ho, p. 42, and Chai, p. 276.

English public school education to the sons of the nobility. This fine school provided a nucleus of highly trained civil servants, but the English language and mores only divorced the graduates from the bulk of the Malay population. While the British undoubtedly did a far better job of education than the Dutch in neighboring Indonesia, there is no question that a large part of the blame for the backwardness of the rural sector of Malaysian society rests with misdirected British paternalism.

A few English-language schools of the highest quality were established by the government, beginning with the Penang Free School (1816), Singapore Free Schools (1834; later Raffles Institution), The Malacca Free School (1826), the Government Central School in Taiping (1883; later King Edward VII), and the Victoria Institution in Kuala Lumpur. These were "free" only in the sense of being open to all races. They charged high fees, and thus catered largely to the British and to wealthy Chinese. The curriculum was geared toward entrance into Oxford and Cambridge. The studies in the first two years of secondary school covered "English history from the landing of the Romans to Henry VII"; in the next years the program covered the Tudors and Hanoverians; study of colonial history stopped before the acquisition of Penang. Until the 1960's the English curriculum emphasized the British epoch more strongly than Malaysian history. Mathematics was still taught in pounds, shillings, pence, and farthings and in English stones and gallons rather than pikuls and gantangs. The literature taught was English up to the eighteenth century. The result was that "the Malay or Chinese child, at two degrees from the equator, read tales of Christmas trees and robins playing in the snow"[6] and could "recite Wordsworth's lines on the daffodils, never having seen them, sail up the Thames in imagination, accompany Bonnie Prince Charlie through Scottish burns and braes."[7] This type of curriculum persisted in Borneo well into the nineteen sixties.

Aside from a few prestige schools, English education was left largely to the missions, in which Americans played a large part.

6 Mayhew, cited by Chai, p. 276.
7 Dr. Ruth Wong, in Wang Gungwu, *Malaysia,* p. 200.

British official policy encouraged the missions, in line with the liberal tradition of permitting education to be handled largely by what the British term public schools rather than by the government. These mission schools filled a large void in education, particularly for the Chinese, and still make a major contribution to breaking down communal isolation by bringing all the races into fairly inexpensive schools.

The American contribution to Malaysian education is difficult to exaggerate. A recent government handbook says that "the Mission Schools—particularly under the direction of the Roman Catholic Christian Brothers and the American Methodist Church —were chiefly responsible for the rapid advances in English education, and by 1914 some three-quarters of the boys receiving education in the English language were at these schools. The Missions were also pioneers in education for girls."[8] American interest in education began with the support of buildings and teachers at the Raffles Institution. Malay schools were started by the American Board missionaries in the 1830's, and the educational pioneer Benjamin Keesberry was trained in the United States.

The interest of the Methodist church dates from 1885 when Rev. William F. Oldham accompanied Bishop James Thorburn from India. Oldham, an English-born American, started the first Methodist school, the Anglo-Chinese School in Singapore in 1886. The next year the American missionary Sophia Blackmore pioneered in women's education by starting the Tamil Girls' School, which is now the Methodist Girls' School of Singapore on Mt. Sophia. From this beginning Methodist work has grown into a system of over 137 English-language schools with about 75,000 students of all races. In the 1890's Methodist schools were founded in Penang (1891), Ipoh (1896), and Kuala Lumpur (1897) which have attained top rank among secondary schools in the country. An indication of the importance of these schools is the list of some of the more famous graduates: Dr. Toh Chin Chye, deputy prime minister of Singapore; the former education minister of Singa-

8 *Malaysia Official Year Book, 1963,* p. 394.

pore, Chew Swee Kee; two Malaysian cabinet members, Khaw Kai Boh and Capt. Abdul Hamid Khan; and some of Malaysia's most eminent scholars: Dr. Thong Saw Pak (physicist), Dr. Robert Ho (geographer), Lim Tay Boh (economist and deputy vice chancellor, University of Singapore), Dr. Shanmugaratnam (pathologist), Chua Boon Lan (dean of Singapore Law School), and the principals of over twenty top schools in Malaysia. It is not true, as is sometimes charged, that the Methodist schools—which did provide an especially important service to the Chinese—barred Muslim Malays. If anything made it difficult for Malays to get an English secondary education, it was the British policy of providing a single-language Malay primary education.

While the British favored Malay education, they did make a concession to the Indians by supporting Tamil-language primary schools, mainly on rubber estates. In the process they created a third communal school, an impediment to integration.

The British colonial policy of ignoring Chinese education was based upon the laudable desire for integration of the Chinese. It was feared that the teaching of dialects would result in "strengthening rather than breaking down the barriers of race, would hinder rather than help these alien races from having any commercial or other intercourse with each other, by preventing them from learning the vernacular of the country of their adoption [Malay] . . . and would be committing the fatal error of tending to keep them aliens, and encouraging them in the idea that China or India is their home."[9]

Ironically, by ignoring Chinese education the British helped to realize their fears. When Chinese nationalism grew following the 1911 Revolution, the Chinese began to establish their own schools. The teaching of Kuo Yü, the national language, unified the Chinese community in a way that it had never been when the people spoke mutually unintelligible dialects. More detrimental was the fact that the teaching was accompanied by political propaganda, of both chauvinistic and Communist sorts, which are still

[9] "The System of Education in the F.M.S.," 1902, in Chai, *Development of British Malaya*, p. 250.

the bane of Chinese communities. British laissez-faire permitted
the schools to be run from the Education Ministry in China, with
regular visits by Chinese inspectors.

The result of the colonial policy was to create by 1945, more
by accident than evil intent, an education system which separated
the races and accentuated social and economic differences. The
Malay-language system insulated the rural Malay from the process
of modernization; the Chinese track was geared to Chinese nationalism and increasing left-wing radicalism; the Tamil track led to
nowhere but frustration; and an English-language system was
directed toward learning the kings of England rather than Asian
history. A surer recipe for communal misunderstanding could not
have been devised.

When the British returned after World War II with a policy of
development for self-government, they brought a new education
policy geared to national education. In 1946 they introduced free
primary education in "national schools" in Malaya. Teaching
was in three languages, Malay, Mandarin, and Tamil, while
English was taught as a subject. Dissatisfaction with this led to
rival recommendations for a better system in 1951. The Barnes
Committee recommended teaching only in Malay and English, a
view which pleased Malays but not the Chinese. A contrasting
recommendation, made by the American educator W. P. Fenn
and Wu Teh-yao of the United Nations, favored schooling in
three languages, Malay, English, and Chinese. The report argued
that Chinese, "one of the great languages of the world," should be
taught in government schools rather than in the private ones
where chauvinism was rampant. The Fenn-Wu Report was advocating a Swiss type of system against an American style system of
the Barnes Report.

Upon achieving self-government, Malaya found a compromise
recommended by the Razak Report in 1956, a solution not unlike
the magnificent accommodation of the Alliance Party's communalism within the national political system. The Razak plan permitted primary education in four languages, Malay, English,
Mandarin, or Tamil, in schools that were of a single national
model with a standard curriculum. Malay and English had to be

taught as subjects. The report set a goal that still holds: "A national system of education acceptable to the people for the Federation as a whole which will satisfy their needs and promote their cultural, social, economic, and political development as a nation, having regard to the intention to make Malay the National Language of the country, whilst preserving and sustaining the growth of the language and culture of other communities living in the country."[10]

This policy was put into effect in 1957. In the sixties the government furthered this policy by implementing the Rahman Talib Report of 1960, which provided for free education through age fifteen. The government's method of bringing about a uniform national system was to use the incentive of increased subsidies to schools which conformed to the government syllabus. Few parents would pay the fees for nonconforming schools if they could get free education from the government. The inducement worked, and by 1963 about 90 percent of the Chinese schools had conformed, most of them going over to English medium. This was a revolutionary event, for in a very brief time it reduced to minor proportions Chinese separatism and the accompanying chauvinism that has threatened Malaya since the Chinese Revolution.

The Razak Report placed a strong emphasis upon modern technical and scientific education. The Peace Corps responded to a request for assistance to relieve the shortage of teachers in these subjects in 1961. Since then several hundred American teachers of science and mathematics have taught in Malayan secondary schools, where they have brought modern scientific method and thinking to the classroom. When these volunteers have trained their replacements, the program can be terminated. Malaysia has also recognized the importance of vocational training and has successfully used Peace Corps volunteers to set up shops and to start teaching practical subjects in the equivalent of American junior high schools, in the Technical Teachers' Training College, in rural vocational schools, in the Technical College, and in the apprenticeship school.

[10] *Report of the Education Review Committee, 1960* (Kuala Lumpur: B. T. Fudge, 1960), pp. 2–3.

Singapore, operating always under a separate education policy, created a public school system at the same time as Malaya, but because of its Chinese population it inclined more toward the Swiss model. Separate Mandarin, Malay, and English institutions are maintained through the secondary level, but there is an emphasis upon national culture with English and Malay as compulsory subjects. The problem of Chinese nationalism in the Chinese secondary schools is thus prolonged.

At the time of the federation proposal, the educational pattern in Borneo was much like that of prewar Malaya. A laissez-faire policy permitted private organizations to take the initiative in education. The Chinese, particularly in Sarawak, were attending Mandarin-language schools that were hotbeds of Chinese nationalism and much Communist agitation. English-language education was carried on largely by Christian missions. The Methodist missionaries played the major role in the big Rajang basin, where Reverend James M. Hoover had founded the first Methodist school, at Sibu in 1904. Today there are over twenty-five Methodist schools in the Third Division with such eminent graduates as the first Sarawak cabinet member, Temenggong Jugah; the first Asian Resident of one of the Divisions of Sarawak (the First Division, the most populous), Yau Ping Hua; and member of parliament and lumberman, Ling Beng Sieu.

Much of Borneo's indigenous population lived in the luxury of its traditional culture largely untouched by modern ideas. After World War II only 2 percent of the indigenous population of Sarawak was literate. By 1960 half of the school-age children in Sarawak and about a third in Sabah were still not in school. Those in school were taught for the most part by people completely without training, recent graduates of the school itself. The system lacked financial support for buildings, equipment, and decent salaries. Opportunities for higher education in Borneo were rare, since few secondary schools went as far as the high school level. Those that did, which were confined largely to the upper classes of the cities, offered an elitist education on the English public school model, scarcely geared to the needs of an independent society. Virtually nothing was done about vocational education. By the sixties the reason for neglect of education was not lack of funds, for Sabah was enjoying a budget surplus with its timber boom, and even relatively poor Sarawak returned part of its educational allotment unspent in a recent year.

The language issue was even stronger in the Borneo states than in Malaya. The fact that the Malays were in a minority and somewhat unpopular in places made the introduction of Malay as the national language difficult, even though it was used in the majority of primary schools. The Chinese and indigenous peoples, with some encouragement from British expatriates, agitated for English rather than Malay. Thus, in the Malaysia Agreement of 1963, the education systems of Sabah and Sarawak were given autonomy and permitted to continue teaching in English. This brought about a curious situation. In Malay areas like Limbang, Malay-language schools were converted to English medium *after* the merger, when the government was trying to promote national unity through the Malay language.

The factor that saved the East Malaysia education system from going in completely the opposite direction from West Malaysia was state dependence on the central government for federal grants. He who controls the purse ultimately controls policy. By 1966 Sabah had accepted the first steps of integration into a national education system. A highly regarded Malayan educator was appointed director of education, and the government declared the goal of universal free primary schooling for which federal support was available. The integration of Sarawak's system will certainly benefit that state, not only in bringing a sense of national community but also by spreading the benefits of the successful Malayan experience of a multiracial and democratic school system geared to national needs in the world of Asia.

The American Peace Corps supplied badly needed teachers to help the Borneo states expand their school systems to meet the needs of popular education. Volunteers first came to the states in 1962 to teach at the junior high school level, and have served both in remote primary schools and in the top teacher's colleges.

Brunei for a long time was the most backward state educationally. The first secular school was established in 1914, and even now more than half the population is illiterate. But recent progress has been rapid and at present about a quarter of the people are in schools ranging from kindergarten to teachers' college.

Higher education in the Malaysian area was considerably retarded by British policy. As at the lower levels, the initiative came from popular pressures rather than from the administration. Popular demand and subscription resulted in the opening of the first institution for higher education, the medical school started in Singapore in 1905. The standards of this institution were materially raised by a grant of $350,000 from the Rockefeller Foundation in 1925. There was no other higher education until 1928 when Raffles College opened in Singapore offering courses in English, history, geography, mathematics, economics, physics, and chemistry. To the ire of its graduates, this school was not permitted to offer a degree until 1949, when the medical school and Raffles College united to form the University of Malaya (at Singapore). A second campus was created in 1957 at Kuala Lumpur, which became autonomous five years later when the original campus took the name of the University of Singapore.

Both universities have maintained high standards from the start and have lived up to expectations that they would be foci of national unity and interracial cooperation. Foreign professors contributed much in the initial years, including a number of Americans who have taught subjects as varied as neurosurgery and seed technology. The language of instruction has had to be English because of the lack of sufficient students trained at the secondary level in other languages. Courses are offered in Malay in the Malay Studies Department of the University of Malaya. The number of such courses will expand as more students enter who have had Malay throughout their previous schooling.

The use of English has placed the graduates of the Chinese-language secondary schools at a disadvantage for entry into the University of Malaya. So, following the pattern of secondary education, where the government did not provide the Chinese community took the initiative. A number of wealthy Chinese in Singapore founded Nanyang University—the University of the

South Seas—in 1957. Initially high hopes were held that it would attract famous scholars who had fled from China and thereby serve as a focus of Overseas Chinese loyalties. The famous Chinese-American scholar Lin Yu Tang became the first chancellor. But almost at once the university ran into problems of Chinese politics since it attracted both nationalists and Communists. The university has also had constant trouble with excessive control by its financial backers and by student agitators, threatening academic freedom. Student demonstrations have forced the government to send riot squads into the campus several times. Difficulty in getting first-rate staff has contributed to low standards and ultimately to problems in placing students. The situation was partly improved when the Singapore government recognized Nanyang degrees and gave scholarships. The university continues as a bulwark of Chinese nationalism against integration into Malaysian society. The opening of the school to non-Chinese-speaking students may mark the path to transforming Nanyang into a national university which emphasizes Chinese studies.

The Malaysian government's plans for a second university campus at Penang have been supported by UNESCO. It has been proposed that eventually a branch be established in East Malaysia, perhaps at Kota Kinabalu.

Another institution of higher education which is outside the university setup is the Muslim College founded in 1950 and now located in Petaling Jaya. The leading schools of technology are Singapore Polytechnic and the Technical College in Kuala Lumpur. The latter has been supported by Peace Corps teachers in architecture, mathematics, physics, and television. The College of Agriculture at Serdang, a suburb of the capital, is such an important source of agricultural teachers and technicians that the Ford Foundation has recently given support to a cooperative arrangement with Louisiana State University to improve the curriculum and teaching. The roster of institutions of higher learning also includes a chain of nine teachers' colleges in Malaysia and Singapore which have been aided by Peace Corps volunteers and American Fulbright lecturers.

National Language and Unity

Language is the most explosive issue in Malaysia. It is at the heart of many of the issues of politics and education. For, as in other countries, language is the symbol of nationalism, whether Malay, Chinese, Indian, Dayak, or Malaysian. The discussion of the language issue arouses all the parochial defensiveness of each group. Language is the thing that most divides Malaysians, for the races are often mixed. Yet, paradoxically, language is the major means of unifying any country as we know from history and political science. Almost everyone will agree that communication in a single language is the best means of achieving national unity. Most people will also agree that they would not want to destroy the identity of the component cultures which are best kept alive through language. The issue remains which language should be the national language of unity and how the others should be treated.

The language argument now centers around Malay versus English. In general, the non-Malays take a strong position in favor of English. The arguments are easily understood by an English-speaking person who has his own pride of language. English is fast becoming the lingua franca of Southeast Asia. It is the language not only of diplomatic conferences, but also of international trade, on which Malaysia so depends, and of science and technology and most aspects of higher learning. English has the added advantage in this multilingual situation that it does not emphasize or seem to favor one culture over the other. Its adoption avoids the choice between competing local languages.

The advantages of Malay are also strong. English is, after all, a foreign language. Malay, on the other hand, has been the language of commerce and government of this area for hundreds of years. The first British administrators like Raffles and Crawfurd learned it. Much of the business of the British, Chinese, and Malays in the nineteenth century was conducted in Malay. It was, and still is, the major link of communication in Borneo among the various dialect groups. In the remotest parts of the country Malay is understood where English is not.

Furthermore, the language is international, being used all the way from southern Thailand to New Guinea by some 125 million people. Even the Filipinos acknowledge the kinship of their languages to Malay and understand many of the words through cognates. The popularity of Malay has led to its adoption as the national language of Indonesia, the largest country in Southeast Asia. In two short decades universal education in Malay had led to its being a major factor in unifying the language groups of Indonesia which are even more diverse than Malaysia's. The dialect adopted as the Indonesian national language was Straits Malay, the same one spoken in Johore. The differences between Indonesian and Malay are no more substantial than between English and American.

Malay has the added advantage of being relatively easy to learn, not because of any lack of subtlety, but because of highly logical and regular spelling, pronunciation, and grammar, something most of us wish English had. To speak Malay well and to understand its nuances, of course, takes many years, but for practical purposes fluency in spoken Malay can be achieved in a few months, as a thousand Peace Corps volunteers have demonstrated. The language does lack scientific terms, but it is highly adaptable to borrowing and coining words as needed because the regularity of construction makes new compositions readily recognizable. Malay is particularly adaptable as a language of literature because of its melodic sounds.

Malayan nationalists of all races have recognized the value of adopting Malay as the national language to achieve unity. The multiracial Alliance campaigned on this plank in the first elections in 1955. When it won in a landslide, the Reid Commission recommended the adoption of Malay, and the 1957 Constitution declared that "the national language shall be the Malay language" (Article 152, Clause 1). However, it was recognized at the time that the language of the colonial regime was still widely used in government, and that many people, particularly the Chinese, would need time to learn Malay. Thus the Constitution also provided that English should be used as an official language for ten years or longer if Parliament wished. Meanwhile study of Malay was made compulsory in all government schools. As a concession to the language groups that feared that their cultures would be suppressed, Mandarin and Tamil were still taught in primary schools where desired. A national language institute, the Dewan Bahasa dan Pustaka, was set up to develop the language by collecting and printing Malay literature, publishing textbooks, standardizing spelling, developing new vocabulary, and compiling a national dictionary.

The 1957 compromise on language has proved to be workable. There were two brief periods of resistance, in 1959 and 1965, which came to the surface in politics through the Chinese wing of the Alliance. Responding to demands for recognition of Chinese as an official language, Malayan Chinese Association president Lim Chong Eu pressed for reconsideration of the national language policy in 1959. This provoked a showdown within the MCA; Lim resigned and was replaced by Tan Siew Sin, a victory of the moderate Chinese who accepted the necessity of a national language. In 1965 a similar but smaller crisis occurred in which lower level leaders agitated for more use of Chinese in the government. This episode, too, was resolved without violence and with a general acceptance of the 1957 decision.

Some of the tenseness of the 1965 crisis was undoubtedly caused by the "Malaysian Malaysia" campaign that preceded Singapore's separation. Although the language issue was not explicitly mentioned, it is always implicit in any racial issue. The implication of the slogan was that one should emphasize Malaysianness by accepting all languages rather than stressing its Malayness in the national language. Much of the tension in 1965 was created by misinterpretation of statements of government leaders whose job it was to promote Malay. For instance, there were those who wished to move much more rapidly to the adoption of Malay as the sole language, like Syed Ja'afar Albar, then chairman of UMNO, and Syed Nasir, whose job as director of the Dewan

Bahasa was to promote the national language. Part of the government's campaign to teach Malay was a National Language Month, of increasing length each year, in which only Malay would be used in government offices. This program stirred up Malay youths who went around the country blotting out with red paint the English names on road signs. The Chinese, particularly in Singapore, were unduly provoked by the Malay statements, which they probably took too seriously.

Actually both the Singapore and Malaysian governments have taken very moderate stands on the language issue. If anything, Singapore made more of its Malay language campaign. Long before the Malayan decision for merger the leaders of Singapore had accepted the need for a national language, and the People's Action Party promoted a drive for "Malayan Culture." Lee Kuan Yew and other Singapore leaders spoke to voters in Malay and promoted an effective National Language Month of their own.

The Malayan government took a very lenient stand on language at the time of merger. Singapore and Borneo were given linguistic autonomy and educational control to support it. The 1963 Malaysia Agreement permitted Sabah and Sarawak to use English as an official language in the national and state legislatures and courts for ten years and thereafter until the state (not federal) legislature decided upon the use of Malay (Article 63). Thus, even after Malay became the sole official language for West Malaysia in 1967, the East Malaysia delegates went on speaking English in Parliament, and English will be used in the state governments until 1973 or as long as they please.

Everyone in Malaysia was apprehensive about what would happen in 1967 and 1973, when official status of English was to be reconsidered. Singapore leaders in particular feared that the advocacy of the national language by Malay nationalists would produce counterreactions from the Chinese, and that this would result in riots even bloodier than those of 1964.

However, in 1967 the Malaysian government handled the situation with consummate skill. A year before the Tunku made clear that "All that is intended is to put Malay as the national and official language and English as a second language, while the others will go on as they have been going on."[11] The whole issue was played down by cabinet members, especially Malays. The minister of education made numerous statements reaffirming the importance of English in the modern world and the need to study all languages. Prestigious Malays urged students not to abandon their English since it was an international language which would help them with science and technology. The public had been very much reassured by the time the bill was presented to Parliament by the Tunku in February 1967. The act stated that "the national language shall be used for official purposes," but provided that the chief of state could "permit the continued use of the English language for such official purposes as may be deemed fit" (Clauses 2 and 4). A safeguard for the other communities was written in by guaranteeing the right to use other languages (Clause 4).

Such a moderate position could hardly provoke opposition of the Chinese or Indians. The main objection came from the Malay right wing which did not feel that the bill went far enough. At a rally Syed Nasir broke into tears and said that he was "overcome with emotion in thinking of the fate of my race. I am about to be destroyed."[12] For this breach of party discipline the Tunku wanted to expel Nasir from UMNO, but let him resign. A few students demonstrated at the Muslim College, but there was no violence and none of the feared race riots. The bill passed the House of Representatives on March 7 with the Alliance deputies solidly in favor. It was implemented on September 1, 1967. There were some minor demonstrations in Penang, but no violent opposition.

The peaceful establishment of the national language was a tribute to the moderation and statesmanship not only of the government but of the Malaysian people. The net effect is perhaps not significant, since it only places Malay ahead of English as the official language, but it is a step toward unity. There is no question that English will continue to be widely used and taught

---

[11] November 10, 1966; quoted in Margaret Roff, "The Politics of Language in Malaya," *Asian Survey*, 7.5:5 (May 1967): 324.
[12] March 3, 1967, in Roff, "Politics of Language," p. 327.

and that the peoples of Malaysia will become increasingly bilingual. The minor languages will probably lose their significance in time, though Mandarin in particular will continue to be studied as a key to an important culture of Malaysia, as will Arabic and Hindi to a lesser extent.

If the same sort of gradual approach can be made to the introduction of the national language in East Malaysia, there is no reason why 1973 cannot be as quiet as 1967, with the same results. Singapore has continued to emphasize the importance of Malay. There is no question that it will be of prime importance in trade and government dealings with Indonesia. Brunei has its own national language campaign. That it is using materials prepared in Kuala Lumpur shows the continued cultural links of the area. Following the end of Confrontation, Indonesia and Malaysia have resumed cooperation on their national languages. The growing use of Malay and English in all the southern parts of Southeast Asia will bring more effective communication and encourage understanding if not integration.

Malaysian Culture

Will a distinctive national culture emerge in Malaysia, combining the best qualities of the major cultures which are represented there? The country is too new to give any final answer, but there are signs of cultural vitality and innovation.

Architecture is one of the first areas where cultural dynamism can be seen. The magnificent National Mosque in Kuala Lumpur is one example. It combines traditional Muslim motifs in its 245-foot minaret, the lacy Arabesque grillwork, and blue reflecting pools, with modern design which uses stressed concrete materials. The architect was a Malay, Baharuddin bin Abu Kassim; the building was completed in 1965 by the Chinese contractors Boon and Cheah.

The National Museum (1963) also reflects innovation. The architect Ho Kok Hoe uses the ancient Malaysian motifs of the pointed roof with crossed peaks in modern materials. A splendid mosaic on the front depicts the history of the races that have come to Malaysia. Other unusual architectural examples in the national capital are the Parliament Building, the campus of the University of Malaya in Pantai Valley (particularly the Faculty of Arts), the new Foreign Office, the Dewan Bahasa, and some of the modern office buildings of downtown Kuala Lumpur.

In Borneo, Brunei is the center of some imposing architecture that follows traditional lines but uses modern materials: the Sultan Omar Mosque and the Religious Affairs Department opposite, and the Sultan's Palace.

The Malaysian National Gallery, started under the direction of the American Frank Sullivan, is full of paintings in which we see considerable originality and what may be called a Malaysian style. For instance, the ancient Malay batik method of dyeing cloth is being used for modern subjects by artists like Chuah Thean Teng of Penang. A number of Malaysian artists are using the traditional Chinese ink brush to paint subjects of modern Malaysia such as the striking latticework of a Chinese tin mine or the stilting of a Malay fishing village. One of the most interesting uses of traditional Sarawak designs in a new medium is the mural on the walls of the library of Batu Lintang Teachers' College in Kuching.

Aborigine tribes have created a completely new form of art where no traditional style existed. One of the artists of the Mah Meri tribe on Pulau Carey in the Straits of Malacca was inspired to carve his conception of a bad dream. The resultant "moyang" was so unusual that other artists on the island have been encouraged to create a whole series of sculptures of striking imaginativeness. The Jah Hut tribe of Pahang is producing some wood sculpture that are modern adaptations of traditional carvings.

Modern Malay literature has shown great vitality since the war. The beginning of a new literature was marked by the founding in 1950 of the Angkatan Sasterawan '50 in Singapore. Strongly influenced by growing nationalism, this literary group wrote on political and social themes. Among the best known artists are the poet Masuri S. N., the short-story writer Keris Mas, and the novelists Samad Said and Salmi Manja. In English, the most famous novelist is Han Suyin of Singapore whose *The Rain My Drink* captures the feeling of the Emergency.

Original research on Malaysian culture and traditions is being carried out in a number of institutions: in history at the universities of Malaya and Singapore; in linguistics and historical literature at the Dewan Bahasa; in archaeology and ethnology at the National, Kedah, and Sarawak museums. All of this is bringing to light new aspects of the national culture that give both Malaysians and foreigners a greater appreciation of its depth and beauty.

8
International Relations

The international relations of the Malaysian area—the states of Malaysia, Singapore, and Brunei—are conditioned by factors of geography, culture, defense, trade, ideology, and personality. Geographical proximity affects relations, making the three neighbors, Indonesia, Thailand, and the Philippines, potential enemies or friends. Indonesia, China, and India have deep cultural influence. Against any threats the area relied in the past on Great Britain, but is now increasingly dependent upon Australia and New Zealand. Trading partners, primarily the United States, Great Britain, and Japan, are important to commerce and aid. Ideology also influences policy. The kinship of Islam is significant for Malaysia and Brunei; anticommunism is an attitude in all three states. There is sympathy with socialism in Singapore; opposition to racism on the part of all; and a deep belief in international organization, particularly the United Nations and regional cooperation.

Personality helps determine foreign policy style. Singapore's shirtsleeves diplomacy, with its hardheaded approach to trade and political realism, is very much a reflection of the personality of Lee Kuan Yew and the hard-boiled politics he fights in Singapore. Malaysia's goodwill and cooperativeness derives in large part from the Tunku, who has been his own foreign minister for most of a decade. One is reminded of the rare statesman in history like Louis IX whose devotion to peace and cooperation made him sought as mediator. Brunei's conservative outlook comes from the example of its sultan.

These determining factors appear clearly when one looks at Malaysia's major foreign policy problems and issues.

Indonesian Confrontation

The most serious problem faced by Malaysia has been the three-year war with Indonesia (1963–1966), euphemistically dubbed by Sukarno a "Confrontation." Malaysia and Indonesia have more in common with each other than they do with any other country: a common culture, national language, Islam as the major religion, similar background of customary law and local government, many trade and personal ties, and a common experience under the Japanese occupation. On the other hand, their postwar experiences have been different. As Malaysia evolved slowly toward political democracy and a mixed economy, Indonesia plunged into a violent nationalist revolution leading to a guided democracy with strong Communist influences. In this difference of recent experiences are the roots of their quarrel.

Each country had a perception of the other different from the image the country had of itself. Indonesia's image of Malaysia, in particular, was distorted by its own experience and ideology. Their colonial experiences had been different. Indonesia's bitter struggle against the Dutch contrasted with Malaysia's happy transfer of power. Indonesia had to fight for New Guinea, whereas the transfer of the Borneo territories to Malaysia was comparatively simple. There were many elements in the Malaysian federation that looked suspicious to Indonesia: (1) that Borneo was thrown in to counterbalance Singapore, (2) the initial opposition of all Borneo political parties to merger, (3) the continuing doubt of the majority of Borneans, as expressed to the Cobbold Commission, (4) the conduct of the first elections in Borneo by indirect method which obscured the issues, (5) the detention of some party leaders who opposed merger, (6) opposition in Brunei expressed in elections, then revolt, (7) that the British first suggested merger, (8) the continuation of the British military presence, especially in the Singapore base, (9) the retention of expatriates in responsible posts, (10) that the Tunku took British foreign policy advice, and

(11) that a moderate nation like the Philippines doubted the legality of Sabah's cession.

Besides these suspicions, there were sharp differences between Malaysia and Indonesia. Indonesia's social revolution had eliminated most of the "feudal" classes that seemed to rule Malaysia. Indonesia's Marxist economic outlook made it far less tolerant of free enterprise. Malaysia's tolerance of the Chinese contrasted with Indonesia suspicions. Malaysia's prosperity no doubt caused some jealousy in Indonesia, particularly when it was based in part on smuggling to avoid Indonesian export duties. Asylum given in Malaysia to Indonesian rebels was another irritant to relations. Indonesia was not consulted about the Malaysian merger; this was taken as a definite affront. Indonesia's injured pride was probably more responsible for its opposition to Malaysia than was territorial ambition.

Domestically, Sukarno found Confrontation to his advantage. It provided a way to play off the ambitions of his two major opponents, the army and the Communists. As a result of this balancing, and his appeal to many factions, a wide spectrum of Indonesian opinion supported Confrontation. But what gave it the most credibility was the suspicion that Malaysia was a British creation.

The course of Confrontation followed three phases: (1) growing Indonesian opposition through 1962 resulting in the first peace efforts in mid-1963, (2) the military phase following the formation of Malaysia in September 1963, with an American peace effort in 1964, and (3) the gradual decline of hostilities from late 1964 to the conclusion of peace and the resumption of full diplomatic relations in 1967.

Indonesian misgivings about the merger idea were aroused in 1962 as various forms of opposition began to appear in Malaysia. Open Indonesian opposition did not begin until the outbreak of the Brunei Revolt on December 8, 1962. Sukarno supported the rebels, and the next month Indonesian Foreign Minister Subandrio declared the policy of Confrontation, which the Tunku called a "virtual declaration of Cold War." The United States gave its support to Malaysia by warning "that if anyone on the outside attempts by force to interfere" it "would create a very serious problem."[1] The first Indonesian military action began in April 1963, with an attack on Tebedu on the border of the First Division of Sarawak.

Peace talks began at the same time, with the first of three summit meetings at Tokyo in May 1963, which produced a Malaysian-Indonesian declaration of peaceful intentions. A second summit, of the leaders of the Philippines, Malaysia, and Indonesia at Manila in June, resulted in two agreements. One established the regional organization Maphilindo; the other, the Manila Accord, agreed to "welcome the formation of Malaysia provided the support of the people of the Borneo territories is ascertained" by the United Nations. The world organization's mission headed by the American-born international civil servant Laurence Michelmore, reported that the Borneo elections had been fairly conducted and that Malaysia was a major issue; the impartiality and correctness of this conclusion was not challenged. Under strong pressure of the unilateral declarations of independence by Singapore and the Borneo states, Malaysia announced the merger before the Michelmore report was out. This provided the excuse for continuation of Confrontation.

The second, the active military, phase of the conflict began after the formation of Malaysia on September 14, 1963, when Sukarno began his campaign to "Ganjang Malaysia"—literally, "Devour Malaysia." The United States, which had welcomed Malaysia and backed the United Nations finding, soon suspended a large part of its aid to Indonesia, but continued some minor aid in an attempt to keep its foot in the door. After the assassination of President Kennedy, this policy was continued by President Johnson, who sent Attorney General Robert Kennedy to attempt to stop the war. Kennedy obtained agreement to a cease-fire on January 25, 1964, but this was never fully effective, in part because of Sukarno's apparent determination to continue. American threats to stop all aid evoked Sukarno's famous cry, "To hell with your aid!"

[1] Secretary of State Rusk, February 13, 1963, *Department of State Bulletin,* XLVIII, 366.

The third and final summit meeting in Tokyo in June 1964 failed to resolve the question of withdrawal of Indonesian guerrillas from Borneo, and then Confrontation began in earnest. In July Indonesia made a large amphibious landing at Pontian in Johore, and in September dropped paratroopers in northern Johore. The invasion was a total failure due to the loyalty of the local people to Malaysia. Nevertheless the case of aggression was taken to the United Nations Security Council. The United States strongly supported Malaysia, but a mild resolution deploring the incident was defeated by a Russian veto, against the wishes of the majority of members. When Malaysia was elected to the Security Council shortly afterward (as had been agreed in 1963), Indonesia withdrew from the United Nations.

The third phase of Confrontation started about this time with a tapering off of Indonesian incursions. The British had made clear that they would commit their full military strength in retaliation against further Indonesian attacks, though the exact nature of the response was not revealed. The Gestapu Coup in Indonesia in October 1965 brought a real letup, but Sukarno's continued opposition to Malaysia prevented any peace moves until March 1966. In the Bangkok Accord of June 1966 Razak agreed with Indonesian Foreign Minister Adam Malik upon a resumption of relations. The conflict was officially ended by a peace treaty signed in Djakarta on August 11, 1966. The treaty also settled the old issue of self-determination of the Borneo peoples by providing for general elections in the Borneo states. Elections were held in Sabah in April 1967; in Sarawak they were delayed past 1968. Indonesia and Malaysia re-established trade relations in late 1966 and full diplomatic relations on August 31, 1967, ending nearly five tense years.

On the whole, the effects of Confrontation on Malaysia were positive. The war came at a time when there were few national symbols to unify the country, and the conflict became a patriotic issue. The loyalty of the majority of the Borneo peoples was confirmed. The left wing in all parts of Malaysia was weakened, either discredited for its opposition or forced to soften its criticism. On the negative side was the diversion of Malaysian funds and energies from the task of economic development. Singapore suffered the most by the loss of its entrepôt trade with Indonesia. From the standpoint of decolonization, British withdrawal was delayed, but this was balanced by the gain in making the Commonwealth acutely aware of its responsibilities for defense of Malaysia.

Ultimately, Confrontation may be regarded as a relatively harmless catharsis of some of the irritants in relations, a catharsis that made effective cooperation possible by showing the countries the differences that separate them. A new relationship was indicated by the formation of joint military patrols on the Borneo border, the resumption of cultural exchange and language cooperation, and the fact that the two countries have joined a regional organization (ASEAN) for the first time. There will continue to be areas of friction such as smuggling from Indonesia to Malaysia, fishing in each other's territorial waters, and refugee elements, but the peaceful solution of these problems will contribute to a sense of community. As long as the governments continue their present moderateness, relations between the countries promise to be good.

Britain and the Commonwealth Defense

The survival of Malaysia, Singapore, and Brunei through Confrontation was almost entirely due to defense aid by Britain and its Commonwealth partners Australia and New Zealand. At the peak of hostilities they had committed 50,000 troops, seventy warships, and all the combat aircraft used. Without these Malaysia could not have repelled Indonesian power.

Military dependence on Britain was foreseen in the Malayan Defence Agreement of 1957, a military alliance that is still in effect. But under pressure of adverse balance of payments and because of interest in joining the Common Market, Britain began a review of its worldwide commitments when Harold Wilson's Labour government took office in 1964. A White Paper released in 1966 announced the historic decision to reduce imperial responsibilities.[2] With Confrontation not officially over, the

[2] United Kingdom, *Statement of the Defence Estimates, 1966*, Cmnd. 2901, Part 1, para. 24.

British promised to "maintain a military presence" in the area, and to hold the bases in Malaysia and Singapore as long as those governments agreed, though reductions of forces would be made as soon as conditions permitted. When hostilities ended in 1966, the British withdrew all troops from East Malaysia. The next year they announced a timetable for complete withdrawal from Malaysia. Defense forces would be halved by 1971, and completely withdrawn by 1975. Following the devaluation of the pound in 1967, the British government was forced to advance the date of full evacuation to the end of 1971. Representatives from Australia, Malaysia, New Zealand, Singapore, and the United Kingdom met in Kuala Lumpur in mid-1968 to discuss ways of meeting the problem of military defense after 1971. Since Britain would not keep any forces in Malaysia or Singapore after 1971 it promised to send troops from Europe in an emergency.[3] Australia and New Zealand did not want to assume the British mantle directly, so primary defense strength would have to come from Singapore-Malaysian cooperation, backed by the three Commonwealth countries. Britain promised to help Singapore build self-defense forces and convert the city's naval base into a commercial shipyard available to all nations.

Following Britain's declaration in 1966 of intention to reduce its military presence, a shift in Malaysian foreign policy was announced by the Tunku. British inability to give substantial aid for Malaysia's Five-Year Plan was taken as a "financial squeeze" to force Malaysia to cooperate with Singapore on economic relations, and evoked an angry "To hell with Britain" from a woman senator in Parliament. The Tunku spoke of the need for Malaysia to avoid being regarded "as a creation or protégé of Britain" in the eyes of its neighbors. After 1966 ties with Britain were loosened by removing Commonwealth preferences on imports and basing the Malaysian currency on gold instead of the pound. British influence continues to be strong, however. British investments are still the largest, and Great Britain will probably continue to be a major trading partner, though of declining importance. Cultural influence will naturally persist through lan-

[3] United Kingdom, *Statement on Defence Policy 1968,* Cmnd. 3700, para. 10.

guage, law, administrative habits, and parliamentary procedures, but when the present English-educated elite passes, the ties to the mother country are bound to lessen.

The most logical successor as the defender of Malaysia is Australia, aided by New Zealand. The two countries have accepted an increasing role in the defense of the area, as shown by their active contributions during World War II, the Emergency, and Confrontation. Australia has taken the lead in economic aid, by its initiation of the Colombo Plan, which has provided over a thousand technicians to Malaysia. Trade between Malaysia and Australia is growing. Cultural contacts are important, as indicated by the 5700 Malaysian students in Australian schools in 1962 and the Australian educators and missionaries in Malaysian schools.

On the negative side are the "White Australia" policy of racial exclusion and Australia's colonial role in the South Pacific. Differences over racial and colonial issues became apparent in meetings of the Commonwealth and the United Nations. New Zealand has escaped some of the racial stigma; the country has few colonies, and has sent a Maori ambassador to Malaya. But New Zealand's role is by necessity junior to Australia.

The British announcement of a timetable for withdrawal from Southeast Asia was met with open "regret" by Australia. Prime Minister Holt made efforts to get them to stay, but reaffirmed his previous verbal guarantees of defense to Malaysia and Singapore, with the suggestion that there might be formal defense pacts. Alliances would undoubtedly be regarded with suspicion by neutralist countries like Indonesia. This will undoubtedly inhibit Singapore, and to a lesser extent Malaysia, from signing formal alliances with Australia and New Zealand. The Australian role may have to continue to be one of informal backing of British defense, made credible by the continued presence of their troops in the Commonwealth bases in Malaysia for the next decade.

The Philippines' Claim to Sabah

The birth of Malaysia was complicated not only by Indonesia's Confrontation but by the hostility of the second of its three neighbors, the Philippines. The two countries have much in common: a cultural heritage which Filipinos often acknowledge by reference to their country as "the First Malayan Republic"; a relatively mild colonial experience, which gave them common Anglo-Saxon government traditions; a bitter experience under Japanese occupation; and successful defeat of Communist insurrections. All of these have given the countries a pro-Western stance. Their attitudes toward economics is also similar. Since the federation of Malaysia they have been divided over the status of Sabah.

The election of Diosdado Macapagal in November 1961 brought to the presidency of the Philippines a man who had long taken personal interest in the claim of the heirs of the sultan of Sulu. They asserted that most of Sabah had been merely leased to the North Borneo Company, and that Sulu's sovereignty had passed to the Philippines. Though the claim has much plausibility, its presentation at this particular time was accidental. The major motivation was probably to assert Philippine independence from the United States. Following Macapagal's inauguration and the unanimous passage in early 1962 of a resolution by the Philippine Congress claiming Sabah, a formal claim was made to Britain. This led to no result before the formation of Malaysia. At the second summit conference in July 1963 at which the three Maphilindo nations agreed to United Nations determination of the wishes of the Borneo peoples, it was also agreed that the formation of Malaysia would not prejudice the Philippine claim, which should be settled in a peaceful manner. The Philippine government was annoyed by the British cutback of Philippine observers of the United Nations survey and by the premature announcement of the federation of Malaysia. It, therefore, withheld recognition from Malaysia and recalled its ambassador. Malaysia retaliated by breaking off diplomatic relations.

Cooperation between Macapagal and Sukarno, who was becoming more erratic as Confrontation increased, seemed rather absurd, and there were many pressures for the Philippines to seek peace. Through the good offices of Norodom Sihanouk of Cambodia, consular relations between Malaysia and the Philippines were re-established in 1964. This contact gave a basis for discussion and reconciliation. The defeat of Macapagal in 1965 took much of the steam out of the claim, and his successor Carlos Garcia re-established full diplomatic ties in June 1966. The Philippine Congress revived the issue in 1968 by reasserting sovereignty over Sabah, which caused Malaysia to suspend diplomatic relations again. Indonesia and other nations used their efforts to bring the disputants to peaceful settlement. Because the problem is essentially legal, it seemed logical to many to submit it to the International Court of Justice, but national pride made it difficult for either side to accept an adverse decision. One obvious solution would be for Malaysia to give the heirs of the sultan of Sulu lump-sum final payment of the rental obligation the British have never denied.

A related problem in the two countries' relations is smuggling from Sabah into the southern Philippines. This age-old trade, dealing mainly in American cigarettes, is complicated by the pirates who prey on the boats in the Sulu Sea. A treaty concluded in 1967 required the Malaysian government to cut off a lucrative trade and the Philippine government to crack down on its own customs officials. Both actions were unpopular with the respective constituents, and the reopening of the Sabah dispute in 1968 provided an opportunity to renew the forbidden trade.

Thailand and Malaysia

On the conclusion of peace with Indonesia the Tunku thanked Thailand for being one of Malaysia's staunchest allies during the "dark period" of Confrontation. Thailand alone of Malaysia's three neighbors was friendly, and played a critical role in stimulating peace negotiations and in proposing solutions. Close cooperation to date does not mean there are not some potential problems between the countries. The overlapping of Malay and Thai peoples in the border area is the most serious of these. There are still 15,000 Thai-speaking Buddhists in northern Malaya, a reminder of the fact that Thailand ruled the four northern provinces until 1909 and again during World War II. This is a source of common interest as well as conflict of course.

For example, the Tunku refers to himself as half Thai and speaks of his birth in Kedah under Thai suzerainty and his education in Bangkok. Thailand has encouraged good relations by refusing to countenance any talk of the lost provinces. Similarly, the Malaysian government rejects the claims of Malay chauvinists to the southern provinces of Thailand, where 600,000 Malays live. The countries have emphasized their common interests, mainly by cooperating in joint patrols against the about four hundred Communist guerrillas who still hide in the rugged mountains of their border. Although Malaysia has rejected Thai suggestions that it join SEATO, the nations have cooperated closely in regional organizations.

Regional Cooperation

Malaysia has been a leader in integration at the national, regional, and international levels. The Association of Southeast Asia (ASA)—the first organization set up by local powers in the region—was initiated by Malaysia. Though many previous suggestions had been made, the Tunku's proposal of a political grouping with the Philippines in December 1958 was the first to bear fruit. The original political character of the proposal was modified to one of economic cooperation, but retained enough of an anti-Communist tinge to limit its acceptance to the three founding members, Malaysia, Thailand, and the Philippines.

The founding meeting in Bangkok on July 31, 1961, set rather vague objectives of cooperation, most specifically in commodity trade, and established a loose institutional arrangement of annual foreign ministers' meetings preceded by working party meetings. Between meetings, work was to be carried on by committees supported by national secretariats. A special ministerial meeting in Malaysia in April 1962 agreed to concrete fields of cooperation. In three of these definite steps were taken in 1962: (1) the ASA express train from Bangkok to Kuala Lumpur, (2) abolition of visa fees, and (3) microwave radio links from Kuala Lumpur to Manila. The second ministerial meeting in Manila in April 1963 reached agreements to establish an ASA fund, to conclude a trade treaty, and to study the establishment of a central secretariat and joint shipping companies and airlines. These, however, were postponed by the Sabah dispute.

In the meanwhile, another grouping emerged as a rival to ASA, in Maphilindo (for MAlaysia-PHILippines-INDOnesia). This had a more political purpose, as declared in the founding document, the Manila Declaration of August 5, 1963. It favored "the common struggle against colonialism and imperialism" by the "new emerging forces." Its only act was an abortive attempt to mediate Confrontation. The association of Maphilindo with Sukarno's ideology and machinations made it anathema to Malaysia, even after the restoration of peace. Tun Razak's pronouncement on Maphilindo as "dead and buried" was confirmed by the Philippine Foreign Secretary Ramos, who said that it had better be left that way. Thereafter, efforts were put into the revival of ASA.

At the third ASA ministerial meeting in Bangkok in August 1966, the three ministers took the initiative to propose an Asian settlement of the Vietnam War. In early 1967 ASA economic cooperation was revived. The association began to look the most promising of all the regional organizations, with its advantages of effective leadership, attractive goals of economic development, an Asian identity, open-ended membership, and flexible structure. Other powers were again approached on membership, but the continuing anti-Communist image of ASA apparently kept them away.

Indonesia could not accept ASA. Shortly after the end of Confrontation it had announced: "It will not be possible for Indonesia to join ASA, just as it may be difficult for Thailand to join MAPHILINDO. The best thing to do, therefore, is to create a new form of cooperation, embodying the ideas underlying MAPHILINDO as well as ASA."[4] At Bangkok on August 8, 1967, such an organization was formed, with the name Association of South East Asian Nations (ASEAN), bringing together Malaysia, the Philippines, Indonesia, Thailand, and Singapore. ASEAN incorporated the main idea of Maphilindo in a mild anti-imperialist declara-

[4] Foreign Minister Adam Malik, October 5, 1966, *Indonesian Embassy News Release* (Washington), no. 31, October 17, 1966.

tion that "all foreign bases are temporary." Otherwise, the association's objectives were almost identical with ASA's desires for cooperation for economic growth and commodity trade. The organization was also like ASA's: annual foreign ministers' meetings with standing committees in the next host country, ad hoc committees, and national secretariats. Proposals for specific projects such as tourism, shipping, fisheries, and trade were discussed at the second meeting in Djakarta in 1968.

The organization was open to other members, but invitations to Burma and Cambodia were politely rejected "because their basic policies make it impossible for them to join any group except for the United Nations."[5] India, however, indicated that it wished to join if the association "is intended to serve economic purposes and has no political or military undertones or overtones."[6] Despite Malaysia's evident preference for the smaller and more manageable ASA, the old body was dissolved by its members in August 1967, and its functions absorbed by ASEAN.

President Johnson's offer of a billion dollars to support regional cooperation in Asia, made at Johns Hopkins University in April 1965, added much impetus to regional discussions. Malaysia has participated in such efforts. Education ministers of the five ASEAN powers plus Laos and South Vietnam first met in Bangkok in November 1965. The meeting was supported by the Ford Foundation. A second conference of education ministers in Manila in 1967 set up regional centers in five subjects: (1) science and mathematics in Penang, (2) English in Singapore, (3) agriculture in the Philippines, (4) technology in Bangkok, and (5) tropical medicine in five countries. The same seven powers plus Japan first met in a Southeast Asian Development Conference in Tokyo in April 1966. The second meeting, at Manila in April 1967, agreed upon a regional fisheries center in Singapore and a transport and communications conference in Kuala Lumpur. Regional integration is an important element in Malaysian foreign policy, and further progress can be counted on.

5 Paraphrase of Adam Malik's remarks at Djakarta, May 30, 1967, *Indonesian News and Views* (Washington), no. 10/67, June 15, 1967, p. 2.

6 External Affairs Secretary T. N. Kaul, August 18, 1967, *India News* (Washington), September 1, 1967.

Malaysia continued Malaya's emphasis on international organization by listing as the cardinal principle of its foreign policy "to uphold the Charter of the United Nations." The Tunku speaks frequently in support of the United Nations. Tun Razak is president of the United Nations Association of Malaysia. And the Malaysian ambassador to the United Nations has always held cabinet rank. Ambassador Ramani has advocated making the world organization "a supra-national authority which wields both moral and physical power"—an idea that has wide acceptance in the country. Malaysia has demonstrated its convictions by sending 1,550 troops of its 10,000-man army to the Congo from 1960 to 1963, and buying a $350,000 bond during the financial crisis. Conversely, Malaysia has gained much from the United Nations. The General Assembly gave its approval to merger after the Michelmore investigation of 1963; a Security Council majority deplored the Indonesian Confrontation, and the various agencies have given Malaysia numerous international loans for development of power, irrigation, and land surveys. Malaysia has joined most of the specialized agencies. It has been active as an associate member in the Economic Commission for Asia and the Far East (ECAFE) since 1948. When Malaya became a full member in 1957, Singapore and Brunei became associate members too.

Malaysia has been vigorous in promoting Asian cooperation beyond Southeast Asia by supporting the Colombo Plan and in founding the Asian Development Bank. In 1966 it joined in ASPAC, the Asian and Pacific Council, started among the anti-Communist East Asian countries, but it is still resisting any explicitly anti-Communist grouping as SEATO.

Asia beyond the Near Neighbors

Because of the large Chinese population and China's cultural influence in Malaysia, China is bound to loom large in Malaysia's policy calculations. Basically, the policy toward China has been the practical one of maintaining trade but not recognizing either regime. Malaysian attitudes toward the Chinese People's Republic have been flexible, depending on China's policies. China's moral support of the Communist guerrillas made it impossible for the Tunku to support admission to the United Nations of "the Communists whom we are fighting" (though he made clear that he had no evidence of material support of the guerrillas). With the end of the Emergency in 1960 Malaya followed a two-China policy and tried to persuade the United States to adopt it too. But then the Chinese occupation of the Indian border, which began during the Tunku's visit to India in 1962 and was called by him "a stab in the back," caused Malaysia to shift back to opposing China's admission to the United Nations. The Tunku has consistently condemned the Chinese actions in Tibet with terms such as "rape" and "genocide." China's support of Indonesia's Confrontation did nothing to reconcile Malaysia. But in recent years there has been a mellowing of Malaysia's views of China, and Razak has advocated bringing mainland China into the United Nations if Formosa can stay. The Malaysian government has made clear that it does not oppose the Communist system as long as it keeps "its hands off our region."

Because the Indian tenth of Malaysia's population originated in South Asia, and because of the millennia-long cultural influences, as well as India's size, India is bound to be important in Malaysian foreign policy. Relations have been continually friendly, aided by a number of common interests: a democratic heritage, planned economies, ties with the Commonwealth, concern about China, opposition to racial discrimination, a multiracial state, and preference for United Nations cooperation over Western alliances.

Malaysia's relations with Pakistan have been complicated by its neutrality on the border fighting in 1965 between India and Pakistan. Pakistan was so offended by this that it broke off relations. This action came as such a surprise that Malaysia regarded it as Pakistan's object lesson to other neutral nations rather than an objection to Malaysia itself. Relations were restored a year later. Pakistan and Malaysia have a common interest in Islam, but relatively small number of Pakistanis in Malaysia makes cultural and economic ties much less close than with India.

Close relations have been maintained with Ceylon, from which a number of Malaysians come, and there is a link with Nepal through the thousands of Gurkhas who have defended Malaysia while serving in the British army.

Japan figures very strongly in Malaysian foreign policy because of its economic leadership in East Asia. But before cordial relations could be established Malaysia had to overcome the bitter memory of the Japanese occupation. The problem of "blood money" reparations was settled in September 1967 by Japan's payment of $8.3 million in the form of two freighters and technical advice on setting up a Malaysian shipping line. Japanese technical assistance has been important to Malaysia, and trade has been growing. With the settlement of reparations, Malaysia has openly encouraged Japan to assume greater leadership in Asia, in political as well as economic fields. The Japanese are cautious to avoid reviving any fears of the wartime Co-Prosperity Sphere and have confined their activities to economic efforts such as the Asian Development Bank and development and education conferences.

Malaysia has established cordial diplomatic relations with the southern half of Korea alone.

Relations with the northern tier of Southeast Asian countries have been conditioned by their respective attitudes toward communism. Malaysia has strongly supported South Vietnam's fight against communism, seeing a parallel in its own Emergency. It has long given Vietnamese training in guerrilla warfare and advice about its own new villages, and in 1966 offered troops and equipment for the war. Laos, farther away and more neutral, has been less important to Malaysia, though it has trained some Laotian policemen. Malaysia has had cooler relations with the neutralist nations, Burma and Cambodia, than Vietnam, though they are only 300 miles away. Cambodia's relations have been friendly and useful in re-establishing ties with the Philippines. Contacts with Burma are distant, in part because of its self-enforced isolation.

The World of Islam

An important factor in Malaysian foreign policy is kinship with the world of Islam. The Tunku has proposed several times a commonwealth of Islamic nations. Scholarly studies, particularly at Al Azhar University in Cairo, are the basis of friendship with the United Arab Republic. Saudi Arabia, as the guardian of the holy places of Islam, is important for the thousands of Malaysians who go on the hegira each year. Sympathy with the Arab bloc led Malaysia to condemn the American invasion of Lebanon in 1958 and the Israeli actions in 1967, and to avoid diplomatic relations with Israel.

The World beyond Asia

Malaysia has not tried to maintain diplomatic relations with every part of the world, though it could better afford to than diplomatically active Indonesia. Indonesian agitation against Malaysian participation in the Afro-Asian conferences during Confrontation made Malaysia aware of the need to present its views more effectively. Lee Kuan Yew did some campaigning in the Afro-Asian states on Malaysia's behalf, which we have seen were thought to help Singapore more than Malaysia. Tun Razak himself undertook some vigorous tours of Africa, and Malaysia joined the Afro-Asian bloc in 1965. Malaysia has reason to be proud of its support of Africa, not only in its Congo force, but in its consistent attack on colonialism and racial discrimination in the United Nations. The Tunku's condemnation of Apartheid at the Commonwealth Conference in 1960 led to South Africa's walkout. Words have been backed by a concrete action in Malaysia's boycott of trade with South Africa.

Malaysia maintains cordial relations with the major countries of Western Europe, particularly the Common Market countries. The federation sends an ambassador to each member of the Common Market except for Belgium and Luxembourg. This is largely a reflection of the substantial trade with these countries, which also have large investments in Malaysia. A Malaysian embassy is also maintained in Canada, an important Commonwealth partner, which provides considerable aid in the form of technical assistance (the Science Faculty of the University of Malaya) and arms (Malaysia's first jet aircraft).

Anticommunism is the heritage of the Emergency, and for most of its independence Malaya followed a hard line of "non-cooperation with the communist countries" which meant no trade or diplomatic relations. However, with the Emergency's end in 1960, the thawing of the Cold War, and Singapore's example, there has been a lessening of Malaysia's hostility. In 1967 the Tunku assured Parliament that he was not anti-Communist but "only against those Communists who use violence."[7] The conclusion of a trade agreement with the Soviet Union in April 1967 made it possible for Malaysia to sell rubber directly. This opened the way to establishing diplomatic relations with the Soviet Union in 1967 and with Eastern European states.

Latin America is the only region of the world with which Malaysia has no relations at all.

Singapore's Foreign Policy

Although independent Singapore's foreign policy has been different from Malaysia's in its ideological content, it has been controlled by similar practical considerations. These are principally problems of relations with neighbors, defense, and trade. Malaysia will remain Singapore's main foreign preoccupation. Even if Singapore's expressed desire for reunification does not materialize, trade and defense links with Malaysia will be important. Defense of the small city-state is obviously the crucial problem. Without an army of its own, Singapore has had to depend upon outside support, particularly of the British. Furthermore, the British bases provided jobs for 40,000 persons, about a tenth of Singapore's labor force, clearly too much to give up at a time of unemployment. Yet these economic and military needs were contradicted by the desire to prove the country's independence. Lee established his claim to independence by making clear at the start that he could give the British twenty-four hours' notice to leave. This action encouraged British uneasiness about the future. They made no formal commitment to Singapore's defense, and include the island state within the general scope of its concluding defense commitment to the area.

The second practical policy of Singapore is to get enough trade to stay alive. Lee has bluntly put it that Singapore must do this even if it means "trading with the Devil." The most immediate

7 Dewan Ra'ayat, January 20, 1967.

attention is given to expanding the entrepôt trade with Indonesia. Although it has gone a long way toward re-establishing trade, the Indonesian government has indicated that it did not want to go all the way back to the pre-Confrontation situation, and preferred to keep control of some of the lucrative entrepôt trade. Restoration of normal relations was retarded in 1968 when Singapore executed two Indonesians who had been caught doing sabotage during Confrontation.

Trade with "the Devil" included that with both the Russians and the Americans. A trade agreement was concluded with Russia; the United States armed forces were encouraged to make purchases for Vietnam in Singapore.

Practical considerations of trade have partly determined Singapore's commitment to nonalignment, but ideological considerations incline it toward neutralism as well. Singapore's first foreign policy statement in 1965 mentioned identity with Cambodia, and put more emphasis upon Burma and the states outside the Afro-Asian bloc than Malaysia's foreign policy. SEATO is explicitly rejected, as are other ostensibly anti-Communist arrangements like ASPAC. On the other hand, Singapore has been enthusiastic about regional economic cooperation in development and education, and in indigenous political cooperation like ASEAN. It had long been a participant in ECAFE, and joined the United Nations and its specialized agencies shortly after achieving independence.

In the United Nations Singapore has taken a different tack than Malaysia on the admission of China. It has consistently advocated admission of the People's Republic without attaching Malaysia's condition of retaining Formosa. While the People's Action Party is strongly anti-Communist due to its fight against the Barisan, it cannot afford to be anti-Chinese in this predominantly Chinese city. The Chinese cultural orientation of the Singapore Chinese is lessening as the time grows longer since immigration ceased. As the proportion of Chinese born in Singapore rises, loyalty to the city-state grows stronger than ties to the distant ancestral country. In the future, relations with China are more likely to be controlled by practical considerations of defense and trade than by cultural ties. As long as China does not directly threaten it, Singapore will be inclined to establish ties for the sake of the trade.

Singapore diverges from Malaysia on other ideological issues. The PAP's socialist ideology leads it to seek cooperation with other socialist parties of the world. Singapore's foreign policy pronouncements have shown it more oriented toward *realpolitik* than Malaysia. For instance, Singapore's leaders are acutely conscious of the strategic location of their state. Lee calls it "the linchpin of Southeast Asia." His colleagues cite Singapore's importance to Western defenses and its location in the Pacific Basin, which they see as the new center of world power, an idea they credit to the American imperialist Theodore Roosevelt. Lee's frank appreciation that "in the last resort, however, it was power which decided things"[8] reflects an approach that was apparent in Singapore's domestic politics.

Brunei's Foreign Relations

As a protected state, Brunei's foreign policy and defense were controlled by Great Britain. The sultan was apparently content with his influence with the British high commissioner, resident in Brunei. Brunei had no formal diplomatic relations abroad.

Malaysia, in which Brunei is an enclave, is its only immediate neighbor. The sultan established an unofficial residence in Kuala Lumpur, which provided a basis for informal contacts. The new sultan did not indicate any immediate interest in reopening negotiations for merger. Informal relations were maintained with Saudi Arabia because of the annual pilgrimage of Muslims. If one had to project the foreign policy of an independent Brunei, under the present dynasty, one would say it would be more conservative than Malaysia's, inclining to friendship with anti-Communist states. Those in the Middle East, especially Kuwait and Bahrein, have much in common with Brunei in their dependence on Britain to protect their huge oil reserves.

Barring any radical change in the governments of Malaysia, Singapore, or Brunei, the foreign policies are likely to continue to be oriented toward peaceful cooperation with the West, with neighbors in the region, and with the United Nations.

[8] "University of the Air" forum, October 31, 1966, *Straits Budget,* November 9, 1966, p. 5.

9
American Relations
with the Area

Relations between the United States and the three states of Malaysia, Singapore, and Brunei have always been friendly. The cornerstone of American policy with the area has long been that it is a "British responsibility." Translated into terms of old-fashioned power politics, this was a recognition that the Malaysian area was primarily in the British sphere of influence and the United States would not assume direct charge of defense of the area. This abnegation of power corresponded to the Malaysian reliance primarily upon the Commonwealth. However, the whole relationship was changed by the British withdrawal from the area.

The old arrangement with Britain had a great many advantages. The United States did not want to take over the burdens of empire, and certainly not its onus. Britain clearly knew more about its ex-colonies than did the United States, and was not disliked. Brunei wanted to continue the British protectorate; Malaysia had no bitterness about British rule; and even Singapore preferred that the British remain in the naval and air bases. Nor did it seem wise for the United States to spread itself too thin in commitments around the globe, particularly during the war in Vietnam. But with the prospect of that war ending, Britain, Australia, New Zealand, and even some leaders in Malaysia began to think about transferring responsibility to the United States.

Malaysia was not always willing to accept the consequences of its being a sole British responsibility, particularly in relation to foreign aid. Not surprisingly, the United States gave far more assistance to countries for which it assumed direct responsibility, such as the Philippines, Thailand, Vietnam, Korea, and Formosa (and earlier, Japan), and even to ones where the responsibility was divided, as in Indonesia, India, and Pakistan.

Acceptance of British responsibility for Malaysia did not mean, however, that the United States had no interests or influence in the area. The many and varied American interests can be summed up under eight points: (1) independence, (2) security, (3) integration, (4) economic development, (5) friendship with neighbors, (6) regional and international cooperation, (7) acceptance of American power, and (8) trade and investment. A survey of these will show that it is to the advantage of the United States to maintain good relations but avoid assuming direct responsibility.

Independence

It has been a cardinal point of American policy to uphold the firmly established popular regimes of Malaysia and Singapore to help them to remain as major barriers against communism. To this end, the United States was willing to back up the continued defense of the area by British Commonwealth forces for the indefinite future.

An expression of this was made by President Johnson during his visit to Kuala Lumpur in 1966: he cited as the first of four common goals held by Malaysia and America to "build democracy and protect freedom."[1] American policy in Asia has traditionally supported territorial and administrative integrity, the liberation of Asian countries from unequal treaties, and their continued freedom. While the United States is concerned with any threat to the independence of Asian nations, since 1947 it has opposed particularly the Communist threat. With the decline of Russian aggressiveness and the development of a Russo-American détente since 1960, this fear of communism has concentrated almost exclusively on China. Since 1949 the major American concern in Southeast Asia has been the possibility of Chinese expansion. Thus, American policy has viewed these countries as "barriers" to

[1] October 30, 1966, *Department of State Bulletin,* vol. LV, no. 1431 (November 28, 1966), p. 834.

Chinese aggression, or at least as "dominoes" to be prevented from falling.

The threat of China probably has been exaggerated, as America's stanchest allies seem to think. There is no evidence of Chinese territorial claim to any part of Malaysia. Nor has there been any Chinese government interference in the area, even in the guerrilla war of the Emergency, as the Tunku has affirmed. The Chinese encouraged the guerrilla movement verbally, but gave no material support. Chinese government influence is relatively small compared to American. American fears about China's interests and intentions may subside. This would not, however, affect the interest in continued freedom and independence for the area.

The United States has a strategic interest in keeping the area free of any hostile power. This has been shown since 1800 by the maintenance of American naval forces to protect American commerce in the seas near Malaysia. The significance of the Straits of Malacca as one of the vital sea lanes of the world is much lessened with the growing importance of airpower, but the United States still has a large commerce flowing through the straits. It would be regarded as contrary to American interests to see a great port like Singapore—or airbases in any part of Malaysia—in the hands of a power that was hostile, or even a potential enemy such as the Soviet Union.

In defense of Malaysian independence the United States played an important back-up role when the British so desired. For instance, during the Emergency it not only gave strong moral support, but supplied ten thousand carbines and ten helicopters. Since 1949 Washington has coordinated its defense planning in the area through the ANZAM group (Britain, Australia, and New Zealand). The United States was bound by the SEATO Pact of September 8, 1954, to defend British territories in Southeast Asia. This applied to Malaya until its independence in 1957, Singapore and the Borneo states until the 1963 merger, and Brunei until its independence. Support in the event of armed attack is limited to action in accord with constitutional practices; this provides a way out if the president wishes to ask Congress for a declaration of war. Under the ANZUS pact the United States has promised to come to Australia's and New Zealand's defense if their forces are attacked. Washington was not asked for help during Confrontation, but American support of resistance to Confrontation was made very clear at the ANZUS conference in 1964.

When the British announced in 1966 their intention to withdraw from Southeast Asia, the United States tried unsuccessfully to get them to stay. When the inevitability of their departure became apparent in 1968, the Johnson administration accepted the speedup in withdrawal without declaring publicly what it would do. People began to ask who would fill the "vacuum" of power when the British left, assuming that the Communists would if the anti-Communists did not. Public discussion in the United States tended to polarize around the alternatives of complete withdrawal from Asia or taking up the balance of power in imitation of the British. Few Americans publicly advocated complete withdrawal.

The principal method of affecting a balance traditionally has been the creation of an alliance system. But both Malaysia and Singapore had long opposed joining any American alliance. The negative reaction to SEATO in the past is a good indicator of Malaysian attitudes. The Tunku once called SEATO "ineffective, negative, outmoded and under the stigma of Western domination."[2] Malaysia and Singapore would be reluctant to alienate their neighbors by joining an organization that was so completely unacceptable to the majority of the nations of the region: Indonesia, Burma, Cambodia, and Laos. Moreover, being proud of their independence, they would not want to become party to other peoples' disputes, even though their sympathies might be with the West. Foreign bases are also a liability, for they become targets for nationalist and left-wing agitation. Indeed, the moderate new regional organization ASEAN has gone on record against foreign bases.

In the absence of a formal alliance, the United States could consider unilateral intervention, as it did in Laos and Vietnam. Whether the American public will permit repetitions of such interventions is dubious, even if the Malaysian and Singapore

[2] George Modelski, ed., *Six SEATO Studies* (Melbourne: Cheshire, 1962), p. 43.

governments were to invite them. One alternative to American intervention is an increased role for Australia and New Zealand, which is acceptable to Singapore and Malaysia. Backing them would be the British strategic forces that have been promised, and behind that the United States power, if desired. Local aggression will be met best by strictly indigenous regional security arrangements, which Tun Razak has said Malaysia favors.

The most promising alternative is to create a truly universal collective security by improving the capacity of the United Nations to act. This is why Malaysia has put so much emphasis upon strengthening the United Nations and expressed its willingness to contribute to an international police force. It was once suggested that the Singapore military complex would make an excellent base for a regional force under the United Nations. The United States might underwrite the financial cost of such a base and thus contribute to local security without involving itself in an imperialist role.

Internal Security

The second point of American policy is related to defense: upholding local efforts to counter Communist threats of subversion. This policy was specifically mentioned by President Johnson when he visited Malaysia in 1966.

A member of the Singapore cabinet has said that there are two ways of achieving internal security: a good police force and an honest government. He added that neither could be supplied by an outsider. Both Singapore and Malaysia have demonstrated the truth of this. The Communist Emergency was defeated by a combination of efficient (and honest) police action and winning the loyalty of the people to popular governments. The Singapore government's effective containment of the Communist menace has been largely its own effort. Had it been obviously foreign, the Communists would have persuaded many people that the government was not truly independent.

American support of Malaysian internal security has included training of officers costing about three million dollars a year in the early sixties, and arms assistance. The arms assistance has in-

volved at least one unfortunate episode. American arms were offered during Confrontation, and in 1964 officials were sent out
from the Pentagon to negotiate the terms. The American negotiators insisted on the commercial interest rate of 5 percent, taking
account of Malaysia's high credit rating and a reserve of two
billion dollars in London. Malaysia, harassed by the growing costs
of Confrontation, then at its height and with no end in sight, felt
that the United States could afford more generous terms such as it
had given such Asian nations as Vietnam, Korea, India, Pakistan,
and—what was particularly galling—Indonesia. Anti-American
riots broke out in the capital, sponsored by the nationalist Afro-
Asian Solidarity Committee, which had some members close to
the government. The rioters took out their wrath on the easiest
target, the United States Information Service library. The malaysian government apologized for the damage. The United States
promptly granted a loan of $11 million at 3 to 4 percent through
the Export-Import Bank for the purchase of arms and a direct
loan of $5 million more. But the "Five Percent Episode" rankled
in the minds of many Malaysians as an example of American nig-
gling.

The United States also indirectly supported the campaign
against the Communist guerrillas remaining on the Thai-Ma-
laysian border by aiding Thailand to improve the efficiency of
operations in the southern provinces. There is relatively little
Washington could do to solve such problems as the Clandestine
Communist Organization in Sarawak or the Communist opposition in Singapore. In fact, its help would make things worse by
subjecting the governments to charges of foreign intervention.

Integration

The United States hopes to see closer relations develop between
Malaysia and Singapore, with the object of reconciliation of the
two, and it wants to reduce racial tensions and see domestic peace
in the area. This is part of the broader American goal to which
Johnson referred during his 1966 visit as the third common goal,
"to end world tensions."

Probably there is not a great deal the United States can do to reduce racial tensions. At least it can avoid increasing communal consciousness, which it may have done in the past by its circulation of Chinese-language materials aimed at attracting loyalties to Formosa. It can encourage reconciliation by quiet diplomacy, such as the "Golf Summit" meeting of the Tunku and Lee in the cooling atmosphere of the Cameron Highlands in 1967. But American influence is greater in Kuala Lumpur than in Singapore, where American diplomats have had to overcome the legacy of the fifties when the People's Action Party leaders got the distinct impression that Washington looked upon them as crypto-Communists who were too naive to see the dangers of using the Communists. The American failure to distinguish between socialism and communism has not been helpful either. But following the CIA episode in 1965, when Lee revealed that a CIA agent had attempted to bribe a Singapore official, American relations with Singapore have gradually improved.

Economic Development

The United States strongly supports the economic development policies of Malaysia and Singapore, particularly since their free enterprise framework presents concrete proof to other nations that such policies can result in national development. President Johnson expressed this interest as the fourth common goal: "we strive to eliminate ignorance and illiteracy, disease and poverty." During his visit he showed his interest in Malaysian economic development by visiting a Federal Land Development Authority scheme. The scheme's name was transformed from Labu Jaya to L.B.J. in his honor. Johnson's administration was clearly impressed with the progress of Malaysian economic development, as stated by the President and his economic adviser Eugene Black, and it has given help where it could. Malaysian leaders have been grateful for the generosity of the Americans, both private and public. This was perhaps best expressed by Professor Takdir Alishahbana, speaking to the Asian-American Assembly in Kuala Lumpur in 1963: "the well-being of mankind has gradually become an international responsibility . . . There is no doubt that the United States of America has been the initiator and champion of this concept of international responsibility and up to now is still the greatest foreign contributor to the development of education, science, technology and economics in the countries of Asia."[3]

Yet the United States has recently found itself less and less able to contribute financially to the developing countries. This caused considerable disappointment in the Malaysian government, which had counted on American aid for a large part of 1.9 billion dollars that it needed for its First Malaysian Five-Year Plan starting January 1966. Washington was highly sympathetic to this plan, but Congress became increasingly reluctant to provide funds for economic development. By the mid-sixties American aid to Asia was largely confined to India, Pakistan, Korea, and Vietnam, and the Agency for International Development sought ways to comply with congressional desires that it phase out of more countries. American financial aid to Malaysia is probably the lowest in Asia, based upon need rather than desserts. Up to 1966 it totaled only $20.4 million: a gift of $400,000 for roadbuilding equipment in the early 1950's, ten million dollars from the Development Loan Fund for the expansion of Port Swettenham in 1958, and the same amount for highway construction in the next year. On the other hand, Malaysia had been spared the adverse effects of a large aid mission, such as the American ghettos with living standards that sharply contrast those of the local population—the problem that inspired *The Ugly American.*

The Peace Corps has been the major American contribution to Malaysian development. Most people have forgotten that "the ugly American" was the quiet technician who lived with the rural people and helped them to improve their standard of living. Otto Hunerwadel has had his counterpart in thousands of Peace Corps volunteers in Malaysia. Malaya was one of the first countries to respond to President Kennedy's offer of volunteers. Shortly after the founding of the corps in 1961, the government asked for high school teachers of science and mathematics, nurses, doctors, and

[3] T. Alishahbana and C. J. Eliezer, eds., *Papers on Cultural Affairs and International Understanding* (Kuala Lumpur: University of Malaya Press, 1965), p. 52.

other technical personnel. The first thirty-six volunteers took intensive training in the Malay language and culture in the fall of 1961 and arrived in Kuala Lumpur on January 12, 1962. Most of these were medical personnel: fifteen nurses, four laboratory technicians, and a volunteer for the Aborigine Hospital at Gombak. There were seven secondary school teachers, an instructor for the Technical College, an architect, two apprenticeship institute instructors, two business school teachers for the Rural and Industrial Development Authority College, two road surveyors, and a soil surveyor. This wide variety and high level of skills has characterized the Peace Corps effort in Malaysia ever since.

Shortly after the first volunteers arrived in Malaya, the British colonies of North Borneo and Sarawak both requested nurses, road surveyors, and laboratory technicians. In addition Sarawak asked for help with an agricultural extension service. A plan was devised to send experienced farm youths to start a 4-H program in Sarawak. The first fifty volunteers arrived in Borneo in August 1962. After the federation of Malaysia what had been separate Peace Corps programs in three parts of Malaysia were united into one.

By 1966 over a thousand volunteers had served in Malaysia. These included three doctors, a dentist, about one hundred nurses, dozens of laboratory technicians and technologists, radio technicians for Radio Sabah, agricultural workers for Sarawak, architects, hundreds of science and mathematics teachers, community development workers, librarians, a variety of technical personnel, and English teachers that have been the mainstay for the Sabah and Sarawak educational expansion.

In addition to providing skills—the first of the Peace Corps's objectives—the program is serving well the need for a growing mutual understanding. Malaysians have an opportunity to become acquainted with Americans. And the volunteers are bringing knowledge of Malaysia back to the American people. Over a thousand Americans now speak Malay fluently, in contrast with a mere dozen in the fifties. With this goes a sophisticated knowledge of Malaysia and its peoples. American attitudes toward Malaysia are bound to be more sympathetic when these former volunteers reach positions of influence in American government and society.

One of the unforeseen benefits of the Peace Corps in Malaysia has been its inspiration to Malaysians to take up the Peace Corps idea. For instance, a few years after the program began, some students at the University of Malaya looked around for a useful vacation activity and found a place in Kedah where they could help in a rural building project. This idea was revolutionary in that it helped break down the barrier between the intellectuals and the rural people. Such practical experiences could help the future leaders of Malaysia to understand popular needs and desires. Direct communication between the educated elite and the rural people, so rare in Asia, may be the answer to agrarian unrest upon which communism feeds. If the idea of a Malaysian Peace Corps takes hold, it increasingly can take over the job the Americans are doing, and ultimately send volunteers to lesser-developed countries. If there were only a few Malaysians, the United States might support their joining with other nations in an international peace corps under United Nations auspices.

For the new Five-Year Plan the United States government supported the meeting of an international consortium, the "Aid to Malaysia Club," and promised more aid for Port Swettenham and other harbors, and for the East-West Highway. In 1967 the Export-Import Bank granted a credit of fifty million dollars for this, and nearly forty million dollars more to buy American jets for Malaysian Singapore Airways.

In addition to American government assistance through loans and grants and the Peace Corps, aid critical to economic development has come from American private foundations and banks. The Ford Foundation gave grants for such projects as development planning, agricultural diversification, economic advice to MARA and the Economic Planning Unit, family planning, and educational reform. Singapore has also received over a million dollars from Ford for its university, technical institute, and Family Planning Association. The Asia Foundation of San Francisco gave over five and a half million dollars to Malaysia and Singapore since 1954 for a wide variety of projects such as graduate scholarships, sports and recreation advisers, support of Singapore and Nanyang universities, agricultural extension programs in Sabah, English teaching in Sarawak, and training of journalists. CARE-Medico Foundation has sent thirty-five medical specialists to Malaysia between 1963 and 1966, including a neuro-surgeon who began training of specialists at the medical school. The Catholic Welfare Relief Organization has given its own funds and staff for the distribution of American surplus food in a school lunch program and for other projects for improving local nutrition. The Hooper Foundation of San Francisco has supplemented the research of the United States Army Medical Unit in the study of malaria. The Rockefeller Foundation has been giving aid in the medical field since the 1920's. Much of the milk distributed through UNICEF comes from American purchases of Christmas cards, and a large part of the financial support for the experts of United Nations specialized agencies comes from the United States. American banks have been active in lending for development; for instance, the Chase Manhattan Bank lent Malaysia five million dollars in 1963 for railways and roads.

Friendship between Neighbors

The fifth objective of American policy is to encourage friendly relations of Malaysia and Singapore with their neighbors, particularly Indonesia and the Philippines. It has been a deliberate policy to foster reconciliation with Indonesia and a re-establishment of diplomatic relations and trade.

As we have seen, Washington was very unhappy about Confrontation and lent every effort to prevent hostilities by sending top negotiators like Robert Kennedy. Confrontation was particularly embarrasing because the United States wished to retain friendly relations with both countries. While its sympathy lay primarily with Malaysia, as Adlai Stevenson made clear in the Security Council debates, the United States was anxious to maintain "a foot in the door" of Indonesia against the day when the government might become more friendly. This policy was not very popular with the British or Malaysians, and was widely condemned in America as toadying to Sukarno, but has been proven correct by events in Indonesia. The United States regained much influence in Indonesia following the 1965 coup. American efforts to foster regional harmony are not spectacular because they are most effective when done without publicity.

One might expect that the Malaysians would be rather touchy about the fact that the United States has resumed large-scale aid to Indonesia. But with the advent of a new regime in Indonesia Malaysian officials have generously encouraged the idea that American economic aid is essential to build Indonesia's economy and achieve stability under the new government. Progress in Indonesia is recognized as so important to Malaysia's security that at the 1966 Commonwealth conference the Tunku argued that Indonesia "needed assistance quickly from all developed countries of the world" to "recover her bearings."

There has been no competition between Malaysia and Singapore over American aid. Eugene Black visited Singapore in November 1966 to extend assistance, but the Singapore government let it be known that it would not ask for aid lest it compromise its nonaligned status. It may be questioned whether Singapore can maintain this stance if its economic plight becomes worse, but the United States clearly preferred to give aid multilaterally, anyway, and Singapore gladly accepted this.

Regional and International Cooperation

It is a major policy of the United States to support actions which lead to closer relations between nations of Southeast Asia and to promote active cooperation in international organizations. Encouragement of regional integration was set forth as a particularly important objective in President Johnson's speech at Johns Hopkins University on June 7, 1965. In that address he called upon "the countries of Southeast Asia to associate themselves in greatly expanded cooperative effort for development," for which he promised a billion dollars. This was a major expansion of an American policy that had been expressed first by President Eisenhower's offer of $200 million for regional economic cooperation in

Asia. Johnson expressed his appreciation of Malaysia's efforts to promote regional integration, and paid particularly high compliments to ASA. In implementing the offer of aid to the region, the United States gave strong support to the founding of the Asian Development Bank in 1966 by an initial contribution of $200 million, and has encouraged regional conferences in education and development. Financial aid through such regional organizations promises to be the main channel of American support of Malaysia in the immediate future, though this does not exclude occasional bilateral efforts.

The American Role in Preserving Security

It is also an American policy to persuade the Southeast Asian countries that American strength is essential to preserving the security of the region, and constantly to reassure them that they can depend on American determination and capability to fulfill its responsibilities. This is clearly related to the primary goal of securing the independence of Asian countries from external and internal threats, and secondarily of protecting American interests. The importance of the United States' role is a point that American diplomats have got across very effectively to the Malaysian government. When Johnson arrived in Kuala Lumpur in 1966 the Malaysian Chief of State spoke for the government in saying that "The part which America is playing has won the highest esteem of small nations . . . which look to your support for their security, in fact for their very survival."

Reflecting this policy is Washington's attempt to win Malaysia's sympathetic support for its intervention in Vietnam. This was made easy by the fact that the Tunku had firmly supported South Vietnam long before American involvement, drawing the analogy to Malaya's own Emergency. As the Vietnam War intensified Malaysia did consistently give strong support to the United States position. Over 3,000 Vietnamese officers had been trained in anti-guerrilla operations in Malaysia between 1961 and 1966, and the training continued at about 120 a year. At the same time, Tun Razak said that he was willing to send combat troops to Vietnam

"If we are asked." Although this offer was not taken up immediately, Malaysia sent an economic mission to Vietnam in 1967 to help with rural and economic development. The Malaysian government also invited American soldiers to come from Vietnam for rest and recreation.

It is perfectly consistent with opposition to aggression that the Tunku has also worked for peace in Vietnam. He represented a widespread popular view in Malaysia when he praised American peace feelers and urged the United States to consider carefully before resuming bombing. The Tunku backed the Thai proposal for an all-Asian peace conference to settle the war (at the ASA meeting in Bangkok in mid–1966). Although the United States approved this initiative for peace, nothing came of it at the time, probably because it was largely a move by pro-Western countries.

The strong Malaysian support of the United States war effort in Vietnam does not mean that the Malaysian population was unified behind the administration. There was considerably more popular uneasiness about American involvement than the Malaysian or American government would be willing to admit. In its extreme form opposition is found in the periodic demonstrations in the cities, such as Kuala Lumpur, where the USIS library was wrecked several times. The First National City Bank of New York was damaged in the anti-Vietnam demonstrations that marked the arrival of the Assistant Secretary of State for Far East, William P. Bundy, in March 1966, because it is on the ground floor of the building where the American Embassy is located. The arrival of American troops on rest from Vietnam in July 1966 was one of the occasions for wrecking of the USIS library. The so-called anti-American riots at the time of Johnson's visit in October 1966 were mainly expressions of opposition to the Vietnam War. One hundred twenty arrests were made when serious riots took place in the major cities of Penang, Malacca and Ipoh, as well as the capital, where a Chinese youth was killed in front of the USIS library. The funeral of this boy, Ong Chang, drew a crowd of 3500 people, probably from the same source as much of the demonstrations, the left-wing Chinese elements, who were undoubtedly encouraged by the Communists.

The demonstrations of this radical minority reflect a wider discontent. Respectable intellectuals in Malaysia, as in America, have entertained serious doubts about the role of the United States in Vietnam. The nationally respected chairman of the Department of History of the University of Malaya, Wang Gungwu, who is basically anti-Communist and sympathetic to the United States, questioned the whole domino theory and warned that: "United States power on the side of anti-communism in Southeast Asia . . . may well confirm the "domino theory" . . . The longer the United States believes that the Southeast Asian countries cannot help themselves, the more dependent it will expect these countries to be on American power and the more likely it becomes that they cannot do without that power if they wish to survive. It is not inconceivable that the communists would wish to drag the United States so far into an ever increasing conflict that there will be . . . no independent or viable states left . . . There may well be no end to the war in Vietnam short of another world war."[4] The novelist-doctor Han Suyin, a long resident of Singapore, has commented: "Many of us in Asia think it would be more dignified to apologize, than to go on, as America is doing, losing not only face but honor, and gaining the world's contempt for the death she rains down upon an unfortuate small country, Viet Nam, because America, so large, so wealthy, is unable to admit to a mistake in judgment."[5]

In Singapore, the ruling People's Action Party was slow to give outright support to the American position in Vietnam. Foreign Minister Rajaratnam has expressed an appreciation of the position of the United States as a Pacific power, and Ambassador Wong, as a historian, spoke of the recognition "that the U.S. had to assume a more positive role in the affairs of the region" as Britain lost "her grip." It was to the surprise of many, though, that the Prime Minister spoke out to say that "What is happening

---

[4] "Communism in Asia," *Journal, Historical Society University of Malaya,* V (1966/1967): 7.

[5] Han Suyin, *A Mortal Flower: China—Autobiography and History* (New York: G. P. Putnam, 1966).

in Vietnam cannot be repeated . . . We cannot allow the same
forces that have emasculated South Vietnam to emasculate the
whole region" and to prevent this Southeast Asia might "prefer a
permanent American military presence" whose "credit-worthi-
ness" would depend on "performance."[6] This did not mean complete endorsement of the American position, for soon after this
statement, Singapore joined India in an expression of concern
over escalation and called for an immediate halt in the bombings
as a "necessary first step" to peace.[7] Uneasiness about the bombings was certainly widespread in the area.

The Singapore government welcomed the arrival of American
troops from Vietnam for rest and recreation—a boon to the tourist
trade—and the rising volume of American military purchases in
Singapore.

Sultan Omar of Brunei joined in the support of the American
presence in Vietnam. The Sultan rarely made public statements,
particularly on foreign policy, which was still a British responsibility. But in 1967 he allowed a New York *Times* correspondent
to write that he had "absolute confidence" in American policy in
Vietnam and that he felt the war was "a question of defending
what is good against what is evil," so that it was the American
duty to stay in the area to protect "the small nations."[8]

This acceptance of the American presence in Southeast Asia
and its aims in Vietnam by all three governments of the Malaysian
area speaks highly for the skill of American diplomats. USIS has
done an effective job of helping to persuade much of the reading
public in Malaysia to the same view.

Trade and Investment

The objective of developing American commerce and protecting American capital is the oldest of United States policies, going
back beyond John Hay's pronouncement of the Open Door Policy

6 Tokyo, March 21, 1967, New York *Times*, March 23 and 29, 1967.
7 May 10, 1967, *Straits Budget*, May 17, 1967, p. 14.
8 April 10, 1967, New York *Times*, April 16, 1967.

to its earliest contacts with Asia. The American government continues to emphasize the advantages of private capital investment, and this is encouraged by the Malaysian government.

Economic ties between the United States and Malaysia are quite important. The fact that the United States is the best customer for Malaysia's goods, particularly tin and rubber, has meant an increasing dependence on American price stability. As we have seen, in recent years Washington has been very sensitive to the problems of Malaysian price dependence, and has released tin and rubber from its stockpiles at a very cautious rate, responding to Malaysian protests.

Malaysia and Singapore frequently assert that the United States can help their prosperity through "aid by trade." A growing problem for these governments, like other developing countries, it to market the manufactures which they produce to avoid dependence on rubber and tin. It is clearly in the interest of the economically advanced countries to encourage the diversification of the economies of the lesser-developed countries. Just as clearly, if the United States is to welcome Malaysian industrialization, it must accept the competition of the new industries, which can often produce goods more cheaply than American manufacturers.

One specific problem in American trade relations with Malaysia and Singapore is incredibly like Rabelais' cake peddlers' war—the battle started over shop towels. Shop towels are very simple cotton textiles woven into long sheets, then cut off into short lengths for wiping grease off machinery. To protect its own exports, the United States joined an international agreement in 1962, the Long-Term Agreement Regarding International Trade in Cotton Textiles (LTA), which put quotas on foreign exports of cloth. Whenever a new nation tries to start industrializing by the manufacture of its own cotton cloth, the developed nations have threatened to invoke a clause of the LTA which permits it to cut off imports which will threaten its own producers. This was usually followed by a "gentleman's agreement" not to export more than a certain amount. The event may go virtually unnoticed in the United States, but cause great bitterness in the nation which is industrializing.

Singapore started producing these simple shop towels about 1965 and Malaysia in 1967. The United States was pressing negotiations for the limitation of Singapore production in Kuala Lumpur when the separation occurred. Negotiations had to start again with the new independent government of Singapore, and finally in August 1966 Lee's government agreed to a limitation of thirty-five million square yards of textile exports to the United States a year for the next three years. The advantage to Singapore was the fact that at least the Americans would accept that amount, which would guarantee work for 3000 laborers in its budding textile industry.

The limitation on Singapore tempted manufacturers to move to Malaysia. A short time after the agreement, cotton goods were being shipped to the United States from Malaysia. The Americans threatened restrictions, which provoked a protest from Malaysia. The pattern was repeated: a gentleman's agreement was proposed to limit the expansion of Malaysia's industry.

Economists are supported by many United States officials in the belief that the better approach would be to retrain and relocate American textile workers rather than hold back industrialization abroad. It seems undeniable that manufacture of cotton textiles does not represent efficient use of American resources and skills.

Understanding Malaysia

To improve understanding between the United States and Malaysia is not one of America's stated policy goals, but it is one of the implied objectives. It is an explicit objective of the Peace Corps and implicit in the USIS and Fulbright programs.

American and Malaysian knowledge of each other has been greatly increased in recent years by the Fulbright program, which provides exchange of professors and students. There is an active American Field Service program which sends American high school seniors to study in Malaysia and Malaysians to American high schools. The 4-H Foundation also has an annual exchange of farm youths. Rotary International is very active in the area, working to promote better understanding among business and professional men of all countries. The floating American University of the Seven Seas calls each year, giving American college students a firsthand acquaintance with Malaysia. Private foundations, especially the CARE-Medico, Ford, and Asia foundations, have financed visits of hundreds of experts.

There have been obstacles to education exchange programs. The most serious one was Malaysia's long refusal to recognize degrees from American universities. This appeared to be a hangover of the old British colonial prejudice against American education, reinforced by protectiveness on the part of British-educated persons. Most educated Malaysians condemned this and recognized that they were wasting the talents of American-educated Malaysians by not allowing them to practice their professions. The policy has already been relaxed for certain scarce skills such as those in chemistry, engineering, mining, and fishing, and presumably will be abolished in time.

Other problems are the cost of sending students to the United States, the loss of so many in the "brain drain," and the inappropriateness of training people in a nontropical environment. Short tours of study in the United States by Malaysian professors have proved ineffective; yet such experts rarely can be spared to do lengthy study abroad. It does not seem likely that these problems will be remedied by American universities establishing branches in Asia, since the American institutions can hardly meet rising financial costs at home. The most effective way for the United States to provide more technical education for Asia is to work through Asian schools. The best Malaysian students can be sent to the United States for training as future professors. In the meantime, American professors can go to Malaysia on short tours to help with curriculum development and administrative organization. This is the pattern that is being followed at the Serdang Agricultural College by arrangement with Louisiana State University, under Ford Foundation sponsorship. This development holds great promise for expansion of knowledge that is necessary to bring the developing countries rapidly into the modern world.

It is apparent that some American goals are more realistic than others. We have seen that there is relatively little the United

States can do about problems which are basically internal, such as security, internal cohesion, and neighborly cooperation. We have indicated serious doubts about the acceptability of American military alliances. But it is clear that there is a great deal the United States can do to achieve its policy goals through cooperative institutions which would deal on an international basis with problems of commodity prices, trade, education, defense, and security. It is for this reason that Johnson's Johns Hopkins address of 1965 is such a hopeful guideline for future American policy.

founding member of the ASA and AsEAN and active supporter of other regional organizations. Within a wider framework, Malaysia has supported the United Nations, giving generously of troops and money. Yet, to the pleasure of the United States, it has openly opposed communism in Tibet and Hungary. Malaysia's friendly relations with the West, and particularly with its former master, Britain, have not compromised its essential independence.

Malaysia's most significant achievement is in racial cooperation. Combining communal parties into an Alliance has worked effectively. A similar compromise on the explosive issue of national language has avoided the violence that occurs in many countries. Malaysia seems to have discovered a way of permitting three ancient cultures to continue their great traditions but to work together in harmony. It is this that makes Malaysia so significant to the world.

Appendix: Facts about Malaysia

Table 1. Area

	Square miles	Comparable area of U.S.
Malaya	50,840	New York State
Sarawak	48,340	Pennsylvania
Sabah	28,490	Maine
Malaysia	127,670	
Brunei	2,226	Delaware
Singapore	225	New York City
Total	130,121	

Sources: *First Malaysian Plan 1966–1970*, p. 3; *Singapore Facts and Figures*, 1966.

Table 2. Population of Malaysia by race, 1965

	Malays and related groups		Chinese		Indians		Others		Total
	Thou-sands	Per-cent	Thou-sands	Per-cent	Thou-sands	Per-cent	Thou-sands	Per-cent	Thou-sands
Malaya	4,011	50	2,968	37	882	11	160	2	8,021
Sarawak	578	69	279	30	3	0	6	1	866
Sabah	394	74	125	24	4	1	5	1	528
Malaysia	4,983	53	3,372	36	889	9	171	2	9,415
Singapore	267	14	1,396	75	154	8	48	3	1,865
Brunei	71	71	25	25	2	2	2	2	100
Greater Malaysia	5,321	47	4,793	42	1,045	9	221	2	11,380

Sources: Malaya from Pierre R. Crosson, *Economic Growth in Malaysia* (Washington: National Planning Assn., 1966), p. 23, with 1965 projected at 2.7 percent growth, and racial proportions as in 1962; Borneo states from L. W. Jones, *The Population of Borneo* (London: Athlone Press, 1966), p. 167, with author's corrections of Sabah "others" figure to exclude Sabah Malays and Filipinos and to include estimates of Indians; Singapore from *Singapore Facts and Figures, 1966* (Singapore: Ministry of Culture, 1966), p. 10.

Table 3. Exports and imports, 1965 (million U.S. dollars)

	Exports	Imports	Balance
Malaysia	1,260.9	1,118.7	+142.2
Singapore	1,002.7	1,269.3	−266.6
Brunei	66.6	38.0	+28.6
Total	2,330.2	2,426.0	−95.6

Sources: *Far Eastern Economic Review*, 1967 Year Book, p. 264 (for Malaysia); *Singapore Facts and Figures 1966*, p. 22; *Brunei: Annual Report 1965*, p. 38. All figures converted at the rate of one U.S. to three Malaysian dollars.

Table 4. Ten major exports, 1965 (government of Malaysia only)

Commodity	(Value millions of U.S. dollars)	1,000 tons	Trend of value
Rubber	484.7	941	Down
Tin	274.3	70	Up
Timber	117.6	3,543	Up
Iron Ore	54.3	6,500	Up
Palm Oil	31.0	132	Up
Pineapple	12.3	49	Up
Pepper	8.3	12.4	Up
Copra	7.3	37	Down
Coconut Oil	3.7	11	Down
Palm Kernels	3.3	23	Down

Source: *First Malaysia Plan*, pp. 23–24. Figures are preliminary, converted at exchange of three Malaysian to one U.S. dollar.

Table 5. Malaysian parliaments, 1963–1967

A. FIRST HOUSE OF REPRESENTATIVES (Nov. 2, 1963–March 1, 1964): 159 Representatives

    107 GOVERNMENT

        74 Malaya Alliance

            52 United Malays National Organization (UMNO)

            19 Malayan Chinese Association (MCA)

            3 Malayan Indian Congress (MIC)

        17 Sarawak Alliance

            4 Sarawak Chinese Association

            3 Party Pesaka Anak Sarawak (Papas)

            2 Barisan Ra'ayat Jati Sarawak (Barjasa)

            1 Sarawak National Party (SNAP)

        16 Sabah Alliance

            6 United Sabah National Organization (USNO)

            5 United National Kadazan Organization (UNKO)

            4 Borneo Utara National Party (BUNAP)

            1 National Pasok Momogun Party

     52 OPPOSITION

        30 Malaya

            12 Pan-Malayan Islamic Party (PMIP)

            8 Socialist Front

            5 People's Progressive Party (PPP)

            5 Others

        15 Singapore

            12 People's Action Party (PAP)

            3 Barisan Sosialis

7 Sarawak
  3 Sarawak United People's Party (SUPP)
  3 Party Negara Sarawak
  1 Independent

B. SECOND HOUSE OF REPRESENTATIVES (May 1964–Sept. 1965): 159 Representatives

122 GOVERNMENT
  89 Malaya Alliance
    59 UMNO
    27 MCA
    3 MIC
  17 Sarawak Alliance
    4 Sarawak Chinese Association
    3 PAPAS
    2 Barjasa
    1 SNAP
  16 Sabah Alliance
    6 USNO
    6 UPKO
    4 BUNAP

37 OPPOSITION
  15 Malaya
    9 PMIP
    2 Socialist Front
    2 PPP
    1 United Democratic Party (UDP)
    1 PAP
  15 Singapore
    12 PAP
    3 Barisan Sosialis
  7 Sarawak
    3 SUPP
    3 Party Negara Sarawak
    1 Independent

C. 1967 HOUSE OF REPRESENTATIVES: 145 Representatives

118 GOVERNMENT
  89 Malaya Alliance
    59 UMNO
    27 MCA
    3 MIC
  19 Sarawak Alliance
    4 Sarawak Chinese Association
    3 PAPAS
    2 Barjasa
    2 Party Negara Sarawak

10 Sabah Alliance
    6 USNO
    4 Sabah Chinese Association

27 OPPOSITION
  15 Malaya
     9 PMIP
     2 Socialist Front
     2 PPP
     1 UDP
     1 Democratic Action Party
   6 Sarawak
     3 SUPP
     1 SNAP
     1 Independent
   6 Sabah
     6 United Pasokmomogun Kadazan Organization

D. DATES OF FIRST STATE ELECTIONS TO NATIONAL PARLIAMENT

State	Dates	Seats
Sabah	Dec. 16, 1962, to May 5, 1963	16
Sarawak	April 26, 1963, to June 25, 1963	24
Singapore	Sept. 21, 1963	15
Malaya	April 25, 1964	104

Table 6. Growth of Chinese representation in Malayan electorate

Community	Voters (Thousands)			Percent of Electorate		
	1955	1959	1964	1955	1959	1964
Malays	1,078	1,217	1,591	84.2	56.8	54.1
Chinese	143	764	1,117	11.2	35.6	38.0
Others	59	163	232	4.6	7.6	7.9
Total	1,280	2,144	2,940	100.0	100.0	100.0

Sources: Vasil, R. K., "The 1964 General Elections in Malaya," *International Studies*, 8.1 (July 1965): 57, 60–61; Ratnam, K. J., *Communalism and the Political Process* (Kuala Lumpur, 1965), pp. 187, 200.

Suggested Reading

The reader seeking more information about Malaysia will find that general descriptions are rare. The best place to start is with *Malaysia: A Survey* (New York: Praeger, 1964) edited by Professor Wang Gungwu. This is a symposium by twenty-seven experts, including four Americans. It is of uneven quality and goes only to the time of merger in 1963. Newer is K. G. Tregonning's *Malaysia and Singapore* (2d. ed., Melbourne: F. W. Cheshire, 1966) which is a sketch of modern Malaysia up to the separation of Singapore in 1965.

For the natural setting there are excellent chapters on the geography of Malaysia by Robert Ho for Wang Gungwu's *Survey* mentioned above, and in Charles A. Fisher's *South-East Asia,* 2d. ed. (London: Methuen, 1966), as well as some recent geographies of parts of Malaysia: Ooi Jin-bee's *Land, People and Economy in Malaya* (London: Longman's, 1963) and Lee Yong Leng's *North Borneo (Sabah): A Study in Settlement Geography* (Singapore: Eastern Universities Press, 1963). A couple of useful atlases are Harold Fullard, ed., *Senior Malayan Atlas,* 8th ed. (London: George Philip, 1963), and Hamzah bin Sendut, ed., *Atlas Menengah Melayu* (Kuala Lumpur: Dewan Bahasa dan Pustaka, 1964), which will soon be supplemented by a more detailed atlas being compiled by the Dewan Bahasa.

There is as yet no book on the varied peoples and cultures of Malaysia. By far the best book on the three major races of Malaya is N. J. Ryan's *The Cultural Background of the Peoples of Malaya* in paperback (Kuala Lumpur: Longman's, 1962). The best source on Malay custom is Sir Richard Winstedt's classic, *The Malays: A Cultural History* (revised ed., London: Routledge and Kegan Paul, 1950), which can be supplemented with works dealing with the effect of modernization of the Malays, such as Judith Djamour's *Malay Kinship and Marriage in Singapore* (revised ed., London: Athlone Press, 1965). For the Chinese of both Malaya and Borneo see the two long sections in the second edition of *The Chinese in Southeast Asia* (London: Oxford, 1965) by Victor Purcell, who spent a quarter of a century in Malaya dealing with Chinese affairs. Several paperbacks by Leon Comber deal more directly with Chinese customs; *Chinese Ancestor Worship in Malaya* (Singapore: Eastern University Press, 1954) and *Chinese Festivals in Malaya,* with Dorothy Lo (Singapore: Eastern University Press, 1958) are examples. S. Durai Raja Singam has collected some random notes about the Indian culture in Malaya in two little pamphlets: *Temple Bells* (Kuala Lumpur: N. T. Pillay, 1964) and *A Malayan Heritage* (Kuala Lumpur: Khee Meng Press, 1962). Supplementing the older scholarly studies of Borneo peoples are a couple of recent paperbacks: *Nine Dayak Nights* (New York: Oxford, 1961) by the ethnologist W. R. Geddes, and *The Dusun* (New York: Holt, Rinehart and Winston, 1965) by the American Thomas Rhys Williams.

The writers of a history of Malaysia are still struggling to overcome two obstacles: the tendency to write from a local viewpoint without taking account of the interrelation of the whole area, and what the Dutch historian Van Leur called looking down at the Indies from "the deck of a ship" or a European fort and business house. The Australian historian K. G. Tregonning has been the leader in reorienting our view to that of Asians in his interesting *A History of Modern Malaya* (London: University of London Press, 1964) and *A History of Modern Sabah* (2d. ed., Singapore: University of Malaya Press, 1965). Archaeological work can be said to have barely begun. The exciting finds are best summarized in M. W. F. Tweedie's pamphlet *Prehistoric Malaya* (3d. ed., Singapore: Donald Moore, 1965) and in Tom Harrisson's "50,000 Years of Stone Age Culture in Borneo," *Smithsonian Institution Annual Report, 1964* (Washington: Smithsonian, 1965). The best history of Malaya prior to European times is by the American, Paul Wheatley, *Impressions of the Malay Peninsula in Ancient Times* (Singapore: Donald Moore, 1964). For the Malaysian period, Sir Richard Winstedt's *A History of Malaya,* (2d. ed., Singapore: Marican, 1962) is still the best. William R. Roff's *The Origins of Malay Nationalism* (New Haven: Yale, 1967) is highly recommended. Tregonning is strong on the British period in Malaya and North Borneo, and Sarawak's history is best described by the British historian Sir Stephen Runciman's *The White Rajahs* (Cambridge: Cambridge University Press, 1960).

The first book on the governments of Malaysia and Singapore has been published in paperback: R. S. Milne, *Government and Politics in Malaysia* (Boston: Houghton Mifflin, 1967). Biographies of political leaders as well as prominent citizens are found in *The Who's Who in Malaysia: 1967,* edited and published by J. Victor Morais (Kuala Lumpur, 1967). *Malaysia: Buku Rasmi Tahunan* (in English; Kuala Lumpur: Government Press), *Singapore: Annual Report* (Singapore: Government Printing Office), and *State of Brunei: Annual Report* (Brunei: Government Printer), the official yearbooks of the governments, are authoritative reference works on government activities but always lag in publication. American scholars have long led in analyses of Malaysian politics, starting with Rupert Emerson's classic *Malaysia: A Study in Direct and Indirect Rule,* reprinted in paperback (Kuala Lumpur: University of Malaya Press; New York: Oxford University Press, 1964). The first commentary on the Malaysian constitution is the American Harry E. Groves' *The Constitution of Malaysia* (Singapore: Malaysia Publications, 1964). The authority on the civil service is another American, Robert O. Tilman, whose major work is *Bureaucratic Transition in Malaya* (Durham, North Carolina: Duke University Press, 1964). Racial issues in elections are well analyzed in K. J. Ratnam's *Communalism and the Political Process in Malaya* (Kuala Lumpur: University of Malaya; New York: Oxford University Press, 1965). Recent Singapore politics are described in Milton E. Osborne's *Singapore and Malaysia* (Ithaca: Cornell University Southeast Asia Program Data Paper no. 53, July 1964).

For the whole process of the creation of the Malaysian nation, one should go first to the lively reports for the American Universities Field Staff by the American professor resident in Singapore, Willard A. Hanna. These reports have been collected into two books, *Sequel to Colonialism: The 1957–1960 Foundations for Malaysia* (New York: A.U.F.S., 1965) and *The Formation of Malaysia* (New York: A.U.F.S., 1964). To these should be added Hanna's biography of the Tunku in *Eight Nation Makers* (New York: St. Martin's, 1964).

For an introduction to economic problems and prospects one should see the works of T. H. Silcock, especially his *The Economy of Malaya* (4th ed., Singapore: Eastern Universities, 1963) and *The Political Economy of Independent Malaya: A Case-Study in Development,* with E. K. Fisk (Canberra: Australian National University, 1963). The best source of information about government activities are the various five-year plans available from government printing offices. Two recent analyses by Americans are Pierre R. Crosson's *Economic Growth in Malaysia* (Washington: National Planning Association, 1966) and Gayl D. Ness' *Bureaucracy and Rural Development in Malaysia* (Berkeley: University of California Press, 1967). The most convenient source of current economic data is the *Far Eastern Economic Review* (Hongkong) and its annual *Year Book.*

Information on social problems can be found in the works on history, geography, and economy cited above. The population explosion is revealed in the first demographic study of Eastern Malaysia, L. W. Jones' *The Population of Borneo* (London: Athlone Press, 1966). Views of the impressive social welfare program of Singapore can be gained from such government publications as *Social Transformation in Singapore* (Singapore: Ministry of Culture, 1963). Ho Seng Ong, *Education for Unity in Malaya* (Penang: Malayan Educator, 1952), is not so current but gives the setting of the race problem: To this should be added the government education reports of 1955 and 1960, available from the Government Printer. Despite its importance, the problem of language is poorly treated, the only book being R. B. Le Page's *The National Language Question* (London: Oxford, 1964). To appreciate the vitality of the Malaysian culture today anyone will enjoy looking at the *Straits Times Annual* which contains full color reproductions of modern artists' works and popular articles on the history and culture of Malaysia.

Malaysia's foreign policy is the subject of only two articles: T. H. Silcock's "Development of a Malayan Foreign Policy" in *Australian Outlook*, vol. XVII (April 1963), and Robert O. Tilman's "Malaysian Foreign Policy" in John D. Montgomery, ed., *Public Policy* (Cambridge: Harvard University Press, 1967). Relations with Britain, of course, are part of history, and recent problems centering around the British withdrawal appear in the British White Papers, which are usually entitled "Defence Estimates" and published in the parliamentary papers by command. The Confrontation with Indonesia received a great deal of journalistic attention, perhaps best summarized thus far by Arnold C. Brackman's *Southeast Asia's Second Front* (New York: Praeger, 1966) and analyzed in Willard Hanna's reports mentioned above. Malaysian regional cooperation is discussed in two recent paperbacks: Margaret Grant, ed., *South Asia Pacific Crisis* (New York: Dodd, Mead, 1964), and Bernard K. Gordon, *The Dimensions of Conflict in Southeast Asia* (Englewood Cliffs, New Jersey: Prentice-Hall, 1966). The period 1963 to 1966 in United States policy toward Malaysia is studied by René Peritz' "American-Malay Relations: Substance and Shadows," *Orbis*, vol. XI, No. 2 (Summer 1967), pp. 532–550.

For students seeking more detailed information on Malaysia, the following will be helpful. H. R. Cheeseman, comp., *Bibliography of Malaya* (New York: Longman's, 1959), the first bibliography published and still the best, goes through 1957. Beda Lim's "Malaya: A Background Bibliography," *Journal of the Malayan Branch Royal Asiatic Society* (vol. XXXV, pts. 2 and 3, 1962) covers the period to 1956. For Borneo, see Conrad Cotter's *Bibliography of English Language Sources on Human Ecology: Eastern Malaysia and Brunei* (Honolulu: University of Hawaii Press, 1965). For material since the compilation of these bibliographies the best source is the annual *Bibliography of Asian Studies* published by the Association for Asian Studies (Ann Arbor, Michigan). To keep up with the news in Malaysia one can subscribe to *The Straits Budget,* which is a weekly selection of the main articles in *The Straits Times* (Kuala Lumpur), the main English language newspaper. Current political analyses can be found in *Asian Survey* (Berkeley, California, monthly) and in the American Universities Field Staff Reports (New York).

The reader may get the most vivid impressions of Malaysia from first-rate novelists. Both Joseph Conrad and Somerset Maugham lived in Malaysia and caught the atmosphere of the colonial period beautifully. The period of World War II is nicely described in Agnes Newton Keith's *Land below the Wind* (Boston: Little Brown, 1939), *Three Came Home* (Boston: Little Brown, 1947), and *The White Man Returns* (Boston: Little Brown, 1951). The feelings during the Communist Emergency are vividly portrayed by Han Suyin's *The Rain My Drink* (Boston: Little Brown, 1956). Anthony Burgess's *The Long Day Wanes— A Malayan Trilogy* is the most popular of the author's works recalling his long residence in Malaysia. Samples of recent writing by Malaysians, short stories, poems, and nonfiction, are collected in "Malaysian Literature," the December 1966 issue of *Literature East and West* (vol. X, no. 4).

Index

The American Foreign Policy Library

The United States and the Caribbean REVISED EDITION Dexter Perkins

The United States and China NEW EDITION—COMPLETELY REVISED AND ENLARGED John King Fairbank

The United States and Japan THIRD EDITION Edwin O. Reischauer

The United States and Mexico REVISED EDITION, ENLARGED Howard F. Cline

The United States and India and Pakistan REVISED AND ENLARGED EDITION W. Norman Brown

The United States and Italy REVISED EDITION H. Stuart Hughes

The United States and Argentina Arthur P. Whitaker

The Balkans in Our Time Robert Lee Wolff

The United States and the Southwest Pacific C. Hartley Grattan

The United States and Israel Nadav Safran

The United States and North Africa: Morocco, Algeria, and Tunisia Charles F. Gallagher

The United States and the Arab World REVISED EDITION William R. Polk

The United States and Canada Gerald M. Craig

The Americans and the French Crane Brinton

The United States and Malaysia James W. Gould